ATONEMENT

MARGARET M. TUREK

ATONEMENT

*Soundings in Biblical,
Trinitarian, and
Spiritual Theology*

IGNATIUS PRESS   SAN FRANCISCO

Cover art: *The Holy Trinity with the Virgin,
Saint John the Evangelist, and Donors* (detail)
Masaccio, Tommaso di Ser Giovanni (1401–1428)
Fresco, Santa Maria Novella, Florence, Italy
In the Public Domain, Wikimedia Commons Image

Cover design by Roxanne Mei Lum

© 2022 by Ignatius Press, San Francisco
All rights reserved
ISBN 978-1-62164-504-7 (PB)
ISBN 978-1-64229-212-1 (eBook)
Library of Congress Control Number 2021940698
Printed in the United States of America ∞

To my students

Contents

7

Acknowledgments

I offer my sincere thanks to Adrian Walker for his careful reading of an earlier version of the manuscript; I profited greatly from his insight, suggestions, and encouragement. Thanks are also due to Angela Franz Franks, Douglas Bushman, and Anthony Lilles, who read and commented on earlier drafts of parts of the book. I am grateful as well for the fine work of my editor, Vivian Dudro, and the supportive collaboration of all the folks at Ignatius Press.

Sections of chapters 1 and 2 were presented as lectures at two symposiums sponsored by the Saint John Paul Center for Contemplative Culture, led by Anthony Lilles; I am indebted to all the participants for their helpful feedback and encouragement. Chapters 1 and 2 are also based on earlier articles: " 'In this way the love of God was revealed' (1 Jn 4:9): Atonement as a 'Patrogenetic' Process: Part 1: The Old Testament", *Communio: International Catholic Review* 47.1 (Spring 2020): 7–47; and " 'In this way the love of God was revealed' (1 Jn 4:9): Atonement as a 'Patrogenetic' Process: Part 2: The New Testament", *Communio* 47.2 (Summer 2020): 399–440.

Finally, I owe a debt of gratitude to my family and friends who supported me with their love and prayers while I was preoccupied with this project. Special thanks to the rascals behind the surprise party when all was finished.

Introduction

The perennial value of a theology of atonement

"In this way the love of God was revealed to us: . . . that he . . . sent his Son as expiation for our sins" (1 Jn 4:9–10). The theme of atonement takes us to the very heart of the mission of Jesus Christ. Revealing the love of God as a mortal man, while bearing the conditions of sin-wrought estrangement, God's Son atoned for the sins of the whole world (1 Jn 2:2). Atonement is the form that the love of God takes in his Son, Jesus Christ, under sin-wrought conditions—a love than which no greater can be conceived.

In John's Gospel, those who observed Jesus weeping over the death of Lazarus correctly interpreted the meaning of his tears: "See how he loved him" (Jn 11:36). This recapitulates the confession of faith in response to Jesus' mission, which culminates in his own Passion and death: "See how much he loves us!" This is the key interpretation of the Cross event, which Jesus reveals to his disciples, whom he calls friends: "No one has greater love than this, to lay down one's life for one's friends" (Jn 15:13). And the apostolic Church makes this central to her profession of faith: "God proves his love for us in that while we were still sinners Christ died for us" (Rom 5:8). "The way we came to know love was that he laid down his life for us" (1 Jn 3:16). A theology of atonement is not complete unless it issues from and serves to elicit the profession of faith: "See how much God loves us!"

Clearly, the love of God made manifest in Christ's atoning Passion stands at the center of Christian witness. Christians in every age should know and witness to the God of Jesus Christ in precisely these terms. Not only that, but this witness is to be directed to all mankind: "The Church, following the apostles, teaches that Christ died for all men without exception: 'There is not, never has been, and never will be a single human being for whom Christ did not suffer.'"[1] In our days, this Christian conviction is poignantly conveyed by Pope Saint John Paul II, in a way that draws attention to the profound existential impact it is meant to have on every human person. "Man", he says, "needs to know that he is loved, loved eternally and chosen from eternity." He needs to be made aware that "the Father has always loved us" in sending his Son to deliver us from evil. When everything would tempt us to doubt the existence of a God who is rich in mercy, precisely then "the awareness of the love that in [Christ crucified] has shown itself more powerful than any evil and destruction, this awareness enables us to survive."[2]

The modern aversion to a theology of atonement

It should be cause for concern, therefore, that a conspicuous characteristic of much of contemporary theology is the absence of efforts to explain the Cross event as a work of atonement. Despite the fact that the Church's Scripture, doctrine, and worship all sanction the faith-conviction that Christ by his Passion and death atoned for sin, once for all (Heb 9:26),[3] this understanding of the Cross event has

---

[1] *Catechism of the Catholic Church*, no. 605; the inner citation is from the Council of Quiercy (853): DS 624; cf. 2 Cor 5:15; 1 Jn 2:2 (hereafter *CCC*).

[2] John Paul II, apostolic letter *Dilecti amici* (March 31, 1985), no. 7.

[3] See, for instance, the *CCC* 601, 615, and 623.

largely fallen out of favor. Among theologians, one can detect an unmistakable reserve—even embarrassment—with
regard to the idea. And things are not hugely different in the
world of parish faith formation. On most occasions when
the Scripture readings at Mass testify expressly to the atoning purpose of Christ's Cross, the priest or deacon proves
masterful in avoiding the subject—even on Good Friday,
when the prophecy of the Suffering Servant (Is 53) is read
as prelude to Saint John's Passion account.

We may assume that behind this pattern of avoidance
is the view that the message of the Cross as atonement
clashes with the sensibility of many today. Nonetheless, just
as Christ had to challenge the expectations and mindsets of
his interlocutors, so Christians may not sidestep the task of
challenging and transforming the perspectives of their audiences.

For his part, Pope Benedict XVI is alert to the trend
among Christians to distance themselves from the doctrine
of the Cross as atonement. Indeed, he challenges it in the
first volume of his masterwork, *Jesus of Nazareth*, where he
observes: "The idea that God allowed the forgiveness of
sins to cost him the death of his Son" is widely seen as
repugnant. Benedict then goes on to identify reasons for
this trend. The first reason he singles out is "the trivialization of evil in which we take refuge".[4] We seem to have
a very small estimate of human guilt, the menace of evil,
and the damage it causes. We presume that we sinners know
all about sin, that we can properly "contextualize" it from
our own point of view; after all, we are its perpetrators.
To the degree that the trivialization of evil holds sway in
our minds, the message that Christ's Passion and death is a

[4] Benedict XVI, *Jesus of Nazareth*, vol. 1, *From the Baptism in the Jordan to the Transfiguration*, trans. Adrian J. Walker (New York: Doubleday, 2007), 159.

work of representative atonement cannot but strike us as an overreaction on God's part.[5]

Besides this inaccurate assessment of sin, another troublesome reason for the modern aversion to the idea of atonement lies in a distorted depiction of God the Father's role in the Cross event. Ever since the seventeenth century, and indeed well into the twentieth, a trend arose among theologians and preachers to portray God the Father as a celestial child abuser vis-à-vis Christ crucified, as someone who unleashes violent fury on his Son for sins of which his Son is innocent. Such a portrayal of the Father gained a foothold in Catholic circles under the influence of Jansenism.[6] Here are but two examples. The first is from a sermon by a Catholic bishop, Jacques-Bénigne Bossuet: God the Father

> beholds him [Jesus] as a sinner, and advances upon him with all the resources of his justice. . . . I see only an irritated God. . . . The man, Jesus, has been thrown under the multiple and redoubled blows of divine vengeance. . . . As it vented itself, so his [the Father's] anger diminished. . . . This is what passed on the Cross, until the Son of God read in the eyes of his Father that he was fully appeased. . . . When an avenging God waged war upon his Son, the mystery of our peace is accomplished.[7]

Our second example is from a conference by Reverend Gay: "Fervently emulous of her holy Son, Mary offers herself

---

[5] See Norbert Hoffmann, "The Crucified Christ and the World's Evil", *Communio: International Catholic Review* 17.1 (Spring 1990): 53.

[6] Jansenism views God one-sidedly as a God of justice, punishment, and wrath—a wrath that demands appeasement through the infliction of punishment.

[7] Bishop Jacques-Bénigne Bossuet, *Oeuvres oratories de Bossuet*, vol. 3 (Lille-Paris: Desclée de Brouwer, 1891), 382–83. Quoted in *What Is Redemption?*, Philippe of the Trinity, O.C.D. (New York: Hawthorn Books Inc., 1961), 22.

with him. . . . She abandons herself without reserve into the hostile and incensed hands of the divine creditor . . . whom only the most drastic shedding of blood can satisfy. . . . Behold her locked in combat with this irritated and hostile God."[8] Regrettably, many more texts could be brought forward that imagine God the Father as thirsty for vengeance and demanding the Passion and death of his Son to calm his rage.[9]

An adequate response on our part must counter the trivialization of sin without erroneously thinking that the magnitude of sin is best measured by the magnitude of divine vengeance. We will argue, instead, that it is above all in encountering the fathomless love of God that "our heart is shaken by the horror and weight of sin."[10] If evil can be known only in relation to the good, this must mean that we cannot know the whole truth about sin apart from the whole truth about the supremely good God—a twofold truth that is consummately revealed in the Cross event.

Closely coupled with the above-mentioned faulty notion of divine wrath is another mistaken view, one that fails to preserve the primacy and generative modality of the Father's love in relation to the work of atonement. In this fallacious view, the Son's role is to win back the Father's love for the human race. But this is at odds with the Johannine proclamation that "God so loved the world that he gave his only Son" (Jn 3:16) and the Pauline passage that declares: "God [the Father] proves his love for us in that while we were still

---

[8] Charles Gay, *Conférences aux Mères Chrétiennes* (Paris, 1877). Quoted by Philippe in *What Is Redemption?*, 24–25.

[9] See Charles Parra, *L'Evangile du Sacré-Coeur* (Toulouse: Apostolat de la Prière, 1931), 43; Louis Chardon, *La Croix de Jesus* (Paris, 1895), 154–55; François Maucourant, *La vie d'intimité avec le bon Sauveur* (Nevers, 1897), 23.

[10] *CCC* 1432.

sinners Christ died for us" (Rom 5:8; cf. 8:31–34). If we are to do justice to the biblical testimony, we must show that the Son's work of atonement is the result *of* the Father's love. It does not result *in* the Father's love being revived or jumpstarted, as it were.[11]

At the opposite pole from (and to some extent in reaction to) these flawed portrayals of the Father are those readings of Christ's Passion that outright reject the idea that it achieved atonement. Typical of this stance are the remarks of Peter Fiedler: "Jesus had proclaimed the Father's unconditional will to forgive. Was the Father's grace, then, insufficiently bountiful . . . that he had to insist on the Son's atonement all the same?"[12] Theologians and preachers in this camp appear unable or unwilling to make understandable Saint John's claim that we have come to know that God is love *precisely in view of* God's sending his Son as atonement (1 Jn 4:8–10). To the sensibilities of many like Fiedler, the two prongs of this claim (God the Father is love *and* the Son's Cross is atonement) are mutually exclusive. They feel compelled to dismiss "atonement" as a religious notion that cannot be squared with the revelation of the love of God in the New Testament.

---

[11] See Thomas Aquinas, *Summa theologica* III, q. 49, a. 4, ad 4 (hereafter *ST*).

[12] Peter Fiedler, "Sunde und Vergebung im Christentum", *Concilium* 10 (1974): 568–71. Quoted by Norbert Hoffmann, "Atonement and the Spirituality of the Sacred Heart", in *Faith in Christ and the Worship of Christ*, trans. Graham Harrison, ed. Leo Scheffczyk (San Francisco: Ignatius Press, 1986), 144n18. Other positions in this category interpret the Cross event as the historical manifestation of God's unqualified will to forgive (see Karl Rahner's *Foundations of Christian Faith* [New York: Crossroad, 1987], 282ff.) or as the unmasking of the scapegoat mechanism (see Raymund Schwager's *Brauchen wir einen Sundenbock?* [Munich: Kosel-Verlag, 1978], 143ff. and 211–12) or as mere "solidarity" (see Edward Schillebeeckx' *Jesus: An Experiment in Christology* [New York: Crossroad, 1981], 310).

An adequate response to this camp must shed light on the question as to why God's merciful love does not one-sidedly effect forgiveness but calls for the atonement of sins. It must uphold the biblical claims while making the mystery of atonement sufficiently transparent to the mystery of God who is *caritas*, and, in the first place, to the mystery of the Father.

Toward a biblical and Trinitarian theology of atonement

Enough has been said to show that there are problems associated with the doctrine of the Cross event as atonement. In our judgment, the nub of the problem lies in the heart of the mystery of God. For this reason, our study will bypass such preliminary areas as the history of religion and culture, philosophical ethics, and related juridical categories. We will focus instead on discerning the hidden "theo-logic"[13] of atonement in Sacred Scripture. Our aim will be to illuminate the mystery of atonement chiefly against the backdrop of God, the Holy Trinity.[14] In endeavoring to do so, we will take seriously the declaration of the *Catechism of the Catholic Church* that "the mystery of the Most Holy Trinity is the central mystery of Christian faith and life . . . the source of all the other mysteries of faith, the light that enlightens them" (no. 234). All the mysteries of faith are rooted in the mystery of the Holy Trinity and therefore somehow have a Trinitarian structure.[15]

---

[13] By the term "theo-logic" we mean an intelligibility, purposefulness, and meaningfulness that derive from the mystery of God, the Holy Trinity.

[14] See Hoffmann, "Atonement and the Sacred Heart", 144–45.

[15] Balthasar, in one of his earliest works, urged that "*all* the theological tractates be given a Trinitarian form". *Razing the Bastions*, trans. Brian McNeil

Additionally, our study will keep in view a set of two criteria: one objective and the other subjective. The objective criterion is rootedness in God's revelation; the theology of atonement presented here should be derived from what God has revealed of this mystery. At the same time, the subjective criterion is governed by the experiences and needs of believers and unbelievers today.[16] Since the Cross event is a perennial challenge to faith (Simon Peter himself stumbled over the *skandalon* of the Passion predictions—Mt 16:22), every generation needs re-presentations of the mystery that are faithful to divine revelation and at the same time are expressed in ways that take into account the culturally transmitted dispositions that are either points of openness or obstacles to faith.

To guide us in this endeavor is a group of four theologians who are masters at this: John Paul II, Joseph Ratzinger/Benedict XVI, Hans Urs von Balthasar, and Norbert Hoffmann. Their approach draws from the riches of Scripture and Tradition, most notably from the theological tradition of the Fathers of the Church (both Greek and Latin). At the same time, they have an eye on their contemporaries, those for whom they are writing and to whom they are preaching. And above all, in articulating a theology of atonement, they depend on the assistance of the Holy Spirit. For without the Spirit's presence, not only in themselves but also in their au-

---

(San Francisco: Ignatius Press, 1993), 29. Our main concern, then, is not to attempt to standardize the use of theological terminology but to sketch a theological understanding of atonement that is sufficiently illuminated by the mystery of the Trinity.

[16] I am indebted to Roch Kereszty, O.Cist., for his clear and concise articulation of these criteria; see his book *Jesus Christ: Fundamentals of Christology*, revised and updated ed. (New York: Alba House/A Communio Book, 2002), 327.

dience, any faith-based articulation may seem to be nothing more than a mental construct.

The unity of a theology and spirituality of atonement

The Holy Spirit's presence is crucially important to the way in which our four guides approach theology. All are extraordinary representatives of the renewal of Catholic theology in the twentieth century. Ratzinger, Balthasar, and Hoffmann are distinguished members of the *ressourcement* movement,[17] while John Paul II (along with Benedict XVI) appropriate the best of this movement in their papal teaching, especially as it contributes to the pastoral exposition of doctrine.

One of the key features of the *ressourcement* movement is its commitment to the unity of theology and sanctity. The two are meant to interpenetrate and mutually determine each other. Theology provides a sure orientation by which to follow the Lord on the path of sanctity; conversely, the lived experience of sanctity aids theology as a means of confirming and verifying—and even enriching—its grasp of revealed truth.[18]

Our study deliberately situates itself within this theological movement and adopts its commitment to the unity of theology and holiness. It recognizes that a theology of

[17] Still, it is notable that Balthasar does not simply identify his theological mission with the *ressourcement* movement but aligns himself most closely with those "who are overwhelmed by the Word of God in the way the beloved is overwhelmed by the declaration of the lover". Among these he mentions by name Louis Bouyer and Heinrich Schlier. Quoted in Rodney A. Howsare, *Balthasar: A Guide for the Perplexed* (London: T&T Clark, 2009), 33.

[18] "If dogma is the perfect norm of all spiritual life, it is only because the authentic spiritual life is nothing other than dogma *in actu*." Henri de Lubac, quoted in Hans Urs von Balthasar, *In the Fullness of Faith*, trans. Graham Harrison (San Francisco: Ignatius Press, 1988), 56.

atonement is simply not faithful to the economy of salvation unless it places the revelation of this mystery at the service of the fulfillment of the divine intention that human beings participate in the atoning mission of Christ. The Church Fathers refer to this as the tropological or moral sense of Scripture, and thus of divine revelation. Divine revelation that is not internalized and lived is in fact not fully known in the biblical sense of "to know", that is, to experience, to become one with. This claim is movingly expressed by Saint Paul, when he prays "that Christ may dwell in [our] hearts through faith; that [we], rooted and grounded in love, may have strength to comprehend with all the holy ones what is the breadth and length and height and depth, and to know the love of Christ that surpasses knowledge, so that [we] may be filled with all the fullness of God" (Eph 3:17–19). Divine revelation in its biblical form is fully known insofar as "one 'lives through' and 'suffers through' the sacred text."[19] This is why, for our four guides, the spiritual life as participation in the mystery of Christ is vital to any complete interpretation of Scripture.[20]

In this light, our study intends to be a contribution to the pastoral goal of overcoming the split between the faith that people profess and the life that they lead. This is the goal to which Balthasar and Hoffmann contributed as Catholic theologians, and that both John Paul II and Benedict XVI

[19] Benedict XVI, *Jesus of Nazareth*, vol. 1, 78.

[20] "There is no authentic spirituality that does not put dogma into action. Nor is there, on the other hand, a mystery to believe in that does not have its translation, its repercussion or even its 'culmination' in the soul. Of the life, death, and Resurrection of the Savior, it must be said: 'All these things are done so that the Christian life might be conformed to him' (Origen, *In Jesu Nave*). Understood in this way, tropology becomes 'spiritual meaning' par excellence." Henri de Lubac, *Theological Fragments*, trans. Rebecca Howell Balinski (San Francisco: Ignatius Press, 1989), 117–18.

indefatigably pursued during their pontificates. Accordingly, everything contained in their theology of atonement is meant to speak to the permanently valid concern that we become "imitators of God as beloved children, and live in love as Christ loved us and handed himself over for us as a sacrificial offering to God" (Eph 5:1–2). If today our condition of estrangement from God, self, society, and the natural world is experienced with particular intensity, then the message that "in Christ" we may now turn the suffering of estrangement into the means of a marvelously deep communion with God and with our neighbor is indeed *Good* News. This is the conviction behind Benedict XVI's impassioned question: "Is it not a grace to be able to participate in the sufferings of Christ, uniting oneself to the action with which he took unto himself our sins in order to atone for them?"[21] And is it not lamentable that today many Christians seem not to recognize the opportunities to participate in Christ's mission of atonement?

The structure of this study

On the basis of the above reflections, it is entirely appropriate that the notions, imagery, and patterns of thought employed in our account of atonement are drawn primarily from divine revelation and the spiritual life. These patterns and images will provide a framework within which we can make prominent certain features of the Trinity's saving activity that might otherwise be overlooked or underplayed. Since a theology of atonement ought to start from what is central to divine revelation as set down in Sacred

---

[21] Benedict XVI, *Christmas Message to Catholics living in the Middle East Regions* (December 21, 2006).

Scripture, we will begin by surveying the biblical data. First (in chapter 1), we will examine the Old Testament to identify factors integral to the process of atonement, and we will explain how these factors fit together. Along the way, we will highlight the patrogen(n)etic structure of this process.[22] Then (in chapter 2), we will discuss how, in the Cross event, the Old Testament process of atonement is "raised to the height of a 'Trinitarian event'".[23] The mystery of the Son's mission from the Father to bear away the sin of the world will become more coherent—if also more marvelous —when we see the lines that converge upon it from the old alliance. Finally (in chapter 3), we will draw out the tropological or moral sense of Scripture and show that God, the Holy Trinity, is not content simply to love us. The Triune God loves in such a way as to enable us to love in turn, and not just in imitation of him, but as participating in the power of his divine love. The theology and spirituality of

---

[22] We use the term "patrogen(n)etic" as defined by R. Schulte in "Die Heilstat des Vaters in Christus", *Mysterium Salutis*, vol. 3/1 (Einsiedeln, Germany: Benziger Verlag, 1967), 53: "In view of the trinitarian and christological structure of the entire order of creation and salvation . . . it is helpful to use the dual term 'genetic/gennetic,' familiar to us from the trinitarian controversies, and to apply it, albeit now in a reverse direction, i.e., from the point of view of God *the Father*, to all things as proceeding from him, the *ex quo omnia*: God the Father is the source of the Word, the Son, whom he begets (*gennao*) . . . and thus the Son's relation to him is seen to be 'patrogennetic'. . . . But since God the Father is always the *ex quo omnia* with regard to creation, it follows that all created reality must be seen and understood in a 'theogenetic,' indeed 'patrogenetic' way. . . . Clearly, then, every person and thing must be held to be patrogen(n)etic (*ad intra* as well as *ad extra*), dependent on God the Father as their origin and originator." Quoted in Hoffman, "Atonement and the Sacred Heart", 172n183.

[23] International Theological Commission (hereafter ITC), "Select Questions on Christology (1979)", in *International Theological Commission: Texts and Documents, 1969–1985*, ed. Michael Sharkey (San Francisco: Ignatius Press, 2009), 200.

atonement that emerges from our study will show that being begotten of God by grace in this sin-marred world inevitably involves us in the Son's mission of atonement. Indeed, we should become convinced of the atoning efficacy and value that can attach to the sufferings and sacrifices of everyday Christian existence. And we should be able to appreciate that our participation in the atoning mission of Christ, far from obscuring the Father's face, actually redounds to the greater glory of God.

As regards the style of our approach, it may be helpful to compare it to a fugue, that is, to a musical composition in which one or more themes (musical patterns) are repeated by successively entering voices at different pitches. As a fugue develops a musical pattern by interweaving different voices reiterating the essential elements, so our study develops a theological pattern of atonement by continuously interweaving the articulations of our four main guides. The pattern (with its essential notions and imagery) will appear in analogous ways at different stages of salvation history: beginning with the Old Testament, advancing to the New, and emerging in the experience and wisdom of the saints.[24]

[24] This approach as practiced by our four main guides is discerning of and resembles the process by which the various texts of Scripture gradually unfold the inner potentialities of their revelatory content. This process is explained by Benedict XVI in *Jesus of Nazareth*, vol. 1, xviii–xix. "The unity of Scripture", he says, "is not simply imposed from the outside on what is in itself a heterogeneous ensemble of writings. [Rather, Scripture is forged by means of a] process of constant rereading of the words transmitted in the Bible. Older texts are re-appropriated, reinterpreted, and read with new eyes in new contexts. They become Scripture by being read anew, evolving in continuity with their original sense, tacitly corrected and given added depth and breadth of meaning. This is a process in which the word gradually unfolds its inner potentialities, already somehow present like seeds, but needing the challenge of new situations, new experiences and new sufferings, in order to open up. This process is certainly not linear, and it is often dramatic, but

Since what our study endeavors to produce is an account of atonement that synthesizes the principal ideas and convictions of our group of four theologians, it stands to reason that we will not be intent on magnifying and analyzing whatever variations may be discernible among them. Variations will be noted but without interrupting the harmonious arrangement under development. Even so, we will not take for granted but rather take pains to show that the harmony of thought among our quartet is real, sustained, and significant. In fact it will become clear that key positions taken here are affirmed and promoted in the papal encyclicals and catechetical audiences of John Paul II and Benedict XVI. Indeed, we consider this study an opportunity to preserve and pass on their theological legacy, precisely at a moment when their legacy is sometimes misrepresented and even caricatured. By providing ample evidence of what our group of four actually teaches about atonement, we can set the record straight—not only in fairness to them, but also in service of the ongoing assessment of their theology.

One final word. Despite the many references to our four main guides, this study is not another work in which a theologian talks primarily about other theologians. To the contrary, it is a work of theology that is unabashedly God-centered, as our guides would have it. It is concerned above all with the glory of God in view of God's gracious involvement on our behalf. And it wants to press home that God's glory continues to be represented in and to the world as we ourselves are configured to Christ's pattern of love.

---

when you watch it unfold in light of Jesus Christ, you can see it moving in a single overall direction; you can see that the Old and New Testaments belong together.''

I

Atonement in the Old Testament

In agreement with our four guides, we espouse the conviction that redemption from sin is essentially a mystery that must ultimately be interpreted by God—or, as the *Catechism* insists, illuminated by the mystery of the Holy Trinity. If we are to arrive at an adequate understanding, therefore, we must allow the Triune God's self-revelation in biblical history to shed light on this mystery. And since the Old and New Testaments in the Bible form an indissoluble unity, we will take as our basis the New Testament interpretation of the Cross event together with its presuppositions in the Old Testament. The event of Christ's Cross did not irrupt suddenly and altogether abruptly into biblical history—like a lightning bolt that struck "out of the blue". There was a preparation for it in Israel's covenant history with God. Indeed, the New Testament sees the Cross event as the historical *culmination* of God's saving action, which should prompt us to look back to the Old Testament to identify precursors to the Cross of Christ. If, in combing through the Old Testament, we can identify constant factors in connection with the process of eliminating sin, these factors may enable us "to go beyond the mere fact of the Cross event, subject as it is to a variety of interpretations, to see what is actually going on deep down within it".[1]

---

[1] Norbert Hoffmann, "Atonement and the Spirituality of the Sacred Heart", in *Faith in Christ and the Worship of Christ*, ed. Leo Scheffczyk, trans. Graham Harrison (San Francisco: Ignatius Press, 1986), 147.

Still, as we proceed, we must be ever mindful that since we are contemplating a mystery, our human thoughts and language can never completely fathom the depths of its content or exhaust it in images and formulae. Nor should this contemplation be undertaken in the realm of abstract analysis alone, remote from the insights gained by means of the concrete experience of Christian discipleship. Benedict XVI, with his flair for clarity and beauty of expression, puts it like this:

> In living out the Gospel and in suffering for it, the Church, under the guidance of the apostolic preaching, has learned to understand the mystery of the Cross more and more, even though ultimately it is a mystery that defies analysis in terms of our rational formulae. The darkness and irrationality of sin and the holiness of God, too dazzling for our eyes, come together in the Cross, transcending our power of understanding. And yet in the message of the New Testament, and in the proof of that message in the lives of the saints, the great mystery has become radiant light.[2]

Here at the threshold of our exploration of biblical revelation regarding this mystery, we are reminded of the vital unity and interdependence of theology and sanctity.

Three factors integral to the process of atonement

When our group of theologians examines the way in which eliminating sin is concretely portrayed in the Old Testament,[3] they find three constant factors in a process that

---

[2] Benedict XVI, *Jesus of Nazareth*, vol. 2, *Holy Week*, trans. Philip J. Whitmore, (San Francisco: Ignatius Press, 2011), 240.

[3] We shall start with a fairly general notion of atonement as "a way of eliminating sin". See Hoffmann, "Atonement and the Sacred Heart", 146n25.

involves the interplay of freedom between God and his covenant partner.[4] Two factors are found on God's side; a third factor lies on the side of God's covenant partner.[5]

God's sovereign initiative

On God's side, atonement for sin is the result of (1) *his own sovereign initiative*. God is the one whose actions are decisive, not only in making atonement possible, but in originating the covenant itself.[6] A brief glance at Deuteronomy reveals that the covenant derives from God's election of this particular people, "for which no reason can be given (Deut 7:6–7), without any merit on the people's part (9:6; 8:17), on the basis of love alone (7:8; 10:15)."[7] It is a love that in initiating the covenant, focuses on mutuality with an unswerving

---

[4] See Hoffmann, "Atonement and the Sacred Heart", 147–48, 156. Balthasar says as much in *Theo-Drama: Theological Dramatic Theory*, vol. 4, *The Action*, trans. Graham Harrison (San Francisco: Ignatius Press, 1994), 229 and 262 (hereafter *TD4*).

[5] The consistency of the appearance of these three factors indicates that the process of eliminating sin may well have this threefold form. In "Atonement and the Sacred Heart", 146n35, Hoffmann acknowledges that "a detailed examination is needed to ascertain whether this presentation of the Old Testament concept of atonement, at the level intended, is correct." Gerhard von Rad, *Old Testament Theology*, vol. 1 (New York: Harper & Row, 1965), 269: "What were the special features of the concept of expiation in the Old Testament? . . . No adequate answer has as yet been given." On the many forms taken by the Old Testament phenomenon of "forgiveness", see Walther Eichrodt, *Theology of the Old Testament*, vol. 2 (Louisville, Ky.: Westminster John Knox Press, 1967), 443ff.

[6] See Fritz Maass, "Sühnen", in *Theologisches Handwörterbuch zum Alten Testament*, vol. 1 (Munich: Chr. Kaiser Verlag, 1984), 842–57.

[7] Hans Urs von Balthasar, *The Glory of the Lord: A Theological Aesthetics*, vol. 6, *Theology: The Old Covenant*, trans. Brian McNeil and Erasmo Leiva-Merikakis (San Francisco: Ignatius Press, 1991), 155 (hereafter *GL6*). See Jon D. Levenson, *The Love of God: Divine Gift, Human Gratitude, and Mutual Faithfulness in Judaism* (Princeton: Princeton University Press, 2016), 42–46.

commitment (Deut 6:5; cf. Ex 6:7; Lev 26:11ff.). Consequently, the relationship that God establishes can live only
by the dynamic process of "word and answer, love and re-
ciprocating love, directive and obedience".[8]

When the answer of obedient love is not given, God himself provides the means for the restoration of the covenant
relationship. Joseph Ratzinger highlights this factor as follows: "In other world religions, expiation usually means the
restoration of the damaged relationship with God by means
of expiatory actions initiated on the part of men. Almost all
religions center around the problem of expiation." In the
Bible, however, God restores the damaged relationship "on
the initiative of his own power to love, by making unjust
man just again . . . through his own creative mercy."[9]

Presupposed here is that sin is not simply excused or
passed over by God; it is not forgiven by God in unilat-
eral fashion without making right that which went wrong.
Rather, in biblical revelation, forgiveness is carried out "not
as 'mere forgiveness' but as atonement."[10] God initiates a
process involving atonement as the means whereby sins shall
be forgiven (cf. Ex 29:35–37; Lev 1:3–4; Heb 9:22). This
process, moreover, has a patrogenetic structure: the work

---

[8] Balthasar, *GL6*, 155.

[9] Joseph Ratzinger, *Introduction to Christianity*, trans. J. R. Foster (San Francisco: Ignatius Press, 2004), 282.

[10] Romano Guardini, *Der Herr* (Mainz: Matthias Grünewald Verlag, 1937),
358. Quoted in Hoffmann, "Atonement and the Sacred Heart", 201n317.
See Benedict XVI, *Jesus of Nazareth*, vol. 2, 214; Hans Urs von Balthasar,
Theo-Drama: Theological Dramatic Theory, vol. 3, *Dramatis Personae: The Person of Christ*, trans. Graham Harrison (San Francisco: Ignatius Press, 1992),
118 (hereafter *TD3*). Also Hoffmann, "Atonement and the Sacred Heart",
157–58; Eichrodt, *Theology of the Old Testament*, vol. 2, 443–48, 453; and
Khaled Anatolios, *Deification through the Cross: An Eastern Christian Theology
of Salvation* (Grand Rapids. Mich.: Eerdmans, 2020), 113–14.

of atonement will ultimately originate from and be engendered by God's own power to love.

God's passionate involvement

In addition, on God's side, atonement for sin entails (2) *his passionate involvement* with his covenant partner. The fact that God, out of a free initiative, guarantees the covenant as the utterly sovereign Lord does not contradict the fact that he "courts the trust of the people with living warmth of feeling and looks for a response that is spontaneous and from the heart".[11] The covenant relationship is the privileged place where God reveals his profound passion of love —his "burning and tender love"[12]—for his chosen partner.

According to J. Levenson, professor of Jewish studies at Harvard University, the language of God's passion of love pervades the Hebrew Scriptures. Of special import is Deuteronomy 7:7-8: "The LORD set his heart on you and chose you. . . . It was because the LORD loved you." The verb translated here as "set his heart on" is *ḥašaq* in Hebrew. This verb (and its associated noun, *ḥešeq*) can be reasonably interpreted as "indicating a love of a particularly intense and passionate character".[13] Thus Israel's status as God's covenant partner "is owing to God's love for them, the fact that he conceived a passion (*ḥašaq*) for them, as it were".[14] Indeed one of Levenson's key claims is that the

[11] Walther Eichrodt, *Theology of the Old Testament*, vol. 1, (Louisville, Ky.: Westminster John Knox Press, 1961), 52.

[12] Balthasar, *GL6*, 240. See also Hans Urs von Balthasar, *Engagement with God: The Drama of Christian Discipleship*, trans. R. John Halliburton (San Francisco: Ignatius Press, 2008), 13-15.

[13] Levenson, *The Love of God*, 176 and 42; see also Deut 10:15.

[14] Levenson, *The Love of God*, 48.

love that God manifests toward his covenant partner, the
people Israel, is a matter of "two dimensions, the active and
the affective". Conceptions of God's covenantal love that
try to separate these dimensions result (more or less) in an
anemic biblical theology.[15]

When, moreover, God's love is rebuffed or betrayed, the
Old Testament tells us that God can be hurt thereby. He suffers the passion of an injured love, comparable to a husband
abandoned by his unfaithful wife (Hos 2) and to a father in
the face of his disobedient and ungrateful children (Is 1:2;
30:9). Isaiah 63:9–10 tells us that "in all their affliction he
[YHWH] was afflicted. . . . But they rebelled and grieved
his holy Spirit."[16] The eleventh chapter of Hosea is particularly poignant in this regard: "When Israel was a child, I
loved him; out of Egypt I called my son. The more I called
them, the farther they went from me. . . . Yet it was I who
taught Ephraim to walk, who took them in my arms. . . . I
drew them with human cords, with bands of love; I fostered
them like those who raise an infant to their cheeks. . . . My
heart is overwhelmed" (Hos 11:1–4, 8). God's passionate
involvement, furthermore, takes the form of anger at the
injustices, wickedness, and hardness of heart on men's part
(Ex 32:7–14; Deut 4:25; 6:15; Is 33:14; Zeph 1:18; Zech
8:2). Israel's infidelity "provokes" the Lord, "stirs" him; "a
fire is kindled by my anger, and it burns to the depths of
Sheol" (Deut 32:21–22, RSVCE).[17] This anger on God's
part, however, is not an irrational, blameworthy, or ego-

---

[15] Ibid., 91; see also 132–38; 173–78.

[16] Translation from the Revised Standard Version, Catholic Edition (San
Francisco: Ignatius Press, 2006). Hereafter RSVCE.

[17] See Hoffmann, "Atonement and the Sacred Heart", 149; Balthasar, *GL*6,
48; Alfons Deissler, "Gottes Selbstoffenbarung im Alten Testament", in *Mysterium Salutis*, vol. 2 (Einsiedeln, Germany: Benziger Verlag, 1967), 267ff.

driven emotion but identical with God's fundamental character of love and righteousness.[18] To be sure, God's affective involvement with his covenant partner is expressed also
as joy and delight (Is 62:4-5). As we read in the Book of
Jeremiah: "Is not Ephraim a precious son to me, my de-
lightful child? Though I often speak against him, I remember him lovingly still. This is why I yearn for him, why I
have great compassion for him," says the Lord (Jer 31:20,
RSVCE). With good reason, therefore, Hoffmann concludes
that God's passion of love stands at the "innermost center
of the testimony intended in the Old Testament".[19]

If, at first glance, these characteristics of God—mercy and
compassion, but also love, kindness, long-suffering, and zeal-
ous commitment (among others)—seem to eliminate God's
transcendent otherness since they are found in the sphere of
human relationships, yet it is not to be forgotten that they are
attributed to the One who, as the only God (Is 43:10-12),
is not a being in the world alongside other beings whose
influence he therefore would have to endure unwillingly.
God's sublime transcendence, in the eyes of Israel's faith,
is seen primarily in the fact that he condescends to become
involved with his covenant partner such that he voluntarily assumes the implications of covenantal reciprocity, yet
without being changed, either for better or worse, by that
involvement.[20]

Inevitably, this raises the theological question of whether
and in what respect God can be said to suffer. Since God's

[18] See Balthasar, *TD*4, 344; and Abraham J. Heschel, *The Prophets* (New
York: HarperCollins, 1969), 219.

[19] Norbert Hoffmann, *Kreuz und Trinität: Zur Theologie der Sühne* (Einsiedeln, Germany: Johannes Verlag, 1982), 22. See Balthasar, *GL*6, 234 and
257.

[20] See Balthasar, *GL*6, 177.

passionate involvement is a factor in the theology of atonement under development here, we will pause to clarify
adequate and inadequate ways in which suffering can be
attributed to God. For this we turn to a document of the
International Theological Commission, "Theology, Christology, Anthropology".[21] Here the ITC lays down the parameters of legitimate theological speculation concerning this
issue. We can summarize these parameters in three points.

1. God is *not passible* (not naturally subject to suffering)
in that God is not subject to suffering by way of being in-
voluntarily overpowered from the outside. Neither is God
passible insofar as the term signifies being subject to blameworthy passions (such as unbridled anger, envy, and disor-
dered love).[22]

2. God is *not mutable* (not naturally subject to change) by
way of increasing or decreasing in perfection (cf. Jas 1:17).
"God has no need whatever for creatures (cf. DS 3002)",[23]
and hence God has nothing to gain or lose by involving himself with us. Saint Thomas Aquinas puts it this way: "God
in himself neither gains nor loses anything by the action of
man."[24]

3. Nevertheless, "God loves us with the love of friend-
ship, and he wishes to be loved by us in return. When this
love is offended, Sacred Scripture speaks of suffering on the
part of God. On the other hand, it speaks of his joy when

[21] ITC, "Theology, Christology, Anthropology", in *International Theological Commission: Texts and Documents, 1969–1985*, ed. Michael Sharkey (San
Francisco: Ignatius Press, 2009), 224–27.

[22] See ibid., p. 225, no. 3.

[23] Ibid., p. 225, no. 4.1.

[24] Thomas Aquinas, *Summa theologica*, trans. Fathers of the English Domini-
can Province (New York: Benziger Brothers, 1947), I-II, q. 21, a. 4, ad 1
(hereafter *ST*). See *ST* I, q. 9, a. 2; and ITC, "Theology, Christology, Anthropology", p. 226, no. 4.1.

the sinner is converted (cf. Lk 15:7)."[25] Furthermore, Scripture everywhere speaks of God's compassion toward human beings. At issue here is an affective involvement that stems entirely from God's un-needy and selfless initiative. It is precisely because God has nothing at stake for himself that he, in loving human beings, can involve himself in suffering without this capacity signaling any lack or imperfection of his being. Equally important is the fact that God, in full control of his passion of love (*passio caritatis*), remains sovereignly active in and wholly unhampered by whatever "passion" he would freely endure.[26]

The ITC brings its document to a close by observing that God's unchanging perfection and God's *passio caritatis* are "two aspects [that] need each other. If one or the other is neglected, the concept of God as he reveals himself is not respected."[27]

In the years following the publication of this document, the papacy champions a theology that holds together these two aspects. John Paul II, for instance, maintains that God,

[25] ITC, "Theology, Christology, Anthropology", p. 226, no. 4.2. "One could often suppose from the Old Testament, the divine transcendence notwithstanding (cf. Jer 7:16–19), that God suffers because of the sins of men. Perhaps not all the expressions can be explained as simple anthropomorphisms. . . . Rabbinic theology is even stronger in this respect and speaks, for example, of a God who abandons himself to lamentation because of the [broken] Covenant . . . or because of the destruction of the Temple. . . . In the New Testament, the tears of Jesus (cf. Lk 19:41), his anger (cf. Mk 3:5), and the sadness he feels are themselves also manifestations of a certain way of behavior on God's part. In other places it is stated explicitly that God gets angry (cf. Rom 1:18; 3:5; 9:22; Jn 3:36; Rev 15:1)." Ibid., 224–25.

[26] ITC, "Theology, Christology, Anthropology", p. 226, no. 5.1. See Norbert Hoffmann, "Atonement and the Ontological Coherence between the Trinity and the Cross", in *Towards a Civilization of Love*, ed. International Institute of the Heart of Jesus (San Francisco: Ignatius Press, 1985), 234.

[27] ITC, "Theology, Christology, Anthropology", p. 226, no. 4.2; see also p. 216, no. 3.

36   *Atonement*

in the sovereign freedom of his passion of love, allows himself to be pained on account of sin. The pontiff asserts this boldly and unambiguously in his encyclical *Dominum et vivificantem* (*On the Holy Spirit in the Life of the Church and the World*):

> 39. It is not possible to grasp the evil of sin in all its sad reality without "searching the depths of God." . . . [If the world is to be convinced concerning sin (cf. Jn 16:8–9), it will] have to mean revealing suffering. Revealing the pain, unimaginable and inexpressible, on account of sin [which Scripture, notwithstanding certain anthropomorphic formulations] seems to glimpse in the "depths of God" and in a certain sense in the very heart of the ineffable Trinity. The Church, taking her inspiration from Revelation, believes and professes that sin is an offense against God. What corresponds, in the inscrutable intimacy of the Father, the Word and the Holy Spirit, to this "offense," this rejection of the Spirit who is love and gift? The concept of God as the necessarily most perfect being certainly excludes from God any pain deriving from deficiencies; but in the "depths of God" there is a Father's love that, faced with man's sin, in the language of the Bible reacts so deeply. . . . [Furthermore] the Sacred Book speaks to us of a Father who feels compassion for man, as though sharing his pain. In a word, this inscrutable and indescribable fatherly "pain" will bring about above all the wonderful economy of redemptive love in Jesus Christ . . . in whose humanity the "suffering" of God is concretized.[28]
>
> 41. If sin caused suffering, now the pain of God in Christ crucified acquires through the Holy Spirit its full human expression. Thus there is a paradoxical mystery of love: in Christ there suffers a God who has been rejected by his own creature: "They do not believe in me!"; but at the same

---

[28] John Paul II, encyclical letter *Dominum et vivificantem* (May 18, 1986), no. 39. Hoffmann concurs: "The 'consequences' of sin extend to the Heart of God." "Atonement and the Sacred Heart", 165.

time, from the depth of this suffering . . . the Spirit draws a new measure of the gift made to man and to creation from the beginning. In the depth of the mystery of the Cross, [divine] love is at work, that love which brings man back again to share in the life that is in God himself.[29]

Straightaway, we should notice that John Paul II situates God's "fatherly 'pain'" in the face of sin, understood as the rejection of God's love. This "fatherly 'pain'" is not only divine compassion in view of the miseries that sin causes in the world of men; it is also "fatherly 'pain'" on account of the separation that sin brings about in God's covenant relationship with men.

Next we note that John Paul II is careful to qualify the way in which God suffers in the face of sin. Clearly he does not limit this suffering to the human nature taken up by God the Son at his Incarnation but traces it back to "the depths of God", to the very heart of the Holy Trinity: to "the inscrutable intimacy of the Father, the Word and the Holy Spirit". At the same time, he insists that this "pain" in God's Heart does not spring from any lack or need. Instead, it derives from God's nature as absolute Trinitarian love (*caritas*). This love God graciously offers to men, and it remains unchangeably perfect even in the face of men's rejection. Indeed, the God who *is* love proves he can suffer in such a way that far from being incapacitated or weakened, his passionate love is *actively at work* and in reality "reveals itself as stronger than sin. So that the 'gift' [of divine love] may prevail!"[30]

[29] John Paul II, *Dominum et vivificantem*, no. 41. "*God* expressed his faithful and *passionate* love for sinful humanity to the point of" the Paschal Mystery. John Paul II, "The Spirit's Presence in the Paschal Mystery" (General Audience, June 10, 1998), in *The Trinity's Embrace: God's Saving Plan: A Catechesis on Salvation History* (Boston: Pauline Books & Media, 2002), 70.

[30] John Paul II, *Dominum et vivificantem*, no. 39.

In yet another of his encyclicals, *Dives in misericordia* (*Rich in Mercy*), which is devoted to the mystery of God the Father, John Paul II affirms that the loving Father suffers in a divine manner when his beloved children distance themselves from him. In the parable of the prodigal son, he says, "the son had not only squandered the part of the inheritance belonging to him but had also hurt and offended his father. . . . It was bound to make him [the father] suffer. It was also bound to implicate him in some way. After all, it was his own son who was involved. . . . There is no doubt that in this simple but penetrating analogy the figure of the father reveals to us God as Father."[31]

Here the pope envisions an analogical relation between human and divine modalities of suffering love. The suffering of love that John Paul II highlights is much more a divine quality that we find imperfectly and distantly echoed in the heart of man than a human quality projected onto God.[32] This position is reinforced in *Dominum et vivificantem*, where he asserts that God's inscrutable "fatherly 'pain'" acquires "its full human expression"—indeed is "concretized"—in the humanity of the crucified Son.

[31] John Paul II, encyclical letter *Dives in misericordia* (November 13, 1980), nos. 5–6.

[32] By the same token, the pope refuses to ascribe univocally to God the suffering of love as creatures experience it. Of course, the unlikeness between divinity and humanity is infinitely greater than the likeness, yet the likeness is not eliminated. As the ITC puts it: "Just as 'compassion' is among the most noble human perfections, it can be said of God that he has a similar compassion without any imperfection and in an eminent degree." "Theology, Christology, Anthropology", p. 225, no. 5.1. Eastern Catholics often quote in this context a passage from Isaac the Syrian: "From the strong and vehement mercy which grips [the holy man's] heart and from his great compassion . . . he offers up tearful prayer continually . . . even for the enemies of the truth and those who harm him. . . . [This he does] because of the great compassion that burns without measure in his heart in the likeness of God." Homily 71, in *The Ascetical Homilies of Saint Isaac the Syrian* (Boston, Mass.: Holy Transfiguration Monastery, 1984), 344–45.

Significantly, in this regard the scope of analogical relation expands to include not only the likeness that reigns between the divine nature and human nature (the infinite ontological difference notwithstanding), but also the likeness that reigns between divine fatherhood and divine sonship (their difference as personal modes or manners of existence notwithstanding).[33] God the Son, after all, is distinguished from God the Father in light of his filial manner of divine existence, which Scripture describes as being the perfect image or reflection or exegesis of the Father (cf. Col 1:15; 2 Cor 4:4–6; Heb 1:3; Jn 1:18). Thus, if the Son assumes a human nature and "suffer[s] in the flesh" for us (1 Pet 4:1), he thereby reveals something of the mystery of the Father's love for men. In other words, the Son's passion of love as man in bearing the sin of the world is not simply the human expression of the Son's divine love; it is just as truly the human expression of the Father's passion of love in enduring man's sin, which it is the Son's mission to reveal or "concretize" as man.[34] (We will explain this point further in chapter 2.)

---

[33] See Hans Urs von Balthasar, *Theo-Logic: Theological Logical Theory*, vol. 2, *Truth of God* (San Francisco: Ignatius Press, 2004), 315–16. Here we also draw on the Trinitarian theology of the Cappadocian Fathers and Maximus the Confessor, who use the language of "mode of existence" and "manner of existing" to refer to what distinguishes the three divine Persons/Hypostases from each other.

[34] This finds support in *CCC* 470: "Christ's human nature belongs, as his own, to the divine person of the Son of God, who assumed it. Everything that Christ is and does in this nature derives from 'one of the Trinity.' The Son of God therefore communicates to his humanity *his own personal mode of existence in the Trinity* [= his filial way of being divine]. In his soul as in his body, Christ thus expresses humanly the divine ways of the Trinity (cf. Jn 14:9–11)." See also Hans Urs von Balthasar, *Epilogue*, trans. Edward T. Oakes (San Francisco: Ignatius Press, 2004), 89–90; and Angela Franz Franks, "Trinitarian *Analogia Entis* in Hans Urs von Balthasar", *The Thomist* 62 (1998): 533–59.

Noteworthy too is Ratzinger's position articulated in an essay on the Sacred Heart.

> In the period of the Fathers it was doubtless Origen who grasped most profoundly the idea of the suffering God and made bold to say that it could not be restricted to the suffering humanity of Jesus but also affected the Christian picture of God. The Father suffers in allowing the Son to suffer,[35] and the Spirit shares in this suffering, for Paul says that he groans within us, yearning in us and on our behalf for full redemption (Rom 8:26f.). And it was Origen also who gave the normative definition of the way in which the theme of the suffering God is to be interpreted: *When you hear someone speak of God's passions, always apply what is said to love. So God is a sufferer because he is a lover*; the entire theme of the *suffering* God flows from that of the *loving* God and always points back to it. The actual advance registered by the Christian idea of God over that of the ancient world lies in its realization that God is love.[36]

Further on in the same essay, Ratzinger offers an interpretation of the eleventh chapter of the Book of Hosea that provides light by which to understand his later remarks on Hosea in his papal encyclical *Deus caritas est*. Here he de-

---

[35] Naturally, this stance is not to be mistaken for "patripassianism", which is a brand of modalism.

[36] Joseph Ratzinger, *Behold the Pierced One: An Approach to a Spiritual Christology*, trans. Graham Harrison (San Francisco: Ignatius Press, 1986), 57–58, emphasis added. In note 11, Ratzinger refers to several Catholic thinkers whose treatment of the question of the suffering of God he recommends. Listed first is Jean Galot's "important book" *Dieu souffre-t-il?* (Paris: P. Lethielleux, 1976). Next he recommends Balthasar's discussion in *Theo-Drama: Theological Dramatic Theory*, vol. 5, *The Last Act*, trans. Graham Harrison (San Francisco: Ignatius Press, 1998), 239–46 (hereafter *TD5*). He mentions as well "a remarkable treatise" by Jacques Maritain entitled "Quelques réflexions sur le savoir théologique", *Revue Thomiste* 77 (1969): 5–27. Finally, he promotes John Paul II's *Dives in misericordia*.

scribes Hosea 11 as "the Canticle of the Love of God",[37] in which "the drama of the divine Heart" is revealed.[38] This drama is centered on "the pain felt by God's Heart on account of the sins" of his people, which amount to their rejection of his love. In the face of this rejection, "God ought to revoke Israel's election . . . but 'My heart recoils within me, my compassion grows warm and tender' [Hos 11:8]."[39] God's love proves undiminished despite exposing itself to heartache. From this vantage point, Ratzinger directs us to see that "the pierced Heart of the crucified Son is the literal fulfillment of the [Hosean] prophecy of the Heart of God." Indeed "here [in the Cross event] we see the upheaval in the Heart of God as God's own genuine Passion. It consists in God himself, in the person of his Son, suffering Israel's rejection." Hence, for Ratzinger, "we can only discern the full magnitude of the biblical message of the Heart of God, the Heart of the divine Redeemer, in this continuity and harmony of Old and New Testament."[40] (Unmistakably

[37] Heinrich Gross, "Das Hohelied der Liebe Gottes: Zur Theologie von Hosea 11", in *Mysterium der Gnade*, eds. H. Rossman and J. Ratzinger (Regensburg: Verlag Friedrich Pustet, 1975), 83–91, quoted by Ratzinger, *Behold the Pierced One*, 62.

[38] Ratzinger, *Behold the Pierced One*, 64.

[39] Ibid., 63.

[40] Ibid., 64. Reinforcing our exegesis of Ratzinger's thought is a homily he gave on December 12, 2003, entitled "God's Weeping and the Promise of Victory", in which he highlights God's almighty love manifesting the capacity to suffer our rejection: "God suffers. Why does he not impose his way on his creature with the strength of his omnipotence? . . . Because he does not want to obtain anything by force, but desires love . . . and thus leaves us our freedom to say yes to his offering . . . or else to say no. . . . Man says no and even ridicules this weak God who seeks his consent. . . . Hence God's sadness and suffering." Joseph Ratzinger/Benedict XVI, *On Love: Selected Writings*, trans. Michael J. Miller (San Francisco: Ignatius Press, 2020), 25–26. Cf. Hans Urs von Balthasar, *The Glory of the Lord: A Theological Aesthetic*, vol. 7,

Ratzinger is very close to John Paul II's teaching in *Dominum et vivificantem*.)

Decades later, Pope Benedict XVI makes the revelation of God's Heart—God's passion of love—a central theme of his first encyclical *Deus caritas est* (God Is Love):

> The one God in whom Israel believes . . . loves with a personal love. His love, moreover, is an elective love: among all the nations he chooses Israel and loves her. . . . God loves, and his love may certainly be called *eros*, yet it is also totally *agape*. . . .[41]

> We have seen that God's *eros* for man is also totally *agape*. This is not only because it is bestowed in a completely gratuitous manner, without any previous merit, but also because it is love which forgives. Hosea above all shows us that this *agape* dimension of God's love for man goes far beyond the aspect of gratuity. Israel has committed "adultery" and has broken the covenant; God should judge and repudiate her. . . . Nonetheless, "How can I give you up, O Ephraim! How can I hand you over, O Israel! . . . My heart recoils within me, my compassion grows warm and tender" (Hos 11:8). . . . God's *passionate* love for his people—for humanity—is at the same time a *forgiving* love. . . .

> [O]n the one hand we find ourselves before a metaphysical image of God: God is the absolute and ultimate source of all being; but . . . [God] is at the same time *a lover with all the passion of a true love*. *Eros* is thus supremely ennobled,

---

Theology of the New Covenant, trans. Brian McNeill (San Francisco: Ignatius Press, 1989), 35 (hereafter *GL7*).

[41] When biblical theology says that in God's un-needy and selfless generosity there is a desiring and erotic dimension, it is acknowledging that the height of God's love for his covenant beloved is realized in a spiritual embrace. Pseudo-Dionysius, for instance, talks extensively about *eros* and jealousy as divine names in *De Divinis Nominibus*.

yet at the same time it is so purified as to become one with *agape*.[42]

To be sure, Benedict XVI and John Paul II want to pre-serve divine impassibility (*apatheia*): the idea that God is not naturally subject to *pathos* (*pathos*, for the Church Fathers, "means involuntary suffering imposed from the outside or as a consequence of fallen nature").[43] Yet they are equally concerned with rendering the notion of divine impassibil-ity compatible with God's self-revelation in biblical history. For them, it is ultimately the Cross event that compels us to deepen our understanding of God's way of being impassible. A notion of God's impassibility that was not informed by the drama of salvation history would fail to present the *full* dimensions of this divine attribute. After all, God reveals himself in definitive fullness only in the unique event of Christ's life, death, and Resurrection. If theological reflec-tion is to do justice to God's self-revelation, it must let itself be governed by the christological narrative. This means that

---

[42] Benedict XVI, encyclical letter *Deus caritas est* (December 25, 2005), nos. 9–10, emphasis added. See also Levenson, *The Love of God*, 172–78; and Fran-cis de Sales, *Treatise on the Love of God* (Rockford Ill.: TAN Books, 1997), 81–85. In the patristic era, Pseudo-Dionysius observed that there are places in Scripture where the biblical writers regard *agape* and *eros* as equivalent. "To those who listen carefully to divine things, the term *agape* is used by the sacred writers in divine revelation with the exact same meaning as the term *eros*." *De Divinis Nominibus* 4.12. Quoted by Robert Louis Wilken, *The Spirit of Early Christian Thought: Seeking the Face of God* (New Haven, Conn.: Yale University Press, 2003), 309.

[43] The decision of the early Church Fathers to apply the term "impassi-bility" (*apatheia*) to the biblical God was directed against pagan mythologi-cal representations of capricious and changeable deities subject to suffering. See ITC, "Theology, Christology, Anthropology", p. 225, no. 3; and John-Pierre Batut, "Does the Father Suffer?", *Communio: International Catholic Re-view* 30.3 (Fall 2003): 390.

it will not suffice to define divine attributes (like impassibility) apart from the revelation of God in Christ Jesus.

Consider, for instance, how Benedict XVI takes his stand beneath the Cross and, in beholding the Pierced One, discerns that God's true omnipotence is manifest in his omnipotent suffering of love. "In the Face of the Crucified Christ, we see *God* and we see true omnipotence, not the myth of omnipotence. . . . In him *true omnipotence is loving to the point that God can suffer*: here his true omnipotence is revealed, which can even go as far *as a love that suffers for us. And thus we see that he is the true God*."[44] For Benedict, just as omnipotence is an attribute of divinity, so too its authenticating characteristic (*ad extra*) "as a love that suffers for us" is here attributed to divinity. In Benedict's view (shared with John Paul II),[45] this capacity—to love to the point of suffering on our account—belongs to the nature of the Triune God and not only to the human nature assumed by the Son. Indeed, the latter is the consummate manifestation of the former.[46] What Benedict sees as a key to discerning "the newness of the Christian concept of God" is the insight that the Son's passion of love in human form is not merely a condescension that disguises or obscures the divine glory; rather, it is truer to regard it as a dramatic in-person "face" or image of the glory of God (2 Cor 4:4–6; Jn 1:1–18; 1 Jn 1:1–2).[47]

[44] Benedict XVI, Address to the Pontifical Roman Seminary (February 12, 2010), emphasis added.

[45] "God's omnipotence is manifested precisely in the fact that he freely accepted suffering. . . . The Man of Sufferings is the revelation of that [divine] love which 'endures all things' (1 Cor 13:7)." John Paul II, *Crossing the Threshold of Hope*, trans. Jenny McPhee and Martha McPhee (New York: Alfred A. Knopf, 1994), 65–66.

[46] See Benedict XVI's Message for Lent 2007.

[47] Indeed, to recognize "the newness of the Christian concept of God" is to perceive "an intimate *passion* in God . . . that even constitutes his

Accordingly, both Benedict XVI and John Paul II go beyond the question whether God is impassible to the question of *the character* of God's impassibility. Seen in the light of the crucified Son, divine impassibility is manifest as God's omnipotent passion of love: the strength of divine love to endure all things without the slightest impairment. This characterization perceives the consistency of the Passion of Christ with the general biblical character of God's passionate love for humanity. If Christ, the Son of God, assumed the role of the Suffering Servant, this was done in accordance with his filial way of being divine—as the Image of the Father. Indeed, for these popes, the Cross event sets forth both the humanity and the divinity of Christ. It sets forth the humanity inasmuch as it was enacted by the Son through his human nature: the Son as man handed himself over to sinners, was crucified, and died as expiation for our sins. But the Cross event also sets forth the divinity of the Son inasmuch as it characterizes the power of love freely to bear all things (1 Cor 13:7–8) as consistent with God's all-powerful passion of love.[48]

---

true essence: *love*." Joseph Ratzinger, *Mary: The Church at the Source*, trans. Adrian J. Walker (San Francisco: Ignatius Press, 2005), 77. Admittedly, Benedict spends little time spelling out a metaphysical explanation of the mystery of God's impassible passion of love. For him what matters most is to meditate on the mystery of God by gazing on Christ crucified, and in the light of christological revelation to re-envision the divine attributes (without circumventing the *via negativa*). In our judgment, Benedict's theological method and aims resemble those of Gregory of Nyssa. See Khaled Anatolios, *Retrieving Nicaea: The Development and Meaning of Trinitarian Doctrine* (Grand Rapids, Mich.: Baker Academic, 2018), 196–98.

[48] I am applying here a method of theological discernment that closely resembles how Anatolios explains Athanasius' perception of the self-humbling love *of God* in view of its characterization in the self-humbling (kenotic) love of Christ *as man*. See Anatolios, *Retrieving Nicaea*, 123. This method finds support in *Dives in misericordia*, no. 6, where John Paul II applies 1 Cor 13:7–8

Discernible in the theology of our pontiffs is an application of patristic thought as it unfolds the logic of the wondrous exchange and reversal accomplished through the Cross event. This logic is summarized by the patristic theologian Khaled Anatolios as follows:

> Through Christ, human suffering becomes perfectly transparent to divine compassion such that the incapacity of this [human] suffering is enfolded by the perfect capacity of divine compassionate love. . . . In this way, we can understand Christ's compassionate suffering as applicable to *both* the divine and human natures, preserving the distinction between them, while affirming their communion or "running together" [= Chalcedon's 'συντρεχούσης'] for our salvation.[49]

Plainly, John Paul II and Benedict XVI (as well as Balthasar and Hoffmann) advance a notion of divine impassibility that is thought anew in light of God's self-revelation in biblical history and consequently is understood in a qualified sense. For them, God is capable of "suffering" as long as we stress that God preserves his sovereignly free initiative of pure charity (in which *eros* and *agape* coincide) and remains active in and unhampered by suffering. It is never a question of attributing ontological deficiency or negativity to God but of perceiving that the interpersonal form of divine activity is such that it can integrate passion positively. If God leaves his creatures free to reject his love, nonetheless, their rejection does not render God less perfect. For God's passion of love in the face of sin is only a voluntary modality of the

---

to the interior form of the Father's love, seeing it as love that "endures all things" and "never ends".

[49] Khaled Anatolios, "The Soteriological Grammar of Conciliar Christology", *The Thomist* 78, no. 2 (April 2014): 165–88, 184–85.

pure *actio* of absolute *caritas* that constitutes God's essence. Precisely because the Triune God is perfect *caritas* in and of himself, eternally and immutably, there is an unchangeable basis in God for the salvific change God brings about through the compassionate suffering of Christ for love of us.[50] (See appendix B for a survey of patristic sources that are consonant with the teaching of our four guides on God's impassible passion of love.)

Man's willing collaboration in the process

The third constant factor in the Old Testament process of eliminating sin lies on the side of God's covenant partner. Atonement for sin requires (3) *man's participation and willing collaboration*.

As we have seen, in the vision of the Old Testament, God's passionate love for Israel is utterly gratuitous; it is given without any previous merit on Israel's side.[51] But as Levenson observes, gratuitousness "does not mean normlessness". While God's passionate covenantal love originates as sheer gratuity, "it must also harbor moral expectations within it . . . one obvious expectation of genuine love [is] that it be reciprocal."[52] So although God remains faithful to Israel even when his beloved breaks the covenant, God's fidelity includes his firm insistence that Israel live up to the terms of the alliance. Thus, the covenant relationship is

[50] More yet, if the God of biblical revelation is both immutable and capable of suffering impassibly vis-à-vis his covenant beloved, the roots of this possibility should be traceable to the mystery of the inner-Trinitarian Fatherhood of God. See Margaret Turek, *Towards a Theology of God the Father: Hans Urs von Balthasar's Theodramatic Approach* (New York: Peter Lang Publishing, 2001), 154–88.

[51] See Benedict XVI, *Deus caritas est*, no. 10; and Balthasar, *GL6*, 155.

[52] Levenson, *The Love of God*, 54–55.

both unconditional and conditional. It is unconditional in that God's love comes into and remains at play even when nothing has been done to earn it. "But the relationship is also conditional", says Levenson, "in that it involves expectations and stipulations, and [degenerates] if they are not met."[53] As for these stipulations and ethical obligations, they boil down to the chief commandment of unreserved love for God, which is expressed with astounding radicality in Deuteronomy 6:4–9.[54]

Yet we would be wrong to think that once God initiates this interplay of love, God's covenant partner is on his own as to his appropriate response. For God gives love in such a way that he not only leaves room for but also empowers his covenant partner to love reciprocally. Hence the covenant is two-sided only because of the generative nature and aim of God's love. It is a love intent on engendering mutuality already in its self-donation. Indeed, the love that the beloved gives to God in return is always *God-engendered* love, *filial* love—love that *depends on and derives from* the love it has first been shown.[55]

But there is still more to it. The beloved's return of love is not only derivative; it is also imitative. The response that God engenders is filial love that mirrors or imitates God's archetypal or exemplary love.[56] Consider, for instance, that

[53] Ibid., 61. As Levenson notes on p. 37: "The relationship is still explicitly one of love; though it is not marked by equality, it is still marked by profound reciprocity." Balthasar agrees: "Grace is given freely and unconditionally on God's side; [yet] since man's election gives him . . . ethical obligations, he must make an appropriate response." *TD*4, 228.

[54] See also Deut 10:12–13; 11:13; Mt 22:37–38; Mk 12:28–34; Lk 10:27.

[55] Of course, if God tenders love to creatures, he does so without neediness, with nothing to gain for himself thereby. What is at stake here is solely the beloved's perfection, not God's own.

[56] On the imitative character of Israel's covenantal love, see Ex 22:21; Deut 5:15; 10:17–19; 15:14–15; 16:11–12; Lev 11:44–45; 11:4; 19:2; in the New

it is because God elects Israel out of love without motive (Deut 7:7–9), which bespeaks the selflessness proper to the transcendent Lord, that Israel is summoned to a response of love without reserve (Deut 6:5)—the mode of selflessness proper to God's chosen beloved. More precisely, the filial love to which Israel is summoned consists above all in obedience. As Balthasar observes, "The response 'I will' resounds through all its songs of praise",[57] professing Israel's grateful resolve to glorify God through a life of filial obedience. "Over the abyss of apparent inadequacy, the [divine] archetype continues to be active in the image. . . . [I]t is God's Spirit who is taking pains to interiorly shape [God's chosen 'son' into] the 'man after God's own heart' (1 Sam 13:14)."[58]

With this we arrive at the heart of Israel's vocational identity. Israel is called by God to function as his living image, willingly to mirror or resemble in action the divine archetype. The "Ten Words" or Decalogue (Deut 4:13; 5:22) are essentially instructions on how the people's conduct must be shaped to be considered authentically "godly". By making room for God's Spirit in order to obey these divine instructions, Israel fulfills itself as God's living image and thereby gives glory to God.[59] (This, Balthasar suggests, is the primary reason "Israel is not permitted to make for itself any carved image of God."[60]) We can see here that God's self-revelation in word and deed intends to engender in his beloved a manner of loving that obediently imitates

---

Testament, see Mt 5:48; Jn 5:19–20; 1 Pet 1:15–16; Eph 5:1. See also Levenson, *The Love of God*, 105.

[57] Balthasar, *GL6*, 204.

[58] Ibid., 109.

[59] See Balthasar *GL6*, 15 and 64; and John Paul II, *Man and Woman He Created Them: A Theology of the Body* (Boston: Pauline Books, 2006), 163.

[60] Balthasar, *GL6*, 211; see also 89–91.

and thereby glorifies the God and Father of Israel. Consequently "sin", in the biblical sense, bears a weight that goes beyond the tragic self-ruination of the covenant partner. Sin opposes God's self-glorification in the world through the life-testimonial of the one chosen to be his filial image. Seen from this angle, sin is a defacing of God, a falsifying of his glory by the people called to be God's "sons".[61]

All the same, sin need not finally thwart God's aim to engender in his covenant partner a filial love that mirrors and thus glorifies the true character of the all-powerful God. Biblical history shows that when Israel sins, God remains faithful to his covenantal love but also respectful of the freedom of his partner. There must be an *interplay*—evincing reciprocal love—in the redemption of his beloved from sin: between *divine* freedom, on whose side lies the initiative and ultimate power over sin, and *human* freedom—a freedom that has been impaired but not eradicated by sin. As we shall see, God indeed has the initiative in what concerns the work of atonement, yet what God initiates is a patrogenetic process whereby he engenders his beloved's willing collaboration in wiping sin away.[62]

The Old Testament notion of sin

According to the Old Testament, sin is not simply an ethical fault. It is not simply a failure to act according to the natural law inscribed in every conscience. There is more to it, for the proper setting in which to understand sin is the

[61] See Balthasar, *GL6*, 16; *GL7*, 271; and cf. Num 27:14; Deut 32:51; Is 29:23.
[62] See Balthasar, *TD4*, 318; Hoffmann, "Atonement and the Sacred Heart", 148–49; and Levenson, *The Love of God*, 97 and 108.

covenant relationship. Already in the old alliance, the fervent emphasis on keeping the commandments signifies nothing less than Israel's response of grateful love expressed in actions. "Good deeds become acts of personal fidelity, faithfulness to the personal God", explains Levenson, "and not simply the right things to do within some universal code of ethics (though they may be that as well). Conversely, bad deeds become acts of betrayal. . . . They are not simply morally wrong in the abstract: they wrong the divine covenant partner."[63] Consider, for instance, the Lord's response to the sin of David, which the prophet Nathan communicates to the king in 2 Samuel 12:7–9.

> Thus says the LORD God of Israel: I anointed you king over Israel: I delivered you from the hand of Saul. I gave you your lord's house and your lord's wives for your own. I gave you the house of Israel and of Judah. And if this were not enough, I could count up for you still more. Why have you despised the LORD and done what is evil in his sight? You have cut down Uriah the Hittite with the sword; his wife you took as your own, and him you killed with the sword of the Ammonites.

Sin, therefore, is a failure to respond with grateful love and righteous conduct to the goodness of the Lord. It is manifest in transgressions (deeds) that bespeak a deliberate turning away from God.[64] Sin is fundamentally a refusal to see and mirror the character of God, whose deeds show his paternal presence and benevolence (Ex 4:22–23; Deut 4:37;

---

[63] Levenson, *The Love of God*, 14 and 59. Aquinas says that the guilty character of sin consists in the fact that it is committed against God. See *ST* III, q. 46, a. 2, ad 3.

[64] Hence Aquinas says: "The essence of guilt consists in voluntarily turning away from God." *ST* II-II, q. 34, a. 2. See also *ST* I-II, q. 84, a. 2.

7:8). It is a refusal to hear and to live according to the words that God personally addresses to his chosen beloved (Zeph 3:2; Bar 1:15–22). As Balthasar points out, "The particular transgressions against the commandments . . . are only the results of a fundamental evil, namely, a falling away from the covenant relationship, betrayal, disobedience, culpable forgetfulness of God, the sinful failure to 'know God'."[65] Sin as deed is thus unmasked as a refusal to exist in intimate co-existence with God. Sin indicates a spurning of the Lord's love; it is a forsaking of God (Hos 1:2, 9; 4:10; Is 1:2, 4).[66]

Moreover, sin is committed by someone whom God regards as his beloved son or child. "I am a father to Israel, Ephraim is my firstborn" (Jer 31:9).[67] Sinners are "children who refuse to listen" (Is 30:9); "their hearts are far from" God (Is 29:13); indeed sinners hide from the Lord (Is 29:15); they rebel against and desert God (Hos 7:13; Dan 3:29–30). They are "unmindful of the Rock that begot" them; they "forg[e]t the God who gave [them] birth" (Deut 32:18; cf. v. 20). "Hear, O heavens, and listen, O earth, for the LORD speaks: Sons I have raised and reared, but they have rebelled against me! . . . They have forsaken the LORD, spurned the Holy One of Israel" (Is 1:2, 4; cf. Hos 8:3).

As a consequence of persistent sin, the covenant relationship is ruptured, and sinners exist in a state of estrange-

---

[65] Balthasar, *TD4*, 174. See *GL6*, 215–16; *TD5*, 275; and *Engagement with God*, 20–21. See also John Paul II, "The Demanding Love of God the Father" (General Audience, April 7, 1999) in *The Trinity's Embrace*, 94; and John Paul II, apostolic exhortation *Reconciliatio et paenitentia* (December 2, 1984), no. 14.

[66] See Hos 2; 11:1–11; 2 Kgs 17:6–23; Is 63:16; 64:7; Jer 31:9; Deut 32:6, 18; Mal 2:10. See also Levenson, *The Love of God*, 101; and *CCC* 386.

[67] In addition, see Ex 4:22; Deut 14:1; 32:1–43; Is 43:6; 45:11. "It is worthy of note that the metaphor of father and son . . . is very much present in Deuteronomy, the book containing the Shema and its commandment to love the LORD your God with all your heart' (6:5; 11:13)." Levenson, *The Love of God*, 20.

ment from God—and God, on his side, is forsaken.[68] If the primary sinful *deed* is idolatry (the first commandment proscribes forsaking the Lord by turning toward idols), the primary *effect* of sin is distance from God, alienation from the Lord.[69] To be sure, other (worldly) effects are acknowledged: exile, hardships, and innumerable ways in which sinners suffer alienation internally and externally. Undeniably, the baneful effects of sin are not limited to the time span of the deed itself. Sin's effects do not simply disappear once the sinful conduct ceases, but the effects continue on; they perdure. The biblical scholar Gary Anderson observes that "the act of wrongdoing has put in motion consequences that not even contrition can wholly undo."[70] In any case, the effects and consequences of sin extend beyond the sinner and beyond the power of the sinner to correct.[71]

Here let us note what the *Theological Dictionary of the Old Testament* has to say about the effects of sin.

---

[68] "The theological message [of the prophets] is essentially the same: Israel's behavior has gravely ruptured their intimate relationship with God." Levenson, *The Love of God*, 112. According to Eichrodt, above all it is the prophets who "convey that the annulment of a wholly personal relationship between God and man" is the chief "punishment". *Theology of the Old Testament*, vol. 1, 432. "The divine love that woos a return of love from man must make it plain that to reject God's love is to forfeit the only salvation." Ibid., 433. And thus they "deal out evil to themselves" (Is 3:9). See Balthasar, *GL6*, 165.

[69] "Actus peccati facit distantiam a Deo." Aquinas, *ST* I-II, q. 86, a. 2, ad 3.

[70] Gary Anderson, *Charity: The Place of the Poor in the Biblical Tradition* (New Haven: Yale University Press, 2013), 119. Anderson adds in note 11: "The reach of sin is long indeed. Not even contrition is sufficient to wipe away its effects completely."

[71] "Of course the deed is done and cannot be undone. But what has been perpetrated and set in motion by it transcends both the deed and the doer and has somehow acquired an existence of its own, so that, whether or not the perpetrator's subjective will has undergone a change, it is *there* now and is continuing to exert a 'power proper to it' in the sinner and in his world, affecting God too. This is the sin that must be . . . 'carried away'."

In the theological reflection of exilic and post-exilic prophecy, . . . the suffering of man, whether it be the individual or the nation, is ultimately and properly separation
from God. In affliction at the hand of enemies, in sickness, and in nearness to death, he experiences remoteness
from God and abandonment by him at the deepest level.
The prophets recognize that the reason for this is sin. . . .
[They recognize too that] only God's free intervention (Is
65:18; Ez 36:26–28) can overcome the intolerable situation of man's separation from God through sin and renew
the heart of man.[72]

In summary, the Old Testament notion of sin is a com-
plex reality consisting of three dimensions: (1) the inner disposition of the evildoer (disobedience, infidelity, callous indifference), (2) the evil deed (the transgression), and (3) the
consequent punishments or effects (chiefly, distance from
God).[73]

Atonement is the bearing of sin in filial love-suffering

As noted above, the situation of separation from God brought
about by sin is not eliminated simply by ceasing to do wrong.
If sin is to be effaced, sin must be "converted" in all three

---

Hoffmann, "Atonement and the Sacred Heart", 150. See also Benedict
XVI, *Jesus of Nazareth*, vol. 1, *From the Baptism in the Jordan to the Transfigu-
ration*, trans. Adrian J. Walker (New York: Doubleday, 2007), 158; John Paul
II, apostolic letter *Salvifici doloris* (On the Christian Meaning of Suffering)
(February 11, 1984), no. 15; and "The Demanding Love of God the Father"
(General Audience, April 7, 1999), in *The Trinity's Embrace*, 194.

[72] Hans Ferdinand Fuhs, *Theological Dictionary of the Old Testament*, vol. 3
(Grand Rapids: Wm. B. Eerdmans Publishing Co., 1974–1975), 207. See
John Paul II, "Fight Evil and Sin" (General Audience, August 18, 1999), in
The Trinity's Embrace, 242–43.

[73] See Hoffmann, "Atonement and the Sacred Heart", 149; von Rad, *Old
Testament Theology*, vol. 1, 265; Eichrodt, *Theology of the Old Testament*, vol.
2, 426; Anatolios, *Deification through the Cross*, 116.

of its dimensions. The sinner must (1) turn *back* his heart toward God, (2) turn *away* from the evil deed(s), and (3) turn *around* the effects of sin.

This threefold process hinges on the disposition of the heart, which turns back to God with the inducement of God's grace. Then, due to his change of heart, the sinner ceases to commit the sinful deed(s). Yet more needs to be done. The converted sinner still has to bring his regenerated love to bear on the effects of sin.[74] Sin is not merely walked away from; sin must be "borne away".[75] Indeed the image of "bearing away" sin is central in the Old Testament.[76] We must note that the "original meaning of *nasa awon* ('to bear away sin' in Hebrew) is not to 'take away' or 'remove' guilt, but . . . to take it *upon* oneself and 'carry' it", to endure its effects or consequent punishments (Hos 13:16, RSVCE; Ezek 4:1–8).[77] Insofar as one is animated by the love of God in bearing the effects of sin, this suffering is expiatory; it is a means whereby forgiveness of sins and reconciliation with God are accomplished.

Levenson provides support for this understanding with

---

[74] See Aquinas, *ST* III, q. 22, a. 3.

[75] Hoffmann, "Atonement and the Sacred Heart", 150; and *Sühne: Zur Theologie der Stellvertretung* (Einsiedeln, Germany: Johannes Verlag, 1981), 23. See John Paul II, *Reconciliatio et paenitentia*, no. 4; and Eichrodt, *Theology of the Old Testament*, vol. 2, 423n8.

[76] Gary Anderson notes that within the Hebrew Bible, the idiom "to bear sin" "predominates over its nearest competitor by more than six to one". *Sin: A History* (New Haven, Conn.: Yale University Press, 2010), 17. See also Christian Mihut, "Bearing Burdens and the Character of God in the Hebrew Bible" in *Character: New Directions from Philosophy, Psychology, and Theology* (Oxford: Oxford University Press, 2015), 369.

[77] Alfons Deissler, "Hingegeben für die Vielen", in *Mysterium Salutis*, vol. 2 (Einsiedeln, Germany: Benziger Verlag, 1967), 341. Quoted in Hoffmann, "Atonement and the Sacred Heart", 150n59. The word *awon* can mean offense, guilt (incurred by offense), or punishment (consequences of offense), depending on the context. Also see von Rad, *Old Testament Theology*, vol. 1, 271.

reference to the midrash given by Rabbi Akiva in *Siphre Deuteronomy 32*. Rabbi Akiva's midrash centers on the figure of King Manasseh, son of King Hezekiah. Manasseh is "an evildoing king", whereas his father, Hezekiah, "is a doer of good . . . and a patron of Torah as well." Significantly, although Manasseh must have learned the Torah from his devout father, it evidently "availed him not"; the royal son became a sinner. Yet after all his sinning, Manasseh entreated the Lord and humbled himself before the God of his fathers (2 Chr 33:12). What, asks Rabbi Akiva, "brought about this reversal, making a righteous man out of a sinner, as the study of Torah obviously did not? It was the suffering Manasseh endured at the hands of the enemies of Israel, who captured him and led him off in manacles and fetters to exile in Babylon." Having to face the consequences of sin spurred Manasseh to come to his senses, such that he opened his heart to receive God's gracious regeneration of filial love. Thereby Manasseh's suffering, undergone in pious submission, was enabled to have a positive expiatory effect. And this resulted in God restoring the king to his throne in Jerusalem. "Hence," Rabbi Akiva concludes, "precious is suffering."[78]

Keep in mind that the disposition of the heart is crucial. Only someone whose heart has turned back to God can suffer sin through to its elimination. Only someone converted from sin can "convert" sin's effects in bearing them.[79] God indeed insists upon conversion, yet not only

[78] Levenson, *The Love of God*, 77. According to the midrash on the love of God in *Siphre Deuteronomy 32* (New York: Jewish Theological Seminary, 1969), without expiatory suffering "no sin will be forgiven." In fact, "sufferings expiate even more than sacrifices." Quoted by Levenson, *The Love of God*, 76. See N. T. Wright, *Jesus and the Victory of God* (Minneapolis, Minn.: Fortress Press, 1996), 583n172.

[79] See Hoffmann, *Kreuz und Trinität*, 24.

in the sense of a re-turning of the heart toward him, and not simply in terms of ceasing the misdeeds, but also in the manner of bearing the effects of sin as an expression of filial love.[80]

Here we need recall that the principal effect of sin is distance from God. Suffering through this separation can be called filial love-suffering, when distance from God is experienced as heartache. For only a heart inspired with a renewed love for God will bear God's distance as painful.

In this connection, let us look at Daniel 3:29–43, which affirms that such love-suffering would carry the same atoning efficacy as sin-offerings.[81] Scholars point to this text as one in which a sequence of steps, moving from sin to reconciliation, is laid out clearly and in concentrated form.[82]

[29] For we have sinned and transgressed
by departing from you,
and we have done every kind of evil.

[80] See Hoffmann, *Sühne*, 26; and Eichrodt, *Theology of the Old Testament*, vol. 1, 164. Anderson recognizes that "sins require not just forgiveness but transformation." *Charity*, 179.

[81] Most scholars date this text between 167 and 164 B.C. The actual *geographical* setting where this text was written is Palestine; the Jewish exiles were liberated from Babylon more than three centuries before. Yet the *literary* setting of chapter 3 of Daniel is the Babylonian exile, which serves as a mirror in which the Palestinian Jews in Daniel's day are to interpret their situation: they are delivered over to their enemies, the Greeks. These verses (29–43) were translated from the Septuagint. The Roman Catholic Church regards them as part of the canonical Scriptures.

[82] See Jacob Neusner, *Judaism When Christianity Began* (Louisville, Ky.: Westminster John Knox Press, 2002); Martin Hengel, *Atonement: The Origins of the Doctrine in the New Testament* (Minneapolis, Minn.: Fortress Press, 1981); Odil Hannes Steck, *Israel und das gewaltsame Geschick der Propheten* (Neukirchen-Vluyn, Germany: Neukirchener Verlag, 1967), 184–86; Wright, *Jesus*, 269–71 and 576–77; John T. Carroll and Joel B. Green with Joel Marcus, *The Death of Jesus in Early Christianity* (Peabody, Mass.: Hendrickson Publishers, 1995).

³⁰ Your commandments we have not heeded or observed,
  nor have we done as you ordered us for our good.
³¹ Therefore all you have brought upon us,
  all you have done to us,
  you have done by a proper judgment.
³² You have handed us over to our enemies,
  lawless and hateful rebels;
  to an unjust king, the worst in all the world. . . .
³⁷ For we are reduced, O Lord, beyond any other nation,
  brought low everywhere in the world this day
  because of our sins.
³⁸ We have in our day no prince, prophet, or leader,
  no burnt offering, sacrifice, oblation, or incense,
  no place to offer first fruits, to find favor with you.
³⁹ But with contrite heart and humble spirit
  let us be received;
  As though it were burnt offerings of rams and bulls,
  or tens of thousands of fat lambs,
⁴⁰ So let our sacrifice [our spiritual sin-offering] be in your
    presence today
  and find favor before you;
  for those who trust in you cannot be put to shame.
⁴¹ And now we follow you with our whole heart,
  we fear you and we seek your face. . . .
  [With regenerated love we endure our state of
  God-forsakenness or God's wrath/self-concealment.]
⁴³ Deliver us in accord with your wonders,
  and bring glory to your name, O Lord.

The steps can be identified as follows: (1) The grave
sins (29–30) committed by God's covenant partner result
in (2) a state of separation from God for the nation and for
individuals (31–32, 37–38). Suffering this state conduces to

(3) repentance for sin (39). Here repentance requires nothing less than God's gracious intervention into the recesses of the human heart. Repentance, in turn, is the precondition of (4) atonement (40–41), which completes the process of (5) forgiveness and restoration (43).[83] Especially striking is how this text portrays sin as deserting the Lord, which results in a God-forsaken state; on the Lord's side, he responds to sin by concealing his face (an allusion to his wrath) such that he must be sought once more; the renewed desire to seek the Lord indicates repentance, which takes shape as the willingness to endure sin's consequences with contrite love; and precisely this love-suffering brings about atonement.

Consequently, a perspective is discernible in the Old Testament that sees the sinner's God-forsaken plight (which the sinner chose for himself by forsaking God) not merely as a state *from* which he would be delivered, but also paradoxically as a means *by* which that deliverance would be accomplished.[84]

In summary: Atonement involves "conversion", not simply in the sense of turning away *from* sin, but also the "conversion" *of* sin itself. The sinner turns back to God with filial love (regenerated by God; in this respect God is near), such that now he suffers the effects of sin (principally distance from God) with a repentant heart, and by bearing in love this sin-wrought distance, he turns sin around: away from a refusal of sonship to an occasion of asserting it. Atonement is a work of sonship that "cleanses" from sin (or "annihilates"[85] sin) by transforming sin into its opposite:

---

[83] See Neusner, *Judaism When Christianity Began*, 154; also Levenson, *The Love of God*, 27–28; 78–79; and Anderson, *Charity*, 132.

[84] See Wright, *Jesus*, 577, 581, and 591; and Balthasar, *GL*7, 45.

[85] To annihilate: to cause something to vanish or cease to exist by changing it into other forms; to destroy the substance of something.

nearness to God in the filial love-suffering of distance from God.[86]

Atonement is a process engendered by God

Atonement, as already noted, is a process initiated and enabled by the loving God. In order to appreciate this adequately, we need recall the first two factors integral to the process by which sin is annihilated.

God's sovereign initiative

While sin is atoned for by one who has turned back to God, nonetheless, this conversion can occur only by virtue of God's initial forgiveness as an antecedent gift of love that begets an answering love in the sinner's heart. "Such forgiveness", as Anatolios notes, "does not simply negate the need for repentance, but rather evokes and animates this repentance. . . . Instead of human repentance bringing about divine forgiveness, it is divine forgiveness that gives rise to human repentance."[87] Thus where God is concerned, the sinner's repentance does not occur merely as a result of some self-initiated "natural" reflection on the idea of a lenient God. It results principally from the self-communication of God, whose forgiving love causes the hardened heart to soften, without resorting to force (cf. Deut 30:6; Ezek 16:59–63; 36:23–32; Ps 80:19–20). God's prevenient, forgiving love enables the sinner to return to God, in order that sin can be borne under the power of fil-

---

[86] See Hoffmann, *Sühne*, 31; "Atonement and the Sacred Heart", 152–55; "Atonement and Coherence", 221.

[87] Anatolios, *Deification through the Cross*, 124. This order of causality—divine forgiveness giving rise to human repentance—is clearly present in the messages of exilic prophets (Hosea, Jeremiah, Ezekiel, etc.).

ial love. Hoffmann puts it this way: "It is only because of
the love the sinner has received in the (initial) forgiveness,
and in virtue of the 'initial conversion' wrought by it, that
he is able to 'bear' his sin under the form of [filial love-]
suffering."[88]

God's passionate involvement

Within the covenant relationship, God freely exposes his
"ardent passion" to suffering in the face of his beloved's
disobedience and infidelity.[89] Certainly there is no damage
to the perfection of the divine essence, but here we are in the
order of moral offense and an affective wounding of God's
passion of love. "When Israel was a child, I loved him, out of
Egypt I called my son. The more I called them, the farther
they went from me. . . . My heart is overwhelmed" (Hos
11:1–2, 8). For this reason, we should see that it is God
who is first to endure in love the absence of his beloved. It
is God who is first to let himself be forsaken in the mode
of a suffering love.

Further, inasmuch as the Lord's passionate love for Israel is paternal, it possesses a generative capacity: that is, a
power to engender or produce a mirroring response. It is
crucial to understand that what God "fathers" is a living
image of his manner of loving. This generative work involves the manifestation of divine glory: God's intimate and

[88] Hoffmann, "Atonement and the Sacred Heart", 155. "The disposition
to conversion comes as a gift and grace from God." Balthasar puts it thus:
"Repentance itself is due to the effective power of God's grace." In *TD*4,
166; see 176. See also *CCC* 1432 and 1989; and Levenson, *The Love of God*,
27–28.

[89] "God suffers under Israel's false love-affairs." Hans Walter Wolff, *Dodeka-
propheten* 1: *Hosea*, Biblischer Kommentar Altes Testament 14/1 (Neukirchen-
Vluyn, Germany: Neukirchener Verlag, 1961), 53, cited in Balthasar, *GL*6,
244. See also *GL*6, 235–36.

efficacious presence to his beloved.[90] Under the conditions
of a sin-ruptured relationship, the manifestation of divine
glory entails God's revealing to his beloved a paternal love
sufficiently powerful to be unfailing as it freely endures the
hurt of rejection and separation.[91] Indeed, the disclosure
of God's (paternal) love-suffering has a potent capacity to
evoke repentance, ignite filial love, and empower his partner
willingly to imitate and reproduce it in turn[92]—unto sin's
atonement. In other words, integral to the manifestation of
God's glory is the disclosure of God's suffering love, which
initiates and accompanies the whole process of atonement.

The power of God's suffering love to elicit a mirroring
response is at the root of the paradoxical character of this
process: in the one atoning, bearing sin as *distance from* God
is transformed into a mode of *nearness to* God. For sin as
separation is now borne in union with God whose suffering love is the *exemplar* and *source* of his partner's reciprocal
love-suffering as it bears sin away. In this light we can understand Hoffmann's claim that "atonement is most closely
correlated with YHWH's holy and injured love. It is this
love that brings itself to bear on the sinner. . . . God's love,
wounded by sin, corresponds in the sinner to atonement,
seen as sin transformed into the suffering of love."[93] Thus,
if earlier we showed that God takes the initiative in engendering his partner's free collaboration in wiping sin away,
now we see that in so doing, the beloved on his side reveals
God's power to shape his filial image under the conditions of

<hr />

[90] See von Rad, *Old Testament Theology*, vol. 1, 182.

[91] See John Paul II, *Dominum et vivificantem*, no. 39. Cf. Num 14:17–19; Ex
34:6–7; Hos 2 and 11.

[92] See Levenson, *The Love of God*, 138; cf. Anatolios, *Deification through the
Cross*, 95, 99, and 103–4.

[93] Hoffmann, "Atonement and the Sacred Heart", 154.

a sin-marred relationship. In effect, the converted sinner is rehabilitated as the living image of God, in whom the glory of God's forgiving love becomes visible in confronting and annihilating sin.

In summary: the grace of God's initial forgiveness gives rise to repentance, which enables God's beloved to atone for sin in such a way that he willingly (in the power of love) bears its essential consequence—separation from God. Since it is God who already endures a love-suffering on the sinner's account, the repentant beloved's role in atoning for sin is an engendered mirror image of God's role in delivering from sin. But let us be clear: if God aims to engender in his beloved a reciprocal willingness to suffer the separation brought about by sin, it is not a case of "tit for tat" (the vengeful infliction of suffering in return for what God endures). Rather, it is a matter of God generating in his beloved a capacity to reciprocate his passion of love by asserting filial love against sin, thereby bringing about his beloved's perfection and sin's elimination. For indeed the filial imaging of God's love-suffering is integral to the perfection of the beloved (be perfect as your heavenly Father is perfect [Mt 5:48; 1 Pet 1:15–16; Lev 11:4; 19:2], "be imitators of God, as his beloved children" [Eph 5:1])—this is the pattern of human freedom's greatest good—albeit under sin-wrought conditions. Thus it would be short-sighted to regard atonement as simply a penalty. It is truly a saving event and, equally so, an occasion for the glorification of God (albeit "east of Eden").[94]

---

[94] See von Rad, *Old Testament Theology*, vol. 1, 271; Hoffmann, "Atonement and the Sacred Heart", 154.

God's wrath as a modality of love

We have already acknowledged that a defective notion of divine wrath can get in the way of the biblical claim that God reveals himself to be love precisely in sending his Son as atonement for sin (1 Jn 4:8–10). Nonetheless, we may not simply ignore or cast aside the many biblical references to God's anger in both the Old and the New Testaments. As Balthasar recognizes: "The Old Testament perceptions of the divine 'wrath' (Rom 5:9) . . . and 'judgment' (Rom 8:3), which are taken up by Paul and the whole of the New Testament in speaking of the Cross, are not to be represented as superseded, anthropomorphic, and incompatible with the God of love who wills reconciliation (2 Cor 5:18; Col 1:20), for this reconciliation is to take place precisely '*through* the death of his Son' (Rom 5:10) . . . in his 'offering for sin' (2 Cor 5:21)."[95] Both Hoffmann and Balthasar tackle head on the subject of God's wrath while attempting to avoid two extremes: on one side, the stance that simply dismisses the biblical testimony to God's anger as primitive thinking; and on the other, the view that imagines God's wrath along the lines of the punitive rage of a celestial child abuser.

The course to take, we suggest, is to regard divine anger as an aspect of the second of the three factors integral to the process of atonement: namely, God's passionate involvement. This will entail striving toward a superior harmony in

[95] Balthasar, *GL7*, 204. The ITC does not condone a facile exegetical dismissal of God's anger. "In the New Testament . . . [Jesus'] anger (Mk 3:5) . . . [manifests] a certain way of behavior on God's part. In other places it is stated explicitly that God gets angry (Rom 1:18; 3:5; 9:22; Jn 3:36; Rev 15:1)." "Theology, Christology, Anthropology", p. 225, no. 4.2.

which every aspect of God's involvement in man's redemption is ultimately explained by God's passion of love.

Thus from the outset we must insist that God's wrath in the face of sin is not an independent power of destruction separate from or set in opposition to God's love.[96] Rather, God's wrath is the form that God's love takes when it encounters whatever is opposed to and threatens the designs of his love, designs that boil down to bringing his beloved to beatitude and perfection as God's true filial image.[97]

In agreement with Balthasar, yet with more consistency and explicitness, Hoffmann discerns that God's wrath and God's "suffering" love are two aspects of one and the same mystery of God's affective involvement with sinners. Indeed, a progression can be detected in the Old Testament in which portrayals of God's wrath appear more and more clearly in association with God's wounded love for sinners.[98] This suffering occurs when the recklessness with which God

[96] God's anger is the "obverse of his love for Israel". Johannes Fichtner, "Der Zorn Gottes im AT", in Gerhard Kittel and Gerhard Friedrich, eds., *Theologisches Wörterbuch zum Neuen Testament*, vol. 5 (Stuttgart: W. Kohlhammer Verlag, 1958), 410. See also 404 and 408. See Walther Eichrodt, "Zorn Gottes", in *Die Religion in Geschichte und Gegenwart*, vol. 6 (Tübingen, Germany: J. C. B. Mohr, 1930); and Hellmut Bandt, "Zorn Gottes IV: Dogmatisch" in Kurt Galling and Hans von Campenhausen, eds., *Die Religion in Geschichte und Gegenwart: Handwörterbuch für Theologie und Religionswissenschaft*, 3rd ed., vol. 4. (Tübingen: J. C. B. Mohr, 1960).

[97] See Balthasar, *TD4*, 344 and *Does Jesus Know Us—Do We Know Him?*, trans. Graham Harrison (San Francisco: Ignatius Press, 1983), 32 and 83; and Aidan Nichols, *Balthasar for Thomists* (San Francisco: Ignatius Press, 2020), 88. This stance has some commonalities with that of Jean-Hervé Nicolas, though the latter refrains from using the language of wrath and instead speaks of God's "severity", "Miséricorde et sévérité de Dieu", *Revue Thomiste* 94 (1988): 204–5.

[98] See Martin Bieler's biblical study of vicarious atonement, *Befreiung der Freiheit. Zur Theologie der stellvertretenden Sühne* (Freiburg im Breisgau, Germany: Verlag Herder, 1996), 155–72 and 208–29. See also Balthasar, *TD4*, 55.

loves his covenant partner encounters a freedom that instead of responding in kind to God's generosity and devotion, retreats into a calculating and guarded self-centeredness.[99]

Now, if indeed God's *wrath* is a modality of God's *love*, and if God's love is not revoked regardless of suffering rejection, it follows that the primary aim of God's wrath is to bring the sinner to conversion and reconciliation (as in Jer 33:5–10).[100] This notion is key to the Book of Isaiah, where divine wrath and divine judgment are virtually synonymous: "I will turn my hand against you, and refine your dross in the furnace, removing all your alloy. . . . Zion shall be redeemed by judgment [*mishpat*]" (Is 1:25, 27). According to Isaiah, redemption takes place *through* God's act of wrathful judgment; it "follow[s] on an event of divine judgment as its *telos*."[101] Redemption and wrathful judgment are not mutually exclusive categories here. Rather, redemption consists of the initiative of divine forgiveness, which operates *through* an event of divine judgment, or wrath, an event that counters the obstacle of sin thrown into the path of God's love. God answers the sinner's refusal to abide in his covenant grace with his own refusal to tolerate sin, for it is impossible that God should be a "father" to sin—that is, the archetype and generative source of sin (1 Jn 3:9). Hence,

---

[99] See Balthasar, *TD*4, 328.

[100] God's wrath "is that righteousness that is essentially oriented to salvation". Bernard Renaud, *Je suis un Dieu jaloux: Évolution sémantique et signification théologique de qineah* (Paris: Cerf, 1963), 148 (my translation). "Even the severest punishment" serves "the purpose of conversion". Eichrodt, *Theology of the Old Testament*, vol. 2, 459. God rebukes and punishes only to persuade the sinner "to create on his side the conditions necessary for forgiveness". Josef Scharbert, "Vergebung", in Heinrich Fries, ed., *Handbuch Theologischer Grundbegriffe*, vol. 2 (Munich: Kösel-Verlag, 1963), 742. Quoted by Hoffmann in "Atonement and the Sacred Heart", 151.

[101] Balthasar, *GL*6, 249. See also *GL*7, 33 and 47; and *TD*4, 176.

God brings about redemption with an unwavering passion of commitment to the covenant. The crucial point here is that God's wrath coincides with his zeal to carry out the work of his fatherly love even against sin: producing images of his own forsaken "Heart" whilst overcoming sin in all its consequences. This side of the eschaton, God's wrath serves his beloved's salvation.[102]

Moreover, if God's wrath is a modality of his love, and since God's love is always considerate of the freedom of his beloved, we can see why God's wrath can take the form of letting his partner "be" to his choice of forsaking him. Inasmuch as God takes the freedom of his beloved seriously, God lets his partner "be" to suffer his absence: the state of Godlessness that the sinner has chosen. The divine love that leaves the creature free to respond, in the event that it encounters an obstinate no, shows itself considerate of the creature's freedom by withdrawing and leaving the beloved alone (cf. Ps 27:9; Deut 32:19–20; Ezek 10).[103] Well, not quite. For God, who cannot be absent from any place, is able nonetheless to conceal his presence. Indeed, time and again in the Bible, God's anger is indicated when he hides his face:

---

[102] "God's anger only 'turns' or 'stands still' (2 Macc 7:38) when sin is overcome in all its consequences, when the sinner is finally 'cleansed' and 'healed' from sin, and forgiveness is fully achieved." Hoffmann, "Atonement and the Sacred Heart", 151. See Jer 24:5–7; 31:31–34; Ezek 36:24–26, 33. See also Scharbert, "Vergebung", 741; Eichrodt, *Theology of the Old Testament*, vol. 1, 160; Fichtner, "Der Zorn Gottes im AT", 408 (cf. Is 51:17, 22).

[103] See Psalm 27:9, where the psalmist associates God's anger with "hiding his face" and "forsaking" his servant. On God's anger in the form of self-concealment, see Hoffmann, "Atonement and the Sacred Heart", 154. On God's anger as the distancing of God from the sinner, see Hoffmann, *Sühne*, 59–60; Fichtner, "Der Zorn Gottes im AT", 402; Eichrodt, *Theology of the Old Testament*, vol. 2, 432.

Why do you make us wander, LORD, from your ways,
and harden our hearts so that we do not fear you?. . .
Indeed, you are angry; we have sinned, we have acted
wickedly. . . . For you have hidden your face from us and
have delivered us up to our crimes. Yet, LORD, you are our
father. (Is 63:17; 64:4, 6–7)

"For a brief moment I forsook you. . . . In overflowing
wrath I hid my face from you, but with everlasting love
I will have compassion on you," says the LORD, your Redeemer. (Is 54:7–8, RSVCE; cf. 8:17; 59:2; Ps 80:4–5)

[In my anger] I hid my face from this city because of all
their wickedness. Look! I am bringing the city recovery
and healing. . . . I will purify them of all the guilt they
incurred by sinning against me; I will forgive all their of-
fenses by which they sinned and rebelled against me. (Jer
33:5–8, cf. Bar 4:5–29)

In every case, observes Balthasar, "it is the sin of man which
is the cause of the concealment. However, . . . God's turning away is not simply the 'result' of sin, but rather a personal decision of God (Is 57:17) that finally does indeed deliver the sinner over 'to the power of his sin' (Is 64:6b).
In this active sense God 'turns his face against' the sinner."[104] Attitudes and conduct that ruin the reflection of
God's glory on the face of his covenant partner must be
discredited by God's withdrawing from association with
gravely false and counterfeit "sons". Thus says the Lord:
"I have forsaken my house; I have abandoned my heritage;

[104] Balthasar, *GL6*, 70. "God's face can be either uncovered or concealed,
turned towards one or averted. . . . [I]n times of grace, God's face is turned
towards Israel . . . , in times of anger, it is . . . turned away." Ibid., 69. "[In]
the old covenant, the real one who abandons is God, and his abandoning
(above all, of Israel) is 'in each case an act of judgment, or an act of divine
wrath' [Popkes]. The one who is handed over in this way is 'abandoned by
God', . . . (cf. 1 Sam 24:5)." *GL7*, 224. See Hoffmann, *Kreuz und Trinität*,
24–26.

I have given the beloved of my soul into the hands of enemies" (Jer 12:7, RSVCE; cf. 7:29; also 2 Kings 17:6–23; Lam 2:3, 14, 18; 4:11–12, 16, 22; Dan 9:16–19; Tob 13:6).

However, just as God's *wrath* is a modality of *love* that serves the salvation of his beloved, so God's *self-concealment* is a modality of God's *accompaniment* that serves the atonement of sin. In the context of a sin-ruptured covenant, God can *remain near* his beloved while *hiding his face*. Consider what occurs between the Lord and Israel in Hosea 2:12–22. Israel forsakes the Lord by running after idols. Indeed "everything begins with God's statement . . . that 'the land commits great harlotry by forsaking the LORD . . . (1:2). . . . The people have 'abandoned' God (4:10) and 'rebelled' against him (7:13; 8:1); they have 'fled' from him (7:13) and 'turned to others' (3:1)."[105] On his side, the Lord lets the people endure the God-forsaken state that they have chosen for themselves. He, the forsaken God, lets his people suffer his absence. In concrete historical terms, the Lord hands over Israel to the power of Assyria, and his people are exiled thereto in 722 B.C. Yet though God *conceals* himself, he nonetheless *accompanies* Israel into exile (2:12). God *withdraws* (5:6; 9:12) in order *thereby to draw* Israel back to himself, for in actuality God's forgiving love goes in advance of his people, albeit incognito, for the purpose of converting hearts and restoring the covenant relationship.[106] This is the Lord's secret plan, which for love of Israel he cannot keep to himself but virtually blurts it out.

I will allure her now;
I will lead her into the wilderness [into exile]
and speak persuasively to her. . . .

[105] Balthasar, *GL6*, 241.
[106] See Hoffmann, "Atonement and the Sacred Heart", 155.

There she will respond as in the days of her youth,
as on the day when she came up from the land of Egypt.
On that day—oracle of the Lord—
you shall call me "My husband" . . .
[and] I will betroth you to me forever. (Hos 2:16–21)

The biblical theme of God's withdrawal should be interpreted within the wisdom of God's salvific pedagogy; it is a "strategic withdrawal" in order to lead his beloved to discover his forgiving presence and power at a yet deeper level. The chief point to grasp here is that God's withdrawal is itself a modality of forgiving love that operates in a hidden manner.[107] Though God's passionate love-as-wrath takes the form of withdrawal (hiding his face), God aims to regenerate love in the heart of his estranged partner, enabling Israel to bear God's self-concealment as the pain of love, and precisely in doing so, to atone.[108]

If it is true that God's wrath and God's suffering love are two aspects of God's passionate involvement, we may view them together, at one glance: (1) God's love as *suffering* is divine love in its exposure to the beloved's no. This is God's love in the mode of letting himself bear the absence of his beloved, there being no limit to love's power to endure. (2) God's love as *wrath* is divine love in its opposition to the beloved's no; for God cannot be a "father" or partner to sin.[109] This is God's love in the mode of hiding his face in judgment against sin, thereby letting his beloved bear his absence.

---

[107] See Balthasar, *GL6*, 242–43 and 274.

[108] See Hoffmann, "Atonement and the Sacred Heart", 155.

[109] "God's wrath is . . . the categorical 'No' of God's response to the attitude that the world takes up over against him." Balthasar, *GL7*, 206. God's wrath "will make no compromises with sin but can only reject it". Hans Urs von Balthasar, *The Threefold Garland*, trans. Erasmo Leiva-Merikakis (San Francisco: Ignatius Press, 1982), 101.

*Forgiveness and atonement are
two sides of reciprocal love*

In all this, the process of atonement is patrogenetic: it originates from and is engendered by God's own power to love.
God exercises his power against sin in such a way that human freedom is not bypassed or overridden by a one-sided
forgiveness. God's power is a forgiving power, but it takes
full effect in his covenant partner only by engendering a free
response of contrite love that yields to and comes to reflect
(and so to glorify) the ardent passion of God's love. God's
forgiving (generative) love brings about a union between
himself and his beloved that takes the form of a shared willingness in love to suffer through and transform the separation wrought by sin. Here is Hoffmann's summary:

> When sin is changed into the pain of God's distance, then
> forgiveness and atonement are one and the same reality—
> it is called "atonement" insofar as it is found in the sin-
> ner (as his act and disposition), and it is called "forgive-
> ness" insofar as it is obtained from God. . . . Under the
> influence of grace, [the sinner] achieves initial conversion
> . . . and then—by virtue of the love thus granted—the full
> conversion that embraces the sinner's whole personal be-
> ing. Consequently, it is God who converts; he enables the
> sinner to atone. . . . In this sense it is true that the sinner's
> conversion, which attains its radical fullness in atonement,
> is YHWH's energetic and sovereign response to sin.[110]

Two illustrations on the human plane

In order to illustrate this reciprocal process of forgiveness
and atonement, let us draw from human experience, albeit
guided by the biblical view that depicts God's covenant love

[110] Hoffmann, "Atonement and the Sacred Heart", 155–56.

with reference to both a spousal relationship and a parent-child relationship. To be sure, these illustrations are not meant to do away with the radical difference between divine love and human love. They aim only to illuminate a certain likeness within that radical unlikeness. When using them, we must have the good sense to limit their illustrative capacity to a couple of points and discard the rest.

A HUSBAND–WIFE RELATIONSHIP

Imagine a married couple with children. Imagine that the wife began to look at pornography on the internet. After a few months, she moved beyond this to finding internet chat rooms and participating in "virtual" affairs. Next she actually started to meet these strangers up close and personal. At first she was discreet about it, going to hotels while her husband was at work and her children at school. But as she grew more and more a slave to her lust, she no longer gave thought to the consequences of her actions. These casual affairs began to consume her attention and time, leading her to neglect her responsibilities to her children and husband.

Eventually her neglect of the children became so obvious that her affairs were discovered. Her husband was profoundly hurt by his wife's infidelity and deeply grieved and angered by her indifference to their children. He told her that he was willing to forgive her, but she proved unwilling to give up this lifestyle. When she continued to have adulterous affairs, he sought a legal separation and custody of their children. But he continued to love her (despite his pained heart) and remained committed to work toward reconciliation.

As for the wife, at first she enjoyed the state of separation. But eventually her heart grew sickened by lust and yearned for love. She asked to visit her children again, which her husband granted. And during these visits she came to realize the extent of her husband's love for her. She saw that he was willing to keep his spousal love alive, even if he had to suffer the separation that resulted from her infidelities. In seeing her husband's willingness to bear separation while continuing to love her, she experienced a rekindled love for him.

Now, with her love revived, she felt the separation from her family as something grievous. Now she was pained by what she had done in spurning her marriage and family. Yet since it was precisely love that enabled her to experience this separation as painful, a love modeled and inspired by her forgiving husband, she was in reality closely united with him. Moved by his love, she was resolved to do whatever it took, for as long as it took, to purge her heart of lust and selfishness. So even though husband and wife continued for a time to be legally separated, the separation was already being transformed into a space reserved for their mutual love, a space in which estrangement was suffered through and nullified by its opposite: communion of hearts. To achieve complete reconciliation required that the unfaithful wife be turned around and re-positioned as a mirroring counterpart to her husband's forgiving love: that is, being *near* to her husband in suffering, out of love, his *absence*.

A FATHER–SON RELATIONSHIP

Imagine an attentive and loving father who strove to be a good role model for his son. He himself walked the talk by exemplifying the virtues that he directed his son to practice. Despite this, his son let himself fall under the influence of a circle of friends who idolized wealth and were lawless in obtaining it. Soon the son spurned his father's virtues and values, rejected his father's affection, and avoided his father's presence. The father, for his part, was pained by the distance (moral, emotional, spiritual) brought about by his son's corrupt heart.

Before long, the son got involved in illegal activities. When law enforcement caught up with him and presented evidence of his many crimes to his father, the father would not lie to keep his son from facing the consequences of his actions. In effect, the father handed his son over. A criminal trial of the son ensued.

On his side, the father, who had already been enduring a deeply felt distance between himself and his son, faced squarely the harm caused by his son's crimes. Whenever the father was allowed to visit his son in jail during the trial, he in no way minimized his son's bad choices or their hurtful consequences. The father saw through his son's feeble excuses, which were still soaked in selfishness and which showed that his son was still evading responsibility for his wrongdoing. Nonetheless, the father did not revoke his love for his son.

The trial ended with the son being sentenced to spend time in prison. The (moral, emotional, and spiritual) distance between the son and his father now took the concrete form of the son's incarceration. The father was not untouched by these circumstances. Yet when visiting his son in prison, the father showed his willingness to endure the pain of this separation until his son bore the penalty to the end. His forgiving love took the form of preceding and accompanying his son on the path from the delusion of sin to the truth of love.

As for the son, at first he seemed impervious to the hurtful consequences of his actions. During his trial, he had been careful to avoid meeting the eyes of his victims, and especially the eyes of his father. This enabled his heart to remain hardened and unrepentant, while his father's heart was pained by his son's callousness.

But the moment came when the son began to see his father's wounded heart, to realize that his father was willing to endure the consequences of continuing to love him. And in seeing that his father was unwilling to put a stop to love in order to put a stop to paternal love's pain, the son's hardness of heart began to soften. The power of the father's forgiving love empowered the son to mirror the love-suffering of his father. A regenerated filial love arose in his heart, which moved him to let himself be led along the painful path of atonement toward reconciliation, that path of suffering that transforms.

Thereafter, by virtue of his regenerated love, the son felt his father's absence as never before. It pained him to face the kinds of separation that had resulted from his wrong choices. And yet he was able to face his wrongdoing and bear its consequences, because his father's love remained near to him, always sustaining him, ever inciting him to love likewise. Paradoxically, the state of separation that the father and son endured together was transformed into a form of union. Though separated by prison walls, they were now united in their mutual willingness to bear out of love (yet in their different ways) the effects of the son's crimes.

Vicarious atonement

Before crossing the threshold to the New Testament where the Passion and death of Jesus is understood as bringing about the *vicarious* atonement of sin, once for all, we must note the shift that takes place within the Old Testament in the subject who undergoes redemptive suffering: from the suffering of the nation to the representative suffering of individuals. The history of Israel shows that the nation of Israel as God's covenant partner is not able to sustain an unreserved answer of obedient love in the long term. This is why, for Balthasar, "the true history of the covenant will be the history of individuals, of representatives."[111]

What concerns us here are the most significant instances of vicarious or representative atonement leading up to Jesus Christ. Of course the mysterious figure of the Suffering Servant of the Lord (Is 53) leaps to mind, but let us begin by examining the mission of a prophet, highlighting those aspects which correspond to the features of the process of eliminating sin that we have discussed thus far.

The God and Father of Israel, in sending a prophet, endows him with his Spirit. The prophet, on his side, is to make himself totally available to the Spirit so that "something like *a fellowship in attitude and destiny* becomes possible" between God and the prophet.[112]

In bringing about a fellowship in *attitude*, the Spirit that rests upon the prophet communicates to him God's passion of love in the face of sin. Balthasar brings forward von Rad's understanding that the prophet "became detached from himself and his own personal likes and dislikes, and was drawn into the emotions of the Deity himself. It was

---

[111] Balthasar, *GL6*, 158. Joseph Ratzinger, for his part, makes a similar point in a variety of ways throughout his writings. In one of his earliest articles, he maintains that God was not content simply to approve of the few while condemning the many. Rather, God "used the few as the Archimedean point, from which to lift the many, as the lever by which to draw them to himself". "Die neuen Heiden und die Kirche", *Hochland* 51 (October 1958): 4–11. Quoted in Peter Seewald, *Benedict XVI: A Life, Vol. 1: Youth in Nazi Germany to the Second Vatican Council 1927–1965*, trans. Dinah Livingstone (London: Bloomsbury Continuum, 2020), 299.

[112] Balthasar, *GL6*, 232 (emphasis added).

not only the knowledge of God's designs in history that was communicated to him, but also the feelings of God's heart: wrath, love, sorrow (Hos 6:4; 11:8; Is 6:8; Jer 6:11)."[113] In this way, God enables the prophet to endure and reproduce the modalities of his love in its exposure and opposition to sin—or, what amounts to the same thing, the Spirit inwardly fashions the prophet to serve as God's image in the confrontation with sin. Anatolios concurs: "Typically, God draws the prophet into his anger and pain" over the people's spurning of his love. "It is part of the job description of a biblical prophet that he accept God's invitation to enter into the divine subjectivity and experience the sins of the people and their rejection of God from God's point of view."[114] Already here we are approaching the threshold to the New Testament, where, according to the ITC, "the tears of Jesus (Lk 19:41), his anger (Mk 3:5), and the sadness he feels are themselves also manifestations of a certain way of behavior on *God's* part."[115]

And just as God's original work of fashioning man in his image integrated the bodily sphere (Gen 1:26–27), so also the bodily sphere of the prophet "is taken decisively into God's service . . . laid hold of as the sphere in which God's emotion and action are expressed. Ezekiel must eat the scroll, he and Hosea are expropriated in their married

---

[113] Von Rad, *Old Testament Theology*, vol. 2, (New York: Harper & Row, 1965), 63. Cited by Balthasar, in *GL6*, 234. Balthasar describes the prophet as "a man who is sym-pathetically open, by divine design, to God's divine pathos toward his world". *TD4*, 344. See Heschel, *The Prophets*; and Emmanuel Durand, *Les emotions de Dieu: Indices d'engagement* (Paris: Cerf, 2019).

[114] Anatolios, *Deification through the Cross*, 133–34. Elsewhere Anatolios corroborates this understanding in his discussion of how Moses internalizes and expresses God's anger against the people worshiping the golden calf (Ex 32:11–20). Ibid., 108–9 and 114.

[115] ITC, "Theology, Christology, Anthropology", p. 225, no. 2.

life so that they become parables of the relationship between God and the people."[116] Increasingly as the history of Israel unfolds, the prophet is called to become "the personified [indeed, embodied] word of God for the people."[117]

Precisely for this reason, the prophet is also drawn into a fellowship in *destiny* with God. The prophet Hosea, for instance, discloses the humiliated love of God when he runs after his unfaithful beloved, only to be expelled from the land. "The prophet is a fool, the man of the spirit is mad!" (Hos 9:7). "Even in this fate," observes Balthasar, "he declares something of the 'foolish' God's love (1 Cor 1)."[118] Jeremiah, for his part, "must share in God's withdrawal: 'Do not enter the house of mourning, or go to lament, or bemoan them . . .' (Jer 16:5). He is separated from other people in loneliness. 'I did not sit in the company of merrymakers, nor did I rejoice; I sat alone, because your hand was upon me, for you had filled me with indignation' (15:17)."[119] Insofar as the prophet exposes the word of God to the sinful people, he himself becomes exposed to their hostility toward God, as is attested by God's warning to Samuel: "According to all the deeds which they have done to me, from the day I brought them up out of Egypt even to this day . . . so they are also doing to you" (1 Sam 8:8, RSVCE; cf. Ps 69:8, 10; Jer 15:15).[120] In this light, Jesus himself will assert that the prophetic mission leads to martyrdom (Lk 13:33). The astounding implication is that "it is God himself who

[116] Balthasar, *GL6*, 234.

[117] Ibid., 268. See also 257.

[118] Ibid., 245.

[119] Ibid., 256.

[120] In the suffering of the martyrs "is a righteousness mirroring that of God which brings about the cruelly premature loss of life". Joseph Ratzinger, *Eschatology: Death and Eternal Life*, trans. Michael Waldstein (Washington, D.C.: Catholic University of America, 1988), 91.

uncovers his heart to blows in the prophets."[121] But this implication will be rendered explicit—beyond all conceivable expectation—only on Golgotha (Mk 15:39; Jn 8:28–29).

The role of the prophet, however, is not only to represent God before sinners; he is also to represent sinners before God. The dialogue between God and his people passes through him. This is readily seen in the case of Moses, where in Deuteronomy we find him lying stretched out for forty days and nights on the mountain "in order to perform penance in substitution for the people (Deut 9:9f., 18f., 25)."[122] Even more, the reason Deuteronomy gives as to why Moses dies outside the Promised Land is that "Moses has to die vicariously for the sake of Israel's sin."[123] "The LORD was angered against me also on your account, and said, You shall not enter there" (Deut 1:37; cf. 3:26; 4:21). Moses "becomes the one who suffers vicariously".[124] Accordingly, Balthasar (with von Rad) regards this portrait of Moses as already converging on that of the anonymous figure of the Suffering Servant of the Lord (Is 53).

We should consider, too, the suffering of Jeremiah (Jer 16:1–3) and Ezekiel (Ezek 4:1–8). The suffering of these prophets alongside the sin-burdened people is in some sense representative. Especially pertinent to our study is the depiction of Ezekiel's suffering in terms of bearing the people's sin:

---

[121] Balthasar, *GL6*, 236.

[122] Ibid., 189.

[123] Von Rad, *Deuteronomy* (Philadelphia: Westminster Press, 1975), 201, cited by Balthasar in *GL6*, 192. See also *GL6*, 296.

[124] Balthasar, *GL6*, 188. The full passage reads: "In the earlier portraits, Moses is punished because of a personal mistake, when he is refused entry into the Promised Land (Num 20:12); but here [in Deuteronomy] he becomes the one who suffers vicariously."

[The Lord instructs the prophet:] Then lie on your left
side, while I place the guilt [*awon: iniquity, guilt, punishment
for iniquity*] of the house of Israel upon you. As many days
as you lie like this, you shall bear their guilt [*awon*]. I allot you three hundred and ninety days during which you
must bear the guilt [*awon*] of the house of Israel, the same
number of years they sinned. When you have completed
this, you shall lie down a second time, to bear the guilt
[*awon*] of the house of Judah forty days; I allot you one
day for each year. (Ezek 4:4–6)

Admittedly, there is no clear indication that by suffering in
solidarity with the people under divine judgment, Ezekiel
atones for their sin, on their behalf, and thus directly advances the process of reconciliation with God. Ezekiel's (and
Jeremiah's) suffering is indeed representative but only (apparently) in a limited, prophetically illustrative way.

At any rate, in the Suffering Servant of the Lord (Isaiah 53) we have an unambiguous instance of an individual
who *vicariously atones*. The Servant bears the sin (*awon*: iniquity, guilt, or punishment for iniquity) of the many in their
place (Is 53:11–12). The suffering is willingly assumed by
the Servant, undergone in righteousness, and deliberately
offered to God (53:10, 12). It renders righteous the unrigh-
teous, cleanses them from sin, and brings about reconciliation (53:5, 11–12). Behind this atoning sacrifice is God's
initiative. God lays upon the Servant the guilt of all (53:5–
6). The whole process bespeaks God's resolute will to redeem through judgment (1:27) by way of commissioning
his Servant (with whom he is pleased, 42:1) to take upon
himself the baneful effects of sin.[125] Though the Servant had

[125] However we view the idea of "punishment" when applied to the Servant (Is 53:5), we should agree that the idea of "solidarity" is insufficient
to express the substance of the biblical affirmation. There is solidarity, it is

done no wrong (53:9, 11), God allowed sinners to seize and condemn him (53:8); in effect, God hid his face or abandoned his Servant so that God's will to forgive and restore (53:5, 11) "shall be accomplished through him" (53:10). The view that this expiatory suffering involved an experience of God's seeming absence is perhaps supported by the Servant's words that describe the feeling of a seemingly useless self-expenditure. Nonetheless, all the while his cause is with YHWH (49:4; 53:10–12). Here too, then, regarding the prophecy of the Servant, Hoffmann suggests that we "see the righteous man's power of *atonement* as a power of *transformation*, inasmuch as his righteousness enables him to *change sin* (i.e., the 'forsaking of YHWH' or 'being forsaken' by him) into the painful renunciation of God's nearness."[126] And finally, inasmuch as his righteousness is the stamp of genuine sonship, the Servant is the one in whom God shows his glory (49:3).

At the same time, we should note that the atoning efficacy of the Servant's suffering is confirmed by the sinners who benefited from it (53:4–6). The fact that they now recognize and confess their own transgressions and iniquities is itself a divinely inspired fruit of the Servant's Passion. Their conversion is a concrete sign that the Servant, the righteous one, by his death renders the many righteous (53:11).[127]

---

true, but it extends as far as substitution (vicarious suffering): the Servant's solidarity with sinners goes as far as allowing the weight of *their* sin to be laid upon *him* (53:6).

[126] Hoffmann, "Atonement and the Sacred Heart", 153 (emphasis original). See Balthasar, *GL6*, 295–97.

[127] See Christopher Seitz, "The Book of Isaiah 40–66", in *The New Interpreter's Bible*, ed. Leander E. Keck (Nashville: Abingdon, 2001), 466; and Anatolios, *Deification through the Cross*, 135.

The Suffering Servant of the Lord doubtless has his successors in the mysterious death of "the pierced one" in Zechariah (Zech 12:10–11; 13:1) as well as the willing "oblations" of the martyrs (Dan 3:29–42; 11:31–35; 12:1–10; and 2 Mac 7:37–38). With these cases, we move beyond the limited sort of representative suffering that the prophets Jeremiah and Ezekiel were called to embody. Here we are in touch with a tradition (under the influence of Isaiah 53) which holds that the suffering and death of certain righteous Jews can atone for the sins of the people, can function within the divine plan to bring about cleansing from sin and reconciliation with God. These righteous individuals are said to bear the consequences of the people's sins in such a way that sin is expiated (at least partially), on behalf of the people.[128]

Notably, all these instances of representative atonement are found in Jewish literature written after the Babylonian exile. Though the Jews have returned to Palestine from a *geographical* exile (from the Babylonian captivity), they continue to endure a *theological* exile, a state marked by God's seeming absence. So long as the Jews are being delivered over to foreign powers (first to the Greeks and then to the Romans), so long as they do not in fact possess their homeland, many believe that God has not yet definitively returned to rule over his people.[129] And hence they interpret their situation as an ongoing state of exile, or what amounts to

---

[128] When John Paul II discusses the emergence of vicarious atonement in the Bible, he collects and links together many of the key points that we make here; see "Fight Evil and Sin", 243–44. See also Wright, *Jesus*, 583–84.

[129] "Judaism never shakes off the suspicion that God did not truly re-establish the covenant after the return of the people from exile." Balthasar, *GL7*, 204. Wright concurs: "For the bulk of first-century Judaism, the exile was simply not yet over. The promises of Isaiah and the rest had not been fulfilled." *Jesus*, 576. See also Benedict XVI, *Jesus of Nazareth*, vol. 1, 12.

the same, a state of God-forsakenness. The *cause* of such a state, according to the prophets, can only be the sins of the people. If God is concealing himself, if God is handing his people over to the power of their enemies, it is on account of their sins. And the only *remedy* for this is God's forgiveness, which, as we have shown, is not given unilaterally but initiates and enables the collaboration of repentant sinners in the form of atonement.[130]

When, moreover, we consider the redemptive suffering willingly endured by these individuals, we should keep in mind that whatever concrete form their suffering takes, the essence of the suffering "is ultimately and properly separation from God. In affliction at the hand of enemies . . . and in nearness to death, [they] experience remoteness from God and abandonment by him."[131] Only if we realize this, will we be able to discern that the representative atoner's suffering not only manifests the God-forsaken plight of sinners but also reveals the power of the forsaken God to "father" his filial image under the conditions of a sin-ruptured relationship. For since it is God who already (freely) endures a love-suffering on the sinner's account, then whoever is enabled by grace to experience remoteness from God as a sin-bearer should be seen as a filial mirror image of the God who forgives. Among the cases of representative atonement that we will discuss below, this key insight is most readily grasped when beholding "the pierced one" in the Book of the Prophet Zechariah.

The death of "the pierced one" in Zechariah (12:10–11; 13:1) is presented as an event in which a prophetic figure is rejected by his own people, that is, by the inhabitants of

[130] See Wright, *Jesus*, 577.
[131] *Theological Dictionary of the Old Testament*, vol. 3, 207.

Jerusalem. In our reflections on the mission of a prophet, we already noted that God sends the prophet to serve as his image in the confrontation with sin. God enables the prophet "to enter into the divine subjectivity and experience the sins of the people and their rejection of God from God's point of view".[132] Just as Hosea and Jeremiah are drawn into God's experience of being rejected by his beloved people, so here the unnamed prophetic figure serves to make known the pain of sin from the point of view of God's subjectivity. This interpretation finds support "in the Masoretic Text, as well as all the notable ancient versions, [where] the one who is pierced is YHWH himself. . . . However, later versions and modern commentators shy away from this conceptually more difficult reading and separate YHWH from 'the one whom they have pierced'."[133] The ancient versions of Zechariah 12:10 read: "They will look on me [YHWH] whom they have pierced and mourn for him as for an only son. They will grieve bitterly for him as for a firstborn son who has died."[134] The references to an "only son" and a "firstborn son" evoke those passages in Exodus where Israel the nation is referred to as YHWH's "firstborn" (Ex 4:22–23). Intimated here is that the unnamed figure plays a twofold role of representation: he represents YHWH who is "pierced" by the people's rejection, and he represents the people whose sinfulness is on display as the cause of his death. Moreover, his Passion and death are not merely illustrative of the people's estrangement from God but also carry an atoning efficacy: they bring about the people's cleansing from sin (Zech 13:1). The early Christians, of course, iden-

---

[132] Anatolios, *Deification through the Cross*, 133–34.

[133] Ibid., 126.

[134] The New Living Translation, cited by Anatolios, *Deification through the Cross*, 127.

tified "the pierced one" with Jesus Christ (Jn 19:37; Rev
1:7), the Son sent by the Father to be his definitive revealer
(Jn 1:18; 14:9-11) and, concurrently, to be expiation for
the sins of the world (1 Jn 2:2; 4:10).

Emerging here in Zechariah is a further aspect, not directly developed in Isaiah 53: namely, the generative nature
of God's love that serves as the model and source of the filial love-suffering that bears sin away. Even if the Old Testament and late Judaism lacked a formal theory of atonement
properly so-called,[135] we may still see God's generative love
as part of the horizon of understanding within which Israel
envisioned God's role vis-à-vis his chosen beloved. In this
perspective, the God-inspired work of atonement can be understood to show not only the *human* suffering of the representative atoner in compassion with the sinful people, but
also "the *divine* suffering caused by Israel."[136] Previously,
we observed that the disclosure of God's passion of love
initiates and accompanies the whole process of atonement.
More precisely, we discerned the power of God's passion of
love to induce repentance in the beholder and to elicit a mirroring response unto sin's atonement. This pattern of reciprocal (paternal-filial) love is at play once again in Zechariah,
where "the pierced one" rehabilitates Israel's vocation as
God's filial image. This occurs in such a way that he does
not simply exclude the people's participation, but in being
beheld as an icon of God's passion of love, he is the means by
which they are moved to contrition and primed to become
co-atoners through and with him—and hence also "sons"
in whom God is once again glorified.

Concerning the willing "oblations" of the martyrs, we

---

[135] See Eichrodt, *Theology of the Old Testament*, vol. 1, 166f.
[136] Balthasar, *GL6*, 410. See also 234 and 257.

have already discussed the sequence of steps discernible in Daniel 3:29–43. Very likely, this prayer was composed under the influence of Isaiah 53. That would account for the explicit way it speaks of the suffering of the righteous (of the three would-be martyrs) as equivalent to sin-offerings. According to Martin Hengel, this prayer, when placed in the mouths of the three men in the fiery furnace (in the Septuagint), suggests a representative atoning death offered by the (almost) martyrs on behalf of God's sin-ridden people.[137] Additionally, the martyrdom of "those with insight" in Daniel 11:31–35 brings to mind the atoning purpose of the Servant's death in Isaiah 53.

Finally, we turn our attention to 2 Maccabees 7:37–38 (RSVCE), which is an account of a young martyr who offers his life in order to advance the process of forgiveness so that the nation may be delivered from its enemies: "I, like my brothers, give up body and life for the laws of our ancestors, appealing to God to show mercy soon to our nation. . . . And through me and my brothers to bring to an end the wrath of the Almighty that has justly fallen on our whole nation." Inscribed in this text is the belief that a martyr, in suffering at the hands of foreign powers who occupy the land, takes upon himself "the suffering of the nation as a whole, so that the nation may somehow escape".[138] The inner meaning of this representative suffering consists of willingly bearing this state of God's seeming absence, his self-concealment—in a word, his wrath—as a consequence of the nation's sin.

[137] See Hengel, *Atonement*, 61.
[138] Wright, *Jesus*, 583. Cf. 4 Mac 6:27–29 and 7:20–22. Wright also notes on p. 581 that the Qumran scrolls provide evidence of Jews believing that the suffering of the righteous carries atoning value; cf. 1 QS 8.1–4; 5.6; 9.4 (Vermes, 1995).

The martyrs' self-sacrifices and the Temple sacrifices

The above-mentioned belief that the suffering and death of righteous ones carries an atoning value first appears with clarity when the Jews are in exile in Babylon. In the absence of the Temple with its Levitical sacrificial system, "where the sacrificial animal is said to 'bear' the iniquities of the people" (cf. Lev 10:17; 16:20–22),[139] the Jews receive the prophecy of the Suffering Servant: the suffering of the Servant "in righteousness of heart" is believed to carry an atoning efficacy to hasten the people's release from captivity. The emergence of this belief, though, does not necessitate that Temple sacrifices be viewed as superfluous. For when the Jews return to Jerusalem, they rebuild the Temple and resume the cult of sacrifice. Before long, however, they are conquered again and forced to submit to occupation by foreign powers. Under these circumstances, some Jews, facing persecution for being faithful to the Lord's law, come to view their suffering and death in the light of Isaiah 53; that is, they offer themselves to God with an inner disposition comparable to what is required of the Jew when he offers a ritual sacrifice, and they believe that the value and efficacy of this self-offering unto death is comparable to a sacrificial sin-offering.

And thus we see (as we noted above), first in Isaiah 53, and then in Zechariah, Daniel, and 2 Maccabees, the transference to the sphere of human suffering and death of a theology that originally arose in the sphere of the ritual cult of sin-offerings. Nonetheless, the suffering and death of the martyrs among them does not warrant the abandonment of the Temple sacrifices. Rather, the process of atonement is

[139] Ibid., 588.

believed to extend to both spheres, without the sphere of human suffering in righteousness simply superseding or re-placing the Temple's sacrificial cult. The two forms of sac-rifice—one a ritual act, the other an existential act—exist side by side and mutually interpret each other.[140]

The sin of the Gentiles

Up to this point, we have been delineating the process of cleansing from sin as it develops in the history of the covenant between God and Israel. But what of the sin of the Gentiles?

In approaching this question, we will begin by situating the human race in relation to God as Creator. God, in cre-ating man, "fashions a creaturely freedom and sets it over against his own."[141] God genuinely hands over and entrusts to man this freedom. It is a freedom, therefore, that is inher-ently marked by a gift character. "Biblically, this situation is evidence of God's generosity: God entrusts the freedom of self-disposing to man, thus making man an '*image* and *like-ness*' of himself."[142] In order that man may freely choose to fulfill his vocation *to image* God in the world, God situates man among finite goods that both point to and conceal God

[140] See Wright, *Jesus*, 585, 588. Noteworthy is Aquinas' view that holy per-sons of the old dispensation could atone for sins in a valid but non-definitive way. Their acts of atonement achieved perfection only in Christ. Hence, for the saints of both dispensations—the old and the new—"it is necessary that individual acts of satisfaction be founded on the condign (perfect) satisfaction of Christ." Quoted by Romanus Cessario, *The Godly Image: Christ and Salva-tion in Catholic Thought from Anselm to Aquinas* (Petersham, Mass.: St. Bede's Publications, 1990), 79. The Latin text of Aquinas is from the *Scriptum super Sententiis* III, d. 20, q. 1, a. 1, qca. 3, ad 3.

[141] Balthasar, *TD4*, 328.

[142] Balthasar, *TD3*, 340.

himself as the infinite Good. Although God communicates himself to human freedom in this latent, covert way, man can nonetheless "recognize in finite goods the hidden presence of the infinite Giver and make an appropriately grateful response."[143] God's latency in the world of finite goods does not prevent man from perceiving the fundamental gift character of his freedom. We may even regard the divine prohibition against eating of the tree of the knowledge of good and evil (Gen 2:17) as serving to remind man of his dependence on God, the infinite Archetype and Giver of freedom.

To eat of the fruit of this tree (Gen 3:6), consequently, indicates that man comes to regard his power of choice, his capacity for self-disposing, as something absolute. It means that he usurps God's proper place while denying his own real indebtedness and orientation to God. It signifies his refusal to acknowledge the Giver in the gifts—including the gift of human freedom itself. Hence, to eat of the fruit of this tree is to choose a state of estrangement from God. This state of God-estrangement is brought about not through mere human carelessness and neglect, but through "deliberately obliterating the difference between God and the creature".[144] Instead of enacting his vocation to image God through a life of obedience, man takes up the "will to power" as his inner stance, the will to determine what is good and evil independently of God ("you will be like gods, who know good and evil", Gen 3:5). Human freedom corrupts itself

---

[143] Balthasar, *Theo-Drama: Theological Dramatic Theory*, vol. 2, *Dramatis Personae: Man in God*, trans. Graham Harrison (San Francisco: Ignatius Press, 1990), 275 (hereafter *TD2*). See also *GL7*, 268.

[144] Balthasar, *TD4*, 162. Ratzinger concurs; see *"In the Beginning. . .": A Catholic Understanding of the Story of Creation and the Fall* (Grand Rapids, Mich.: Eerdmans, 1995), 70–71. Also see John Paul II, *Reconciliatio et paenitentia*, no. 10.

by acting as if it has the good *in* its power, whereas authentic absolute freedom—the freedom of God—acts in the power *of* the Good.[145] "In seeking to arrogate power to itself," Balthasar observes, "human freedom does two things: it *separates* power *from* self-giving goodness [that is, from God's archetypal way of being powerful], and it sets itself up *against* the absolute Good."[146] Temptation is always based on a lie, and in sinning the one created to be a living icon of God debases himself to be a counterfeit idol.

After he sins, man tries to keep hidden the lie he is living. "At the beginning of the Letter to the Romans, Paul explicitly speaks of the pagans 'not acknowledging' God's divinity; this failure to ac-know-ledge presupposes a prior (and persisting) 'knowing.' If evil is the lie, it necessarily implies that there must be a primary consciousness of what is fundamentally true, of what should be the case; and there must be a constant attempt to reassure oneself that it is *not* true and is *not* the case."[147] This evil and the lie that maintains it are what incur the judgment of God. God's judgment on the corrupt hearts and works of the Gentiles reveals that they have in fact usurped the power of God, who is almighty goodness. From here we can understand Saint Paul's assertion that all men, Gentiles and Jews alike, are "liars" (Rom 3:4), "under the domination of sin" (3:9); "all have sinned, and are deprived of the glory of God" (3:23). Nevertheless, Paul is aware of a significant difference between the sin of Gentiles and the sin of Jews. As Balthasar points out, "Sin arises in the case of Gentiles (in biblical terms, those who

---

[145] See Balthasar, *TD*4, 163. Indeed, "the divine power *is* goodness and *calls for* goodness, if man is to exercise his own power in a pure manner." Ibid., 175.

[146] Ibid., 165 (emphasis added).

[147] Ibid., 164.

have not come into contact with God's historical revelation) because, while they are bound to know God—this is a basic law applying to all men—they do not want to acknowledge him (Rom 1:18ff.)."[148]

To be sure, the Gentiles exhibit an awareness of guilt and the need for atonement, but insofar as their efforts to atone for faults and evil deeds proceed solely from their own power, they repeat the basic pattern of man's original sin. For even in dealing with their guilt, they regard themselves as empowered to draw divine power over to their side. Here again, fallen human freedom appears bent toward the "will to power" and acts as if the good to be gained from godly power (overcoming guilt) were *in* its power.[149]

Now, at this juncture, how are we to situate the Gentiles in relation to the vocation of Israel? Hardly anyone disputes the fact that the Old Testament connects the original "fall" of the human race with the divine mission of Abraham. God chooses Abraham to be the head of a new people, whose vocation is to become through obedience the authentic filial image of God in the world and thereby to renew human life in history. This renewed humanity is itself intended to be a gift, a source of blessing, for all the nations. "In your descendants all the nations of the earth will find blessing, because you obeyed my command" (Gen 22:18). In the footsteps of Abraham, the people of Israel are called to prolong this obedience on behalf of the human race (cf. Gen 18:18–19). God, for his part, is priming his "firstborn son" (Ex 4:22–23; Zech 12:10) to act as the image of his glory in this sin-marred world. God's beloved is to be lifted up as a testament to the power of God's forgiving love to evoke repentance

---

[148] Ibid., 168.
[149] See ibid., 170.

and enable atonement. "That is why," says Balthasar, "in the whole of history, Israel is the place where the nature and the burden of sin is most directly manifested."[150] And it is why God's definitive exposure of the nature and burden of sin will reach its climax in Jerusalem with the Crucifixion of God's only-begotten Son, where we will witness both Jews and Gentiles taking a stance against God's reign in Christ Jesus. This is in accordance with the teaching of Saint Paul, who says that the Son of God comes to unveil sin in all its depth and breadth (Gal 3:19–23; Rom 5:20; 7:7ff.).[151] Here in the Passion and death of Christ, the perfect unity of God's goodness and power—more precisely, the power *of* God's goodness—has to "show itself in the form of wrath [that is, God's self-withdrawal, hiding his face], so that the power of his goodness can be seen as his mercy upon sinners".[152]

One final remark on the concrete shape of Israel's sinfulness and guilt on the eve of Christ's appearance. Certainly Israel, after it returns from exile in Babylon, has given up its open idolatry and attempts to purify its piety from adulterating influences. Nevertheless, more subtle, hidden dangers come to light. There is a covert tendency to take a stance of prideful creaturely autonomy precisely in keeping the commandments. The power to act according to the Law is credited to oneself, which is a subtle way of usurping God's power for the purpose of one's own self-perfection. This form of self-righteousness is accompanied by the propensity to regard oneself as guiltless in contrast to the "godless". The self-deception that underlies this attitude will be

---

[150] Ibid., 173. See also *GL7*, 38.
[151] See Balthasar, *TD4*, 173.
[152] Ibid., 167.

exposed by Christ Jesus when, for our sake, he comes to lay bare and bear the sin of the world.[153]

> Jesus scandalized the Pharisees by eating with tax collectors and sinners as familiarly as with themselves (cf. Lk 5:30; 7:36; 11:37; 14:1). Against those among them "who trusted in themselves that they were righteous and despised others," Jesus affirmed: "I have not come to call the righteous, but sinners to repentance" (Lk 18:9; 5:32; cf. 7:49; 9:34). He went further by proclaiming before the Pharisees that, since sin is universal, those who pretend not to need salvation are blind to themselves (cf. Jn 8:33–36; 9:40–41).[154]

Concluding remarks

In this chapter, we focused our attention on the Old Testament and traced the gradually emerging pattern of a process of atonement that is patrogenetic: it originates from and is engendered by God's own power to love. God exercises his power against sin in such a way that human freedom is not merely bypassed by a one-sided forgiveness. God's power is a forgiving power, but it takes full effect in his chosen beloved only by engendering a response of repentant love that willingly bears sin's consequences. The sinner turns back to God with filial love (regenerated by God; in this

[153] "All the faithfulness to the law, including Pharisaism, was perhaps only a new and more dangerous kind of breaking of the covenant. Jesus and Paul confirm this suspicion, and draw away the veil: this religion is 'hypocrisy' and a 'whited sepulcher' (Mt 23:27f.), and 'the anger of God from heaven' is 'revealed' against it (Rom 1:18) just as much as against the godlessness of the Gentiles." Balthasar, *GL7*, 206. See also *GL7*, 412; *TD4*, 176–77 and 179; and John Paul II, *Reconciliatio et paenitentia*, no. 6.
[154] *CCC* 588.

respect God is *near*), such that now he endures the effects of
sin (principally *distance* from God) in filial love-suffering, and
by bearing this sin-wrought distance, he turns sin around:
away from a refusal of filiation to an occasion of asserting
it. Atonement is a work of sonship that "cleanses" from sin
by transforming sin into its opposite: nearness to God in
the filial love-suffering of distance from God. Hence God's
generative (fore-giving) love brings about a union between
himself and his beloved that takes the form of a shared willingness in love to suffer through and transform the separation wrought by sin, thereby enabling his beloved to fulfill
his vocation as the image of God's glory in this "fallen"
world.

As we arrive at the threshold to the New Testament, the
main lines of our sketch point toward a convergence in the
atoning mission of God's Son incarnate. Yet this point of
convergence cannot be foreseen by reason alone. "It remains
an 'utterly strange work' (Is 28:21), an 'offence' (Is 8:14),
'something unheard-of' (Is 52:15)."[155] All the same, the constellation of features presented here may indicate a hidden
"theo-logic" that can cast a penetrating light on the tran-
sition from the Old Testament to the New. We will continue our attempt at uncovering this "theo-logic" in our
next chapter on the Cross as atonement, and in the process
illuminate the Cross event in view of its closeness to and
distance from the old covenant history of eliminating sin.

---

[155] Balthasar, *GL6*, 400. See also *GL7*, 33 and 36–37. Also see Wright, *Jesus*,
591–92.

Atonement in the New Testament

Crossing the threshold to the New Testament

At the threshold to the inauguration of the new covenant, we can discern a mounting sense of powerlessness in the face of sin. There is an unshakable suspicion among the people that the exile is not yet over. Though the people have returned to Palestine from Babylon (the *geographical* exile has ended), they are still being delivered over to the power of their enemies who occupy the land, and consequently they continue to endure a *theological* state of exile.[1] "Israel is living once more in the darkness of divine absence", says Benedict XVI about this state. "God is silent. . . . God seems to have abandoned his people. For that very reason, the land is full of unrest."[2] Israel's atmosphere of disappointment and unrest is surely related to its belief that God's absence signals the presence of a burden of sin that must be borne away. Further, Israel is acutely aware that the process of dealing with sin involves an interplay between God's forgiving love, on

---

[1] See Norbert Hoffmann, "Atonement and the Spirituality of the Sacred Heart", in *Faith in Christ and the Worship of Christ* (San Francisco: Ignatius Press, 1986), 156–57; Balthasar, *GL7*, 204; N. T. Wright, *Jesus and the Victory of God* (Minneapolis, Minn.: Fortress Press, 1996), 576; and Walther Eichrodt, *Theology of the Old Testament*, vol. 2 (Louisville, Ky.: Westminster John Knox Press, 1967), 396 and 455.

[2] Benedict XVI, *Jesus of Nazareth*, vol. 1, *From the Baptism in the Jordan to the Transfiguration*, trans. Adrian J. Walker (New York: Doubleday, 2007), 12; see also 3.

whose side lies the initiative and ultimate power over sin, and his covenant partner's contrite and obedient love, which cooperates by making atonement (cf. Ex 29:35–37; Lev 1:3–4; Heb 9:22).[3] On Israel's side, however, the people are experiencing a deepening sense of inadequacy.[4]

Accordingly, when Jesus appears announcing the inauguration of the reign of God—in other words, the people's definitive release from theological exile—his mission encompasses this two-sided process: both the proclamation of God's *forgiveness* and, inseparably, his work of vicarious *atonement*.[5] That Jesus' teaching and conduct convey the (initial) offer of divine forgiveness is incontestable (Mk 2:1–12; Mt 9:1–8; 18:23–34; Lk 15). With comparable clarity, the New Testament correlates God's (definitive) granting of forgiveness with the atoning efficacy of Jesus' Passion and death (Mt 26:28; Acts 10:43; 13:38; 1 Jn 2:1–2; 4:10; Rom 8:23–25; Gal 1:3–4; 1 Cor 15:3; 2 Cor 5:21; Col 1:13–14; 1 Pet 2:24; 3:18). Indeed, the central claim of the New Testament is that the Old Testament promise of divine forgiveness has been finally fulfilled because in the Passion and death of Christ Jesus atonement has been definitively achieved (Mt 1:21; Lk 1:77; Acts 2:38; 5:31).[6]

Now since that which brings fulfillment must be under-

[3] Hoffmann puts it bluntly: "Forgiveness must take place in the form of atonement." "Atonement and the Sacred Heart", 157. See Balthasar, *TD*3, 118; and Eichrodt, *Theology of the Old Testament*, vol. 2, 443–48 and 453.

[4] See Benedict XVI, *Jesus of Nazareth*, vol. 2, *Holy Week*, trans. Philip J. Whitmore (San Francisco: Ignatius Press, 2011), 234.

[5] On the question of Jesus' human understanding of his mission as entailing the abolishment of the world's estrangement from God, see Benedict XVI, *Jesus of Nazareth*, vol. 1, 26–27 and 331; and Balthasar, *TD*3, 110–11 and 166.

[6] This claim is reinforced by the astonishing fact that in view of the Cross event, straightaway Christians believe the Temple sacrifices to be definitively surpassed. See Benedict XVI, *Jesus of Nazareth*, vol. 2, 230.

stood together with what it fulfills, our task in this chapter is to show how the three factors that we identified as integral to the Old Testament process of atonement remain operative in the Cross event: God's sovereign initiative, God's passionate involvement, and man's willing collaboration.[7] At the same time, we must account for "the staggering newness" of the Cross event.[8] In this case atonement is made not by a mere man whose work is engendered by God's grace but by the human work of the "only Son", whom the Father sends as expiation (1 Jn 4:9-10). Operating here is the reciprocal love of God the Father and God the Son incarnate (in the unity of God the Holy Spirit) asserting itself against sin.

Already we can begin to perceive that the interpersonal matrix within which God counters sin is of a truly *theological* kind. The interpersonal polarity of Lover-beloved, Father-son, Lord-servant that marks the old covenant is now seen to be both affirmed and transcended in being transposed into the Trinitarian relations in God when the beloved Son of the Father *is* atonement for the sins of the whole world (1 Jn 2:2). The two-sidedness of the covenant (Lover-beloved, Father-son, etc.) is "raised to the height of a 'Trinitarian event'"[9] and so proves to be underwritten by the communion in love that constitutes the eternal life of the Blessed Trinity.

With this insight, however, more questions beg to be answered. Why is atonement for the sins of *human beings* the

[7] See Hoffmann, "Atonement and the Sacred Heart", 147-48 and 156; and Balthasar in *TD*4, 229.

[8] Hoffmann, "Atonement and the Sacred Heart", 160. See Balthasar, *GL*7, 33, 104, and 203-4.

[9] ITC, "Select Questions on Christology (1979)", in *International Theological Commission: Texts and Documents, 1969-1985* (San Francisco: Ignatius Press, 2009), 200. See Hoffmann, "Atonement and the Sacred Heart", 158-59.

Passion and death of *God the Son* incarnate? "Where is the sense of proportion here?"[10]

To answer these questions, we must explore the constellation of mysteries that are fully revealed only in view of the Son's redemptive mission: the creation and deification of human persons in Christ as "sons in *the* Son", the inner nature of sin, and indeed the inner life of the Godhead as an interpersonal communion of *caritas*.[11]

The New Testament notion of creation and divinization "in Christ"

Only in the New Testament does the ultimate origin and end of human persons come fully to light. God creates us "*in* Christ" (Col 1:16; 2 Cor 5:17), that is, in the "place" of the only-begotten Son, who is closest to the Father's heart (cf. Jn 1:18). For "being totally dependent on divine freedom, creatures can receive the gift of existence nowhere else but in the eternal Son", who eternally receives the divine being from the generating Father.[12] And we are created *for* one ultimate end: to become sons, children, of God by divinizing grace. This is affirmed unmistakably in the Council

---

[10] Hoffmann, "Atonement and the Sacred Heart", 160.

[11] See Norbert Hoffmann, "Christ and the World's Evil", *Communio* 17.1 (Spring 1990): 53; and Balthasar, *GL7*, 36.

[12] Balthasar, *TD2*, 261; see *TD3*, 326. This theological insight is supported by Athanasius as early as the fourth century A.D. Athanasius sees that the Father's *ad intra* generation of the Son serves as the immutable basis in God for the *ad extra* creation of human beings. See Athanasius' *Orations against the Arians* II.2; and Khaled Anatolios, *Retrieving Nicaea: The Development and Meaning of Trinitarian Doctrine* (Ada, Mich.: Baker Academic, 2018), 116; also Peter Widdicombe, *The Fatherhood of God from Origen to Athanasius* (Oxford: Clarendon Press, 1994), 180–84.

of Trent's *Decree on Justification*[13] and Vatican II's *Gaudium et spes*[14] as well as in the *Catechism*[15] and John Paul II's encyclical *Redemptoris mater*, in which the pontiff states that the opening verses of Saint Paul's Letter to the Ephesians (1:3–7) "reveal the eternal design of God the Father, his plan of man's salvation in Christ. It is a universal plan, which concerns all men and women created in the image and likeness of God (cf. Gen 1:26). Just as all are included in the creative work of God 'in the beginning,' so all are eternally included in the divine plan of salvation, which is to be . . . destined in love 'to be his sons through Jesus Christ'."[16] The

---

[13] "The heavenly Father, 'the Father of mercies and God of all comfort' (2 Cor 1:3), sent to men his own Son Jesus Christ. . . . He was sent that the Jews, who were under the law, might be redeemed and that the Gentiles 'who were not pursuing righteousness' (Rom 9:30) might attain it and *that all 'might receive adoption as sons'* (Gal 4:5)", Council of Trent, *Decree on Justification* (1522) in Heinrich Denzinger, *Compendium of Creeds, Definitions, and Declarations on Matters of Faith and Morals*, 43rd ed., Latin-English, ed. Robert Fastiggi and Anne Englund Nash (San Francisco: Ignatius Press, 2012) (hereafter *DH*).

[14] Vatican Council II, Pastoral Constitution on the Church in the Modern World *Gaudium et spes* (December 7, 1965), nos. 22 and 92–93.

[15] See *CCC* 50–52 and 600–601.

[16] John Paul II, encyclical letter *Redemptoris mater* (March 25, 1987), no. 7. Elsewhere the pope asserts the same: "Man is created in the Incarnate Word, the Lord Jesus dead and risen . . . and in view of him, because the Father—in his utterly free plan—has wanted man to participate, in the only-begotten Son, in the Trinitarian life itself." Quoted in John Saward, *Christ Is the Answer: The Christ-Centered Teaching of John Paul II* (New York: Alba House, 1995), 59. See also John Paul II's apostolic letter *Mulieris dignitatem* (August 15, 1988), no. 9, and his General Audiences on April 9 and May 28, 1986. Additionally, see Norbert Hoffmann, "Atonement and the Ontological Coherence between the Trinity and the Cross", in *Towards a Civilization of Love*, ed. International Institute of the Heart of Jesus (San Francisco: Ignatius Press, 1985), 239–40; Balthasar *TD2*, 266–68 and 330; *TD3*, 35–37 and 516; *TD4*, 372; *GL7*, 310–11, 393–94, 405, 409, and 422; and ITC, "Select Questions on the Theology of God the Redeemer [1995]", *Communio* 24.1 (Spring 1997): 203.

proclamation of the gospel, therefore, should not restrict the scope of the Father's plan; "God wants to communicate his own divine life" to each and every human being he has created; he wants everyone to be "born of God"—and not merely some.[17]

This means that God creates human beings for the purpose of drawing us into the mystery of divine generation. Or what amounts to the same: God creates human beings for participation in the Son's personal relation to the Father within the Trinity (Gal 4:4–6; Col 1:16; Rom 8:14–17, 29; 1 Tim 6:16; 1 Jn 3:1f.). And this means, further, that God's supernatural gift of divinizing grace conforms us to the Son (Rom 8:29).[18] Hence, Balthasar rightly insists that "grace has not imparted some general, vague 'supernatural elevation' to us but a participation in the personal existence of the eternal Word of God. . . . The grace which the Father gives us is christoform: it assimilates us to the Son."[19]

In a letter to the bishops of the Catholic Church, (then-) Cardinal Ratzinger puts forward an excellent summary of the grace of divinizing adoption in the eternal Son:

> In order to draw near to that mystery of union with God, which the Greek Fathers called the "divinization" of man . . . one must recognize that the human person is created in the "image and likeness" of God (Gen 1:26), and that

[17] *CCC* 52.

[18] See *CCC* 398 and 1999; and 1 Cor 8:6; Jn 1:1–14; Heb 1:3f.; Rom 11:36.

[19] Hans Urs von Balthasar, *Prayer*, trans. Graham Harrison (San Francisco: Ignatius Press, 1986), 58. See also *GL*7, 407. The eminent Thomist Gilles Emery agrees completely: Filiation by grace entails "a participation in the natural Sonship of the Son, a participation in his personal relation to the Father". Through the gift of his Spirit, the Son "enables us to participate by grace in his filial relation to the Father. . . . The Christian vocation is thus *filial* by essence." *The Trinity* (Washington, D.C.: Catholic University of America, 2011), 127.

the prototype of this image is *the Son* of God, in whom and through whom we have been created (cf. Col 1:16). This prototype reveals the greatest and most beautiful Christian mystery: . . . "God is love" (1 Jn 4:8). This profoundly Christian affirmation can reconcile perfect "union" with the "otherness" existing between lover[-Father] and loved[-Son], with eternal exchange and eternal dialogue. God is himself this eternal exchange and we can truly become sharers of Christ, as "adoptive sons" who cry out with the Son in the Holy Spirit, "Abba, Father." In this sense, the Church Fathers are perfectly correct in speaking of the divinization of man who, having been incorporated into Christ, the Son of God by nature, may by his grace share in the divine nature and become a "son in the Son" ["*filii in Filio*" (Rom 8:15–17)]. Receiving the Holy Spirit, the Christian glorifies the Father and really shares in the Trinitarian life of God.[20]

What this means for the authentic realization of human freedom is that it must take its bearings from its divine prototype: the Son's personal way of exercising divine freedom. Insofar as the Son is *God*, he is eternal and infinite freedom; yet insofar as he is *the Son* of the Father, he is divine freedom in the filial form of receptivity and mirroring correspondence.[21] The Son exercises divine freedom —he disposes of himself as God—only and always as the Father's perfect Image and Expression (Jn 1:1, 18; 5:19–20). Precisely here a crucial insight is uncurtained: the Son's

[20] Joseph Ratzinger, Congregation for the Doctrine of the Faith, *A Letter to the Bishops of the Catholic Church on Some Aspects of Christian Meditation* (October 15, 1989), nos. 14 and 15.

[21] See Balthasar, *TD2*, 267. For a robust Thomist endorsement of Balthasar's notion of sonship as divine love subsisting in the mode of receptivity and mirroring correspondence, see W. Norris Clarke, *Person and Being: The Aquinas Lecture 1993* (Milwaukee: Marquette University Press, 1993), 82–89.

existence as the perfect Image of the Father entails more than
his personal possession of the one and the same divine nature
with the Father. It involves as well the Son's eternally generated correspondence to the Father; the Son is the Father's
Image *in imaging* the Father's self-giving in love.[22] This, of
course, has implications for man's creation and vocation as
the image of God. Since the Son's way of exercising divine
freedom is perfect according to the filial form of receptivity
and imaging response vis-à-vis the Father, it follows that human freedom authentically realizes itself by following this
filial pattern: by doing only what it sees the Father doing.[23]
Human freedom's perfection, in other words, entails participating in the Son's divine imaging of the Father in the human
form of obedience.[24] Thus if it would be perfect, it must renounce the temptation to determine good and evil for itself.
Human freedom is perfected only through grace-enabled
obedience, by which it images and hence glorifies God the
Father and, just so far, is itself glorified in God the Son.

If we then ask what it means for the Triune God that
human beings are created and called to reflect the glory of

[22] See Balthasar, *TD2*, 266, and *Theo-Logic: Theological Logical Theory*, vol.
3, *The Spirit of Truth*, trans. Graham Harrison (San Francisco: Ignatius Press,
2005), 404. In addition, see Margaret Turek, *Towards a Theology of God the
Father: Hans Urs von Balthasar's Theodramatic Approach* (New York: Peter Lang
Publishing, 2001), 38–39, 61–67, 136–41.

[23] See Balthasar, *TD2*, 268; *The Christian State of Life*, trans. Mary Frances
McCarthy (San Francisco: Ignatius Press, 1983), 78–79. See also John Paul
II, "The Son of God Brings the Fullness of Salvation" (General Audience,
February 18, 1998), in *The Trinity's Embrace: Our Salvation History: Catechesis
on Salvation History* (Boston: Pauline Books & Media, 2002), 28.

[24] These insights are indebted to the patristic theology of the East. See
Anatolios' astute analysis of Athanasius' doctrine of the Son's *imaging* the
Father, both divinely and humanly, in *Retrieving Nicaea*, 107–8; see also
Christoph Schönborn's illuminating treatment of the Trinitarian Christology
of Maximus the Confessor, in *God's Human Face: The Christ Icon* (San Fran-
cisco: Ignatius Press, 1994), 113–20.

the Father as beloved "sons in the Son", our answer must convey a mystery of Trinitarian proportions. God the Father wishes to be Father to his Son in all human persons. God the Son wishes to be Son to (and Image of) the Father in all human persons. God the Holy Spirit wishes to be the Spirit of Sonship in all human persons.

The New Testament notion of sin

Like our divinization as "sons in the Son", sin too is a mystery of Trinitarian proportions. In order to see the real nature of sin, we need to be enlightened by divine revelation. John Paul II states it plainly: "Faced with the mystery of sin . . . it is not enough to search the human conscience . . . but we have to penetrate the inner mystery of God, those Trinitarian 'depths of God'."[25]

As noted above, the Son's "place" within the Trinity is vis-à-vis the Father. We may even, with Balthasar, speak of the Son as existing "op-posite" the Father. By this we mean that the Son exists as the imaging Beloved vis-à-vis the archetypal Lover. Of course in the Triune God this interpersonal "op-position" is entirely positive, since it is a necessary condition of the interplay of *caritas*, which is eternally realized in the most intimate manner conceivable.[26]

[25] John Paul II, encyclical letter *Dominum et vivificantem* (May 18, 1986), no. 32. See *CCC* 387–88.
[26] All four of our guides align themselves with those Church Fathers (Athanasius, Gregory of Nyssa, Hilary of Poitiers, Maximus the Confessor, among others) who see the Father's eternal act of generating the Son as an act of archetypal and generative love. Further, they enhance this traditional view by envisioning the patrogen(n)etic dynamic of the Trinitarian Godhead within the framework of a metaphysic of *caritas*, of interpersonal love. This metaphysic of *caritas* received a strong endorsement by the

(Ratzinger affirmed the same point in different words, when he spoke of God's Trinitarian mystery as "reconcil[ing] perfect 'union' with the 'otherness' existing between lover and loved, with eternal exchange and eternal dialogue.") Moreover, this wholly positive "op-position" between the Father and the Son makes possible the "op-position"—and hence the interplay of *caritas*—between God and human persons. Balthasar suggests that we think of human persons as "standing opposite" God in virtue of creation coming to exist within the Son's being begotten by the Father.[27] God has eternally "made room" for human persons in the "place" that belongs to the Son within the Trinity.[28] In fact, without this interpersonal "op-position" between the begetting Father and the begotten Son, it would be impossible to understand the human person's vocation to adoption into divine life everlastingly, since this can only be tenable if it is founded on the ontological (divine) Father-Son relation.[29]

ITC in "Theology, Christology, Anthropology" in *International Theological Commission: Texts and Documents, 1969–1985* (San Francisco: Ignatius Press, 2009). See also John Paul II, "The Spirit Is the Source of Communion" (General Audience, July 29, 1998), in *The Trinity's Embrace*, 90; see also Turek, *Towards a Theology of God the Father*, 91–206.

[27] See Balthasar, *TD2*, 268; and *Epilogue*, trans. Edward T. Oakes (San Francisco: Ignatius Press, 2004), 35–38.

[28] See Balthasar, *TD3*, 340. Anatolios' commentary on St. Athanasius' theology brings to light the strong resemblance it bears to Balthasar's: "There is a place for the world in God, and that place is the Word and Image of the Father, in which the world comes to be, 'according to the Image'." *Retrieving Nicaea*, 154. In fact, "Athanasius depicts the relation between the Father and the Son in terms that can be styled as 'inter-personal'." Ibid., 153.

[29] See Anatolios, *Retrieving Nicaea*, 84–85, where he explains the Trinitarian doctrine of Athanasius' mentor, Alexander of Alexandria, for whom "salvation as adoption into divine life can only be secured if it is founded on the ontological (divine) filiation of the Son."

By the same token, without this wholly positive paternal-filial "op-position" within the Trinity, it would be impossible to perceive the deepest theological character of sin. Seen from this Trinitarian vantage point, sin "is an inter-personal event between 'Father' and 'son'". Sin in its "objective intentionality" implies a refractory stance in relation to God, not merely inasmuch as God faces us as Creator, but also inasmuch as God faces us as Father-Begetter.[30] Sin turns man's originally *positive* "op-position" into *negative* opposition. Instead of letting our "space" of human freedom be the place in which God begets us by grace (our only true and final salvation), we sinners let sin usurp this place. Sin usurps the place in which the divine Father-Son relationship wishes to extend itself to and in human persons.[31] Sin, in other words, spurns God the Father, who wishes to be Father to his Son in all human persons (Jn 15:21–24). It rejects God the Son (Jn 16:8–9; 1 Jn 2:22), who wishes to be Son to (and Image of) the Father in all human persons. And sin resists God the Holy Spirit (Acts 7:51), who wishes to be the Spirit of Sonship in all human persons.[32]

Since the ultimate end of human persons is to be a recipient of and participant in the love that the Triune God *is*, then sin as opposition to this love "has superhuman rank".[33] Sin possesses an infinite quality inasmuch as it is the rejection of a gift of infinite magnitude: the passionate love with which

[30] See Hoffmann, "Christ and the World's Evil", 58–59; "Atonement and Coherence", 240–41; also Balthasar, *TD*4, 328–29; and Anatolios, *Retrieving Nicaea*, 125.
[31] See Hoffmann, "Atonement and the Sacred Heart", 165; Balthasar, *TD*4, 329 and 333–34; and *CCC* 398.
[32] See Hoffmann, "Atonement and the Sacred Heart", 198–99; Balthasar, *GL*6, 64; and ITC, "Select Questions on the Theology of the Redeemer", 39.
[33] Hoffmann, "Christ and the World's Evil", 59. See ITC, "Theology, Christology, and Anthropology", 216.

the Father wants to beget (divinize) us as adopted sons in his Only-Begotten. John O'Donnell, S.J., explains in *The Mystery of the Triune God*: "The one addressed by God . . . [is] loved with that very love which the Father has for the Son from all eternity. The measure of God's love for the world is not the world but the eternal Son. Thus in God's relating himself to the world, the world is not the terminus by which God's love is measured. The measure is the eternal love of Father and Son."[34]

Moreover, sin, as the rejection of this infinite love, has a "repercussive effect" on the Triune God that "exceeds the bounds of what is human and creaturely".[35] For the love offered and the love rejected are one and the same—love without measure. By way of distant analogy, consider what occurs on the plane of human relationships. The magnitude of the heartache when one's love is rejected is in direct proportion to the measure of the love tendered. (This is borne out when, in order to lessen the pain, one is tempted to diminish one's love; in order to take away the heartache, one is tempted to take back one's heart.) Since the Father's love is infinite, his passion of love in the face of sin takes the form of infinite love-suffering.[36]

---

[34] O'Donnell concludes: "Hence the constitutive term of God's love for the world is the inner-divine terminus of the divine Son into which the world is drawn." *The Mystery of the Triune God* (Sheed & Ward, 1988), 25. This way of measuring the magnitude of sin is meant not to replace but rather to complement the approaches taken by Anselm and Thomas Aquinas; see *ST* III, q. 1, a. 2, ad 2.

[35] Hoffmann, "Atonement and the Sacred Heart", 165. Indeed, "the 'consequences' of sin extend into the Heart of God." Also see "Atonement and Coherence", 241–42.

[36] Recall our discussion of God's impassible passion of love in chap. 1: the love-suffering of the Triune God involves no involuntary passivity, but rather a voluntary assumption of the implications of covenantal reciprocity, which by reason of that assumption changes us without being changed in itself.

If these remarks show that sin has a meaning for God, they also indicate to what extent atonement—God's countermovement against sin—matters to God. As we shall discuss below, the Cross event as vicarious atonement demonstrates the Trinity's determination to stick to the ultimate aim of creation: the extension of the divine Father-Son relationship to human beings in the order of divinizing grace (Gal 4:4–6; Eph 1:3–6; Col 1:16; Rom 8:14–17, 29; 1 Jn 3:1f.). For us and for our salvation, the Father made the Son "to be sin" (2 Cor 5:21) because those who became sinners were made to become sons.

This brings us to a final point. The pattern of an "exchange of places" implied in our last remark invites us to circle back to our reflections on the original positing of human beings within the Father's eternal generation of the Son. Those reflections set the stage and provide the justification for the Son's mission to atone for sins "in our place". The point we want to accentuate here is that it belongs to the Son and not the Father or the Holy Spirit to "exchange places" with humanity. This is because, paradoxically, the Son does not need to leave his own "place" within the Trinity in order to represent humanity before the Father.

Since the world cannot have any other locus but within the distinction between the Hypostases [i.e., between the Persons of the Father and the Son], the problems associated with [humanity's] sinful alienation from God can only be solved at this locus. The creature's No resounds at

Pertinent too is the stance of Jean Galot: "It is possible to grasp the immensity of sin only in the agony of Calvary. . . . In the anguished oblation of the Cross which possesses infinite value, we discern to what degree the offense wounded God in his infinite love." *Jesus, Our Liberator* (Rome: Gregorian University Press, 1982), 262. See also Galot, "La réalité de la souffrance de Dieu", *Nouvelle Revue Théologique* 101 (1979): 224–45.

the "place" of distinction within the Godhead. The Son, the "light" and "life" of the world, who enters into this "darkness" of negation by becoming man, does not need to change his own "place" when, shining in the darkness, he undertakes to "represent" the world.[37]

Fundamentally, this means that the work of vicarious atonement for the sin of the world is the Son's business qua son.

Atonement "once for all" is the bearing of sin by God the Son incarnate

Our discussion until now has stressed that sin is committed by one who is "more than" a mere creature.[38] Nevertheless, sin is the work of human freedom alone, and thus it should be dealt with by human freedom. Indeed, as we observed in our reading of the Old Testament, sin cannot be merely walked away from; it must be *borne away*, effaced, eliminated. Sin is borne away by being transformed or converted into its opposite. If sin is to be transformed into its opposite, then that which is the opposite of sin—filial love —must take up and bear sin away. But filial love can bear sin only insofar as filial love is willing to bear the effects of sin, primarily separation from the Father (in a word: God-forsakenness). And given the enormity of sin, its complete

---

[37] Balthasar, *TD*4, 334. Notable too is the explanation given by François-Xavier Durrwell, that if God the Father has not entered the world as incarnate, it is because "the one who is without origin does not come to the interior of the world where everything has an origin. Rather, he enters creation by exercising his Paternity there . . . appearing in the Son." *Le Père. Dieu en son mystère* (Paris: Les Éditions du Cerf, 1988), 33. My translation.

[38] Inasmuch as sin means the refusal of the vocation to be adopted sons in the eternally begotten Son, it bespeaks the rejection of the divine Father-Son relationship in its gracious extension to human beings.

and definitive transformation calls for a filial love infinite in
efficacy,[39] capable of plumbing the Trinitarian proportions
of sin. And there's the rub: although the work of atonement
must involve human freedom, human freedom alone cannot turn around the repercussions of rejecting the extension
of the divine Father-Son relationship to and in human persons. Alone it cannot convert sin's effects into material for
the expression of a filial love infinite in quality that perfectly
images—and thus perfectly glorifies—the Father's passion
of love in the face of sin. This can be accomplished only
by the divine Son, who, taking up human freedom in his
Incarnation, makes it the place in which a return of love
—precisely in the form of an infinite filial love-suffering—
can be made to God the Father.[40] Atonement for the sin of
the world, simply put, is the assertion of incarnate sonship
against sin. Sonship takes sin upon itself—without ceasing
to be itself—in order to *transform* sin into the suffering form
of filial love, thereby *annihilating* it.

In Hoffmann's words:

> The crucified Son . . . occupies the "place of sinners" and
> allows God to be "Father" there . . . as he stands *in* their

[39] Aquinas argues for the "infinite efficiency" of the act of Christ's atonement in *ST* III, q. 1, a. 2, ad 2; and for its "infinite worth" in III, q. 48, a.
2, ad 3. Moreover, he sees charity as the principle that renders the suffering
of sin's effects efficacious as atonement. III, q. 14, a. 1, ad 1.

[40] "If sin is to be 'wiped out,' 'borne,' something far beyond human powers must take place. True, God is a match for sin, but only he is so." Hoffmann, "Atonement and the Sacred Heart", 165. Balthasar concurs: "For
how could the man Jesus have borne away the world's sin, except as God?",
*TD*4, 319. Elsewhere he says that only the Son of God made man, "through
his distinction-in-relation vis-à-vis the Father, can expiate and banish that
alienation from God that characterizes the world's sin." *TD*5, 260. See also
*GL*7, 211 and 304: *TD*3, 530; *TD*4, 349; and Hans Urs von Balthasar, *Does
Jesus Know Us—Do We Know Him?*, trans. Graham Harrison (San Francisco:
Ignatius Press, 1983), 33. See *CCC* 616.

sinful estrangement from the Father and endures it. . . . And this signifies the *conversion of sin*. . . . As the incarnate Son experiences the nature of sin, sin is converted in its very nature: the proud self-assertion against God, the sinful desire to be free from God, is changed into pain, a pain that is as great as this Son's love. . . . The incarnate Son takes our sinful estrangement into his own relationship with the Father. Here sin is fashioned as in a furnace until all that is left is the Son's suffering love, that is, that form of love that is the exact opposite of sinful rebellion, that *converts and nullifies* it.[41]

In other words, "it is on the Cross that the real transforming miracle takes place: sin is transformed into its opposite; now it has become the negative image of filial love, suffering sonship."[42]

Once again, albeit with deepening insight into its innermost reality, we can affirm that vicarious atonement "once for all" (*ephapax* in Heb 7:27; 9:12, 26; 10:10) is indeed the Son's business qua son. To neglect to see this is to miss what is specifically Christian—Trinitarian—in the mystery of atonement.[43]

Balthasar enriches this Trinitarian soteriology as he tackles a central theme in the New Testament understanding of the Cross event: the "handing over" of Jesus to his en-

[41] Hoffmann, "Atonement and the Sacred Heart", 167–70.

[42] Ibid., 168. Hoffmann describes the relation of atonement to sin as a "*negatio negationis*". *Kreuz und Trinität: Zur Theologie der Sühne* (Einsiedeln: Johannes Verlag, 1982), 45. Balthasar uses the same formula, "the negation of a negation", to describe Christ's work of atonement. *GL*7, 409. See Balthasar, *Epilogue*, 120–21; and Gregory of Nyssa, *Contra Eunomium* III, 10.

[43] See Hoffmann, "Atonement and the Sacred Heart", 168–69; and Balthasar, *TD*5, 277. This claim is in accordance with the biblical texts that regard the Cross event as the definitive disclosure of Jesus' divine sonship (Mk 15:39; Jn 8:28; Phil 2:6–11; Gal 2:20; Col 1:18–20).

emies. (*To hand over* is the English rendering of the Greek *paradidómi* and the Latin *tradere*.) For Balthasar, the primary sense of the "handing over" of Jesus applies to the Father, which Balthasar interprets in view of the Old Testament: God, in an act of judgment, withdraws from his sinful people and thereby delivers them over to their enemies. In like manner, the Father delivers Jesus over to his enemies (Rom 8:32: *parédoken*; Jn 3:16: *édoken*; Acts 2:23; Mt 17:22; 20:18) by withdrawing from the one he has made "to be sin" (2 Cor 5:21).[44] To be sure, one ought not to say that the Father willed that men should crucify his Son. The Father permits this evil to occur as a result of the free action of sinners. Nonetheless, God's permissive will is not limited to mere non-activity in the face of this sinful action; rather, God actively brings a greater good out of it. The Father permits sin only to deal with it actively by judging the sin that the Son, the Lamb of God, bears in our place.[45] Hence, Jesus announces at the start of his Passion: "Now is the time of judgment" (Jn 12:31). Yet as we shall see presently, on God's part, the Cross event is not only an act of divine *judgment against* enemies; it is also, simultaneously, the consummate act of divine *love of* enemies. It is an event that evokes the prophecy of the Suffering Servant of the Lord in which

[44] Jesus "is abandoned 'into the hands of men,' or 'of sinners,' or 'of the Gentiles.' From the Old Covenant, the real one who abandons is God, and his abandoning (above all, of Israel) is 'in each case an act of judgment, or an act of the divine wrath' (Popkes). The one who is handed over in this way is 'abandoned by God' . . . (cf. 1 Sam 24:5)." Balthasar, *GL*7, 224. "Jesus, the 'servant of God' (Acts 3:13, 26; 4:27), the 'just one' (Acts 3:14), was delivered by God, like the just in the Old Testament, into the hands of sinners." Hans Urs von Balthasar, *Mysterium Paschale*, trans. Aidan Nichols (San Francisco: Ignatius Press, 1990), 110–11 (hereafter *MP*). See also *MP*, 108; *TD*4, 241; and *CCC* 599 and 604.

[45] See Balthasar, *TD*5, 251; and *TD*4, 334; also Aquinas, *ST* III, q. 15, a. 6, ad 4; and the *CCC* 600.

God's *judgment upon* sin has *redemption from* sin as its goal (Is 53:5–12; cf. 1:27).[46]

Moreover, there is a second sense of *paradidonai* that applies to Jesus himself. Jesus willingly hands himself over to the power of his enemies, in full accord with the will of the Father (Jn 10:18; Gal 2:20).[47] This self-handing-over reveals the Son's free collaboration with the Father's act of judgment upon sin.[48] It, too, can be traced back to the Old Testament, where certain individuals voluntarily gave themselves to suffering at the hands of their enemies in order to expiate the sins of the people.[49]

Thus, both the Father's handing over of the Son and the Son's willingness to be handed over are in reality two (paternal and filial) manners of willing that operate in the closest unity of action. As Balthasar says, "the entire act of judgment remains contained within the love of the Father who gives up (Jn 3:16) and the love of the Son who places himself at his [Father's] disposal."[50]

In expounding the Cross event, Balthasar interprets this twofold "handing over" of Jesus in connection with one of the most difficult texts in the New Testament: namely, Saint Paul's assertion that "for our sake, he [the Father] made him [the Son] to be sin who knew no sin, so that in him we might

[46] See Balthasar, *GL7*, 36, 47, 227, and 337; see also *TD5*, 261 and 266.

[47] "The words of institution show that Jesus' eucharistic self-surrender is prior to any action on men's part to send him to his death and that God's final and definitive covenant with men is sealed in the self-surrender of Jesus (Mt 26:28 parr.; 1 Cor 11:25)." Balthasar, *TD4*, 241.

[48] See Balthasar, *TD3*, 119–20; *TD4*, 237; and the chapter "Momentum of the Cross" in *GL7*, 202–35, particularly 223f.

[49] See Balthasar, *MP*, 108–9; see also *CCC* 606–9.

[50] Balthasar, *GL7*, 225. See also *TD4*, 243 and 334, and Thomas Kryst, *Interpreting the Death of Jesus* (Washington, D.C.: Catholic University of America, 2009), 221–23.

become the righteousness of God" (2 Cor 5:21, RSVCE). Balthasar's key move is to understand this text in light of Mk 15:34 and Mt 27:46: "My God, my God, why have you forsaken me?" Insofar as the Son is made "to be sin", he bears the chief consequence of sin—separation from God. The Son incarnate, says Balthasar, endures "that darkness of alienation from God into which the sinner falls."[51]

To be sure, the Son incarnate does not identify with (in the sense of echoing) the actual no of sin. Jesus is always and only an obedient and loving yes to the Father, and so his vicarious experience of distance from God cannot be simply identical with that of rebellious sinners. This is surely indicated, for instance, in Jesus' cry of dereliction (Mk 15:34; Mt 27:46), which cannot bespeak the suffering of the damned, since the damned cannot say "my God". To the damned, God is a detested stranger, whereas Jesus' profound expression of God-forsakenness remains pure filial prayer to the Father.[52] This in no way lessens his suffering, however. Up until this "hour", Jesus experienced the Father as ever present and intimately near. But now, in taking the place of sinners before the Father, he bears subjectively their state of alienation from God. It is in fact Jesus' singular intimacy with the Father that, when it is experienced as withdrawn, leaves in its wake an utterly incomparable sense of desolation. The matchless depth of this interior suffering is actually the hallmark of the inimitable filial love stamped on Jesus' human soul. Balthasar puts it like this:

---

[51] Balthasar, *TD*4, 334. See also *Prayer*, 214.

[52] "We cannot say that Jesus . . . feels 'damned' by God and placed in 'hell'. For we associate the state of 'hell' with a hatred of God." Balthasar, *Does Jesus Know Us?*, 36. Indeed, "it is possible to maintain that Jesus' being forsaken by God was the opposite of hell." Balthasar, *TD*4, 336.

The crucified Jesus suffers, in our place, our experience of estrangement from God. . . . For him, there is nothing familiar about it; it is all that is alien and horrible to him. Indeed, he suffers something more deeply than an ordinary man is capable of suffering . . . because only the Son incarnate knows who the Father really is and what it means to be deprived of him, to have lost him (to all appearances) forever. It makes no sense to call this suffering "hell", for there is no hatred of God in Jesus, only a pain [of love] that is deeper than what an ordinary man could endure. . . . Nor can we say that the Father "punishes" his suffering Son in our place. It is not a question of punishment, for the work accomplished here between Father and Son with the cooperation of the Holy Spirit is utter love, the purest love possible.[53]

Concerning the use of "punishment" language in regard to Jesus' sufferings on the Cross, Balthasar clarifies his own stance. It is plain to him that there are notions of "punishment" that must *not* be attributed to the Crucified. "If we say that an innocent man as such cannot be 'punished', even if he is atoning for the guilty"—if "punishment" in the strict sense can fall only on the guilty—"then we shall avoid the term." (This Balthasar does in the text quoted above.) Nonetheless, it is permissible to follow Saint

---

[53] Hans Urs von Balthasar, *You Crown the Year with Your Goodness* (San Francisco: Ignatius Press, 1989), 85 (hereafter *YCY*). Balthasar criticized Karl Barth's doctrine of predestination for being "too close to the view that the sufferings of the Cross were punishment, a view [I, Balthasar] rejected in *Theo-Drama* IV, 284–316; the crucified Son does not simply suffer the hell deserved by sinners; he suffers something below and beyond this, namely, being forsaken by God in the pure obedience of love. Only he, as Son, is capable of this, and it is qualitatively deeper than any possible hell." *TD*5, 277. See Hans Urs von Balthasar, *To the Heart of the Mystery of Redemption*, trans. Anne Englund Nash (San Francisco: Ignatius Press, 2010), 34; and *Epilogue*, 120–21. See also *CCC* 603.

Hilary of Poitiers in distinguishing "between the *sensus poenae*, which Christ experienced, and the *vis poenae*, for *pietatis est susceptio peccatorum ista, non criminis*."[54] Jesus can assume and experience consequences of sin *pro nobis*, while being wholly innocent himself.[55]

For Balthasar, moreover, the effects of sin penetrate deeply into Jesus' rational soul. This inner penetration is indicated, Balthasar says, by Jesus' reference to "the cup" during his agony in the Garden of Gethsemane. The cup is none other than the cup of God's wrath, often referred to in the Old Testament, which "enters into the one who drinks it".[56] What does it mean for Jesus to drink from this cup willingly? For love of the Father, the Son "renounces all *perceptible* contact with the Father in order to experience in

[54] Balthasar, *TD*4, 337. The ITC puts it like this: "Without being personally guilty or being punished by God for the sins of others, Jesus lovingly identifies with sinful humanity and experiences the pain of its alienation from God." "Select Questions on the Theology of the Redeemer", 39.

[55] It is noteworthy that Thomas Aquinas, when discussing the Passion of Christ, occasionally speaks of *poena* (punishment, penalty). "The Son of God took flesh and came into the world, in order to satisfy for the sin of the human race. Now one person satisfies for the sin of another by taking on himself the punishment [*penalties*] due to the sin of the other." *ST* III, q. 14, a. 1. In ad 1, he continues: "The penalties one suffers for another's sins are the matter, as it were, of the satisfaction for that sin. But the principle [or formal element] of it is the attitude of soul which makes someone want to atone for another. It is from this that atonement gets its effectiveness." See also q. 14, a. 4, ad 2; q. 47, a. 3, ad 1; and q. 50, a. 1. All the same, says Aquinas, "Meritum satisfactionis non consistit tantum in caritate, sed requirit passionem Christi." *Commentary on the III Book of the Sentences* d. 18, q. 1, a. 6, qca. 3, ad 1.

[56] Balthasar, *TD*4, 338. See Is 51:17, 22; Jer 13:13; 25:15–17, 27ff.; 48:26; 49:12; 51:7; Ezek 23:32–34; Hab 2:15–16; Obad 16; Zech 12:2; Lam 4:21. According to André Feuillet, the cup Jesus must drink is the eschatological "chalice of the wrath of YHWH". *L'Agonie de Gethsémani, enquêtes exégétiques et théologiques* (Paris: Gabalda, 1977), 87. Quoted by Balthasar in *TD*4, 315. The chalice is offered to Jesus, yet he must accept it voluntarily (see Feuillet, 99, 212f., and 254).

himself the sinner's distance from God".[57] Or, what amounts
to the same, the Son consents to experience the Father's
love in its mode as wrath: paternal love in the form of self-
concealment.[58] If sin is the creature's no to God, divine
wrath bespeaks God's no to sin.[59] Thus, when the Father
wills that his Son drink from the cup of wrath, the Son on
his side becomes the bearer of the world's no to God. *To
that no*, borne by the Lamb, the Father responds by "hiding
his face". On his side, the Son makes his human heart a
place in which the Father is allowed to work (Jn 14:10–
11), albeit as the loving Father who conceals himself from
his beloved Son for the forgiveness-atonement of sin. Hence
the paradox that the dereliction that Jesus suffers is actually
the form that the Father's presence takes in the experience
of the sin-bearing Son.

> The relationship of the Outflow [the sent Son] with its
> Source [the sending Father] *appears* to be interrupted; [this
> "hour" in which the Lamb bears the sin of the world] is
> *experienced* by him as his abandonment by the Father. . . .
> [As the sin-bearing Lamb], he has identified himself with
> what God must eternally reject from himself. And yet he
> is the Son, who can only proceed and live from the source
> that is the Father, and this is the reason for his unfath-
> omable thirst for the inaccessible [hidden] Father.[60]

---

[57] Balthasar, *Unser Auftrag: Bericht und Entwurf*, (Einsiedeln, Switzerland:
Johannes Verlag, 1984), 54. My translation and emphasis. See also Feuillet, *L'Agonie de Gethsémani*, 199.

[58] "The Son experience[s] on the Cross the Father's love in the form of his
anger." Balthasar, *TD5*, 267. See also *TD3*, 450.

[59] "This wrath is no 'pretense,' but fully real: the categorical 'No' of God
to the attitude that the world takes up over against him. God owes it to his
loving covenantal righteousness to utter this 'No' and to maintain it as long
as his will is not done on earth as in Heaven." Balthasar, *GL7*, 206. See also
TD4, 338–51.

[60] Balthasar, *The Threefold Garland*, trans. Erasmo Leiva-Merikakis (San

Yet all the while, Jesus bears this with an attitude of un-wavering obedience. He remains the pure yes of filial love, even when he is plunged into the painfully experienced in-terior void of the Father's seeming absence. This experi-ence does not contradict the last words of the dying Jesus in Luke's Gospel, 23:46, "Into your [unfelt] hands I com-mend my spirit." For Jesus' self-entrustment to the Father is always and resolutely the fundamental attitude of his filial existence.[61]

Ratzinger, for his part, envisions Jesus' atoning Passion and death in a similar light. This vision gains remarkable clarity when viewed against the horizon of the Old Testa-ment and its (developing) understanding of *death*. In its early period, Israel's "phenomenology of death" was increasingly coupled with "an elucidation of *death's spiritual content*."[62]

Francisco: Ignatius Press, 1982), 100. See also *GL7*, 216 and 223; *TD4*, 320, 334–35, and 349–50.

[61] See Balthasar, *Explorations in Theology*, vol. 5, *Man Is Created*, trans. Adrian J. Walker (San Francisco: Ignatius Press, 2014), 58 (hereafter *MIC*). We cannot explore, within the limits of this study, Balthasar's proposals re-garding the incarnate Son's "immediate vision" of the Father. One path to investigate would consider whether the Son's experience of absence is a kind of vision-in-negative of the (felt-as-absent) Father. This path would entail a paradoxical deepening of the idea of the God-forsaken Son having the Beatific Vision on the Cross. For now, a helpful introduction to Balthasar's view is found in Aidan Nichols, *Balthasar for Thomists* (San Francisco: Ignatius Press, 2020), 140–43. Among Balthasar's texts, see *The Glory of the Lord: A Theo-logical Aesthetic*, vol. 1, *Seeing the Form*, trans. Erasmo Leiva-Merikakis (San Francisco: Ignatius Press, 1982), 329 (hereafter *GL1*). Also *GL7*, 216; *TD3*, 166–82, 195–96, and 200; *TD5*, 256–64 and 408–10. Joseph Ratzinger, in his turn, indicates a direction to take with his references to "the mysticism of a darkness in which only love can see" in "The Paschal Mystery as Core and Foundation of Devotion to the Sacred Heart", in *Towards a Civilization of Love*, 52.

[62] Joseph Ratzinger, *Eschatology: Death and Eternal Life*, trans. Michael Wald-stein (Washington, D.C.: Catholic University of America, 1988), 81, em-phasis added.

For the Israelite, death involved not merely the cessation of bodily life but also the loss of contact with the Lord. "Death", explains Ratzinger, "was synonymous with non-communication between the Israelite and Israel's God."[63] The dead man descended into Sheol, into the silence of the Pit, into "the God-forsaken land of darkness, a realm of distance from God."[64] Indeed the full extent of what made death dreadful was "seen from the fact that YHWH was not there."[65] Suffering and sickness, accordingly, were viewed as extensions of the sphere of death insofar as they too destroyed relationships and communication. Significantly, Ratzinger identifies the life of prayer as the primary means whereby Israel advanced in uncovering the "deepest spiritual ground and content" of the phenomena of suffering and death.[66] Communion with the Lord through prayer provided the principal perspective from which Israel deepened its discernment of "the connection between death and sin." The cause of this deadly rupture of relationship was traced back to sin, that is, to "a turning away from YHWH."[67]

---

[63] Ibid., 83; see also 80. Balthasar concurs: "The classic theology of the Old Testament characterizes death as the loss of the living relationship to God." If Jesus is to bear the sin of the world, "this act of bearing can be accomplished only in solidarity with the death that is the lot of all." *GL*7, 229.

[64] Ratzinger, *Eschatology*, 93.

[65] Ibid., 81. Ratzinger explains further that death was regarded as "a non-communication zone where life is destroyed precisely because relationship is impossible. . . . YHWH is not there. In relation to him there is a complete lack of communication in Sheol." Ibid. See Hoffmann, "Atonement and the Sacred Heart", 151; and Gerhard von Rad, *Old Testament Theology*, vol. 1 (New York: Harper & Row, 1965), 388.

[66] "Above all in her life of prayer, Israel developed a phenomenology of sickness and death wherein these things were interpreted as spiritual phenomena. In this way Israel discovered their deepest spiritual ground and content." Ratzinger, *Eschatology*, 81.

[67] "Death, being linked with [sin, that is,] a turning away from YHWH, throws light on what such separation entails." Ibid., 84.

Ratzinger's next step is to accentuate the breakthrough that is evident in the Servant Songs of Isaiah. This breakthrough to a new level of spiritual insight brought forth an interpretation of suffering and death now seen as material for vicarious atonement.[68] Suffering comes to be understood as "not simply the duly apportioned punishment for sins. It can be the proper path for someone who belongs to God and, treading that path of suffering, the Servant of God can open for others the door to life. . . . Suffering for God's sake and that of other people can be the highest form of allowing God to be present."[69] Precisely here Ratzinger brings out the paradoxical pattern of forgiveness-atonement. The Servant of the Lord willingly takes on suffering and death for others and—without suppressing the experience of God-forsakenness that these evince—converts it all into a form of filial prayer. Thus, death as God-*estrangement* is transformed into a mode of *communion* with God. Death as "*punishment* for sins" becomes a vehicle of God's *forgiving* power. Through the suffering and death of the righteous, the effecting of God's *justice* "become[s] so profound that it turns into the *mercy* of vicarious service."[70]

When next we turn to the New Testament, "the first thing to note", says Ratzinger, "is that [it] quite clearly preserves the basic thrust of the Old." Its newness does not consist in the formulation of different ideas concerning suffering, death, and vicarious atonement but "in the new *fact* which gathers acceptingly to itself all that went before and gives it its wholeness. This new fact is the martyrdom of Jesus . . .

---

[68] "We have the interpretation of the painful experience of the Exile in the Servant Songs of Second Isaiah. . . . There, sickness, death, abandonment are understood as vicarious suffering, and in this way the realm of death is filled with a novel, positive content." Ibid., 86.

[69] Ibid.

[70] Ibid. See also 93.

and his resurrection."[71] Jesus, in dying our sin-conditioned death, takes upon himself the full depth dimension of death as the wages of sin (Rom 6:23). Hence he "dies in tears. On his lips is the bitter taste of abandonment and isolation in all its horror."[72] All the same, Jesus' death cry (Mk 14:34; Mt 27:46) is in essence a prayer, signaling that in him the experience of God-forsakenness for sinners' sake becomes truly and definitively "the highest form of allowing God to be present." As Ratzinger contends:

> We must not forget that these words of the crucified Christ are the opening line of one of Israel's prayers (Ps 22:1 [21:2]). . . . This prayer that rises from the sheer misery of God's seeming eclipse ends in praises of God's greatness. This element, too, is present in Jesus' death cry, which has been recently described by Ernst Käsemann as a prayer sent up from hell, as the raising of a standard, the first commandment, in the wilderness of God's apparent absence.[73]

More recently, in *Jesus of Nazareth*, Pope Benedict maintains that Jesus' cry on the Cross

> is no ordinary cry of abandonment. Jesus is praying the great psalm of suffering Israel, and so he is taking upon himself all the tribulations, not just of Israel, but of all those in this world who *suffer from God's concealment*. He

---

[71] Ibid., 92 (emphasis is Ratzinger's). See Hoffmann, "Atonement and the Sacred Heart", 157; and Balthasar, *GL7*, 402.

[72] Ratzinger, *Eschatology*, 93. Jesus enters "the sphere of death [which] is dereliction, isolation, loneliness, and thus abandonment". Ibid., 81.

[73] Ratzinger, *Introduction to Christianity*, trans. J. R. Foster (San Francisco: Ignatius Press, 2004), 297. Similarly, Servais Pinckaers wrote, "The Passion account, especially in Matthew, describes a progressive despoilment and impoverishment . . . The drama culminates in the *supreme spiritual despoilment*, owned in the words: 'My God, why have you abandoned me?'." *The Pursuit of Happiness God's Way: Living the Beatitudes*, trans. Mary Thomas Noble (Eugene, Ore.: Wipf & Stock, 2011), 48.

brings the world's *anguished cry at God's absence* before the heart of God himself. He identifies himself with . . . all who *suffer "under God's darkness"*; he takes their cry, their anguish, all their helplessness upon himself—and in so doing *transforms* it.[74]

Benedict does not leave room for a stance that would see Jesus' atoning death as a merely exterior substitution for sinners. For him, plainly, Jesus' work of atonement is a process of *transformation* that entails an *interior* assumption of sin's estrangement from God. This is evident not only in the texts quoted above, but in numerous additional passages from *Jesus of Nazareth*. Commenting on Jesus' Baptism as anticipating his atoning death on the Cross, Benedict explains that "because of his equality with God, [the Son] can take upon himself all the sin of the world and then *suffers it through* to the end—omitting nothing . . . [in his identification] with the fallen."[75] "He must *go through, suffer through*, the whole of it, *in order to transform it*."[76] Further on, when interpreting Jesus' agony in the Garden of Gethsemane, Benedict avers that the process of transforming sin begins when "the abyss of sin and evil *penetrate[s] deep within [Jesus'] soul*."[77] Indeed, the abyss of . . . evil and enmity with God "he now takes directly upon himself, or rather *into* himself, to the point that he is 'made to be sin' (cf. 2 Cor 5:21)."[78] Yet this process of transformation cannot

---

[74] Benedict XVI, *Jesus of Nazareth*, vol. 2, 214, emphasis added. "Psalm 22 is Israel's great cry of anguish, in the midst of its sufferings, addressed to the apparently silent God. . . . We can hear the great anguish of the one suffering on account of God's seeming absence." Ibid., 204. See also Balthasar, *TD*4, 338.

[75] Benedict XVI, *Jesus of Nazareth*, vol. 1, 20 (emphasis added). See also 30.

[76] Ibid., 26 (emphasis added).

[77] Benedict XVI, *Jesus of Nazareth*, vol. 2, 149 (emphasis added).

[78] Ibid., 155.

be efficacious without the "filial will" of Jesus surrendering itself totally to the Father's will.[79] Hence we have Benedict's brief summary of the process as the Son "taking men's
'no' upon himself and drawing it into his 'yes' (cf. 2 Cor
1:19)."[80] Thereby sin "is truly absorbed, wiped out, and
transformed in the pain of infinite love".[81] Or, as he phrases it
elsewhere, the Son "*transforms evil in suffering, in the fire of his
suffering love*".[82] This manner of envisioning Jesus' work of
atonement bears a strong resemblance to, and is clearly compatible with, Hoffmann's and Balthasar's view that sonship
takes sin upon itself—indeed into itself, without ceasing to
be itself—in order to transform sin into its opposite, thereby
wiping it out. Only the Son incarnate who is closest to the
Father's heart (Jn 1:18) can, as the sin-bearing Servant (Jn
1:29), suffer God's concealment such that the abyss of enmity with God is converted into material for a new and
unparalleled covenantal intimacy with the Father.[83]

John Paul II agrees that what the Son incarnate suffered
entailed a profound subjective experience of separation from

---

[79] Ibid., 156. Significantly, Benedict pauses to insist that it is "quite mistaken on the part of some theologians to suggest that the man Jesus was ad-
dressing the Trinitarian God in the prayer on the Mount of Olives. No, it
is the Son speaking here [to the Father in the Spirit], having subsumed the
fullness of man's will into himself and transformed it into the will of the Son."
Ibid., 162. Benedict's stance reinforces the interpersonal quality (Father-Son,
Lover-Beloved) of the theology of atonement under development here.

[80] Ibid., 123. See also 225.

[81] Ibid., 231, emphasis added.

[82] Joseph Ratzinger, Homily at the Mass *Pro Eligendo Romano Pontifice* (April
18, 2005). Compare this with Balthasar. The Cross event is the hour "when
the eternal Triune plan is executed to clear out all the refuse of the world's sin
by burning it in the fire of suffering love". *The Threefold Garland*, 99. Christ
gathers "up into himself . . . the world's sin, which offends the goodness of
the Father, in order to burn it utterly in the fire of his suffering". Ibid., 71.

[83] See Benedict XVI, *Jesus of Nazareth*, vol. 1, 20–21.

his Father. While John Paul II follows Thomas Aquinas in
affirming that Christ "at the summit of his human spirit had
a clear vision of God", he differs from Thomas in holding
that "the most acute pain for the soul of Jesus" involved an
experience of the Father's absence proportionate to the sin
he bore.

> At the summit of his human spirit, Jesus has a clear vision
> of God and the certainty of his union with the Father. But
> in the areas bordering on the sensitive sphere . . . Jesus' hu-
> man soul is reduced to a wasteland, and he no longer feels
> the presence of the Father, but undergoes the tragic expe-
> rience of the most complete desolation. . . . [T]he Father
> is silent now. That silence of God weighs on the dying
> Jesus as the heaviest pain [or penalty (*la pena*)] of all. . . .
> In the sphere of his feelings and affections, this sense of
> the absence of, and abandonment by, God was the most
> acute pain for the soul of Jesus, who drew his strength and
> joy from union with the Father. This pain rendered all the
> other sufferings more intense. That lack of interior conso-
> lation was his greatest agony. But Jesus knew that by this
> final phase of his sacrifice, which had reached the inmost
> fibers of his heart, he was completing the work of repa-
> ration that was the purpose of his sacrifice for the atone-
> ment of sins. If sin is separation from God, Jesus had to
> experience in the crisis of his union with the Father a suf-
> fering proportionate to that separation.[84]

In this way, John Paul II revises Thomas' interpretation
of Jesus' abandonment by God. In his *Summa theologica*,

---

[84] John Paul II, General Audience (November 30, 1988) nos. 4–6. Translated by Adrian Walker. See also his General Audience (April 27, 198). Notably two Doctors of the Church teach something quite similar to John Paul II
on this subject: see John of the Cross, *The Ascent of Mount Carmel*, bk. 3, chap.
6, and Francis de Sales, *Treatise on the Love of God*, bk. 5, chap. 5. See also
Balthasar, *TD3*, 522.

Thomas mentions it only once, in order to say that the Father did not shield his Son from the power of his enemies.[85] John Paul II, for his part, takes pains to assert that this abandonment does not consist only in the "external" non-intervention of God when Jesus is tortured and killed by his enemies. There is more to it. The Father conceals himself from Jesus internally, which results in an acute feeling of the absence of the Father in his soul. Jesus' soul thus enters into a "night", a darkening of his psyche in its relation to the Father. He no longer feels the paternal presence.

Likewise, John Paul II's theology of atonement agrees with that of Hoffmann and Balthasar in interpreting Matthew 27:46: "My God, my God, why have you forsaken me?", in light of 2 Corinthians 5:21: "For our sake he made him to be sin who knew no sin."[86] These two passages interpret each other, explains the pontiff. The "entire evil" of sin is unveiled when the incarnate Son is made "to be sin", that is, when the Son is made to endure separation from the Father, estrangement from God. John Paul II's words merit quoting at length:

> The words uttered on Golgotha . . . bear witness to this depth—unique in the history of the world—of the evil of the suffering experienced. When Christ says: "My God, My God, why have you abandoned me?" . . . these words on abandonment are born at the level of that inseparable union of the Son with the Father, and are born because the Father "laid on him the iniquity of us all" (Is 53:6). They also foreshadow the words of Saint Paul: "For our sake he made him to be sin who knew no sin" (2 Cor 5:21).

---

[85] In the view of Aquinas, Jesus is abandoned "externally" by his Father but does not suffer the internal experience of the Father's self-concealment. *ST* III, q. 47, a. 3. See q. 46, a. 8; and q. 50, a. 2, ad 1. For Balthasar's remarks on Aquinas' treatment of this question, see *TD*4, 264.

[86] Translations from RSVCE.

Together with this horrible weight, *encompassing the "en-tire" evil of the turning away from God* which is contained in sin, Christ, through the divine depth of his filial union with the Father, perceives in a humanly inexpressible way *this suffering which is the separation*, the rejection *by the Father*, the estrangement from God. But precisely through this suffering he accomplishes the Redemption, and can say as he breathes his last: "It is finished" (Jn 19:30).[87]

What, then, is God's answer to sin? Sin is "annihilated", says John Paul II, in virtue of the love of Christ who vicariously accepts to suffer the experience of separation from the Father proportionate to "all human sin in its breadth and depth."[88]

Atonement is a work engendered by God the Father

If our quartet of theologians is united in affirming that the Son, in vicariously bearing sin, suffers an acute feeling of the absence of the Father in his human soul, they are equally united in affirming the inseparable union of the Son with

[87] John Paul II, apostolic letter *Salvifici doloris* (On the Christian Meaning of Human Suffering) (February 11, 1984), no. 18 (italics are the pope's). Elsewhere the pontiff stresses that the Son's cry of God-forsakenness was not one of despair or protest: "In Jesus' 'Why' there is no sentiment of resentment that would lead to rebellion or be an indulgence in desperation. There is no shadow of a reproach addressed to the Father. Rather, [this 'Why'] expresses the experience . . . of solitude, of abandonment to himself that Jesus undergoes in our place." General Audience (November 30, 1988), no. 3. Translated by Adrian Walker. See also his apostolic exhortation *Reconciliatio et paenitentia* (December 2, 1984), no. 7, and *Crossing the Threshold of Hope* (New York: Alfred A. Knopf, 1994), 66.

[88] "Sins are cancelled out precisely because he alone as the only-begotten Son could take them upon himself, accept them with *that love for the Father which overcomes* the evil of every sin; in a certain sense he *annihilates* this evil." John Paul II, *Salvifici doloris*, no. 17 (italics are the pope's).

the Father throughout his work of atonement. Doubtless it would be a serious mistake to regard the Father's forsaking of Jesus on the Cross as signaling a real rupture of the Father-Son relationship. After all, to be the Son means to be always dependent on the Father (Jn 5:19–20, 31; 15:9). Indeed the Son's historical mission unto the Paschal event should be seen as the graciously free extension of his eternal generation by the Father.[89]

This consideration already implies another point. According to John 14:9–12, Jesus maintains: "Whoever has seen me has seen the Father. . . . The Father who dwells in me is doing his works. . . . Believe . . . because of the works themselves . . . the works that I do." Here Jesus avers that *the Father* is at work in the works that *the Son* performs. Paternal work engenders filial work, such that the Father's work is accomplished in the work of the Son. Inasmuch as the Son's work is to atone for the sin of the world (Jn 1:29; 1 Jn 2:2; 4:10), this work is not performed of himself (Jn 5:19, 30; 8:28), as if the Father, in sending the Son, kept himself back at an uninvolved distance, leaving the Son to act quite alone. Rather, in sending the Son, the Father remains *immanent in* the work of the Son. Put differently, the Father's *sending* of the Son is always at the same time his *accompanying* of the Son; his sending-forth remains always a being-with (Jn 8:16, 28–29; 16:32).[90] Hence for someone (truly) to hear and see

---

[89] "Thomas Aquinas . . . teaches that the Son's being sent, his mission (*missio*), into finite, passing time, is only the extension, the economic form, of his eternal procession (*processio*) from the Father." Balthasar, *MIC*, 56. For Balthasar, "the Son's *missio* is his *processio* [freely] extended in 'economic' mode." *TD4*, 356. See Aquinas, *ST* I, q. 43, a. 2, ad 3; and Balthasar, *GL7*, 213.

[90] "Jesus, who was sent out by the Father, was yet accompanied on his 'journey' by the One who sent him." Balthasar, *Does Jesus Know Us*, 77. See Margaret Turek, "'As the Father Has Loved Me' (Jn 15:9): Balthasar's

Jesus in the performance of his mission would mean, at the same time, "to understand Jesus' deeds as the work of the Father, for they are 'performed with the power of my Father' (Jn 10:32), indeed they are 'the works of my Father' (10:37)."[91] Nothing in the mission of Jesus is separate from the Father's involvement. Nothing in his mission is beyond the reach of the Father's action, for in this respect he *is* the Father's action, inasmuch as he acts always by and with and for the Father.[92]

Thus there are solid biblical grounds for asserting, with Hoffmann, that "in Christ's atoning work, God the Father is acting with his *generative* power."[93] And again: "Christ's atoning work on the Cross . . . is effected by the Father's *generative* power and carried out by the incarnate Son in free, obedient love."[94] If Jesus, with all his love, experiences the distance that exists between sinners and God as an

---

Theodramatic Approach to a Theology of God the Father", *Communio* 26.2 (Summer 1999): 298–300.

[91] Balthasar, *GL*1, 668. The Father "is seen to be present in the One who is sent (Jn 12:45), witnessing to himself in him (5:37; 8:18); he dwells with him (8:16, 29; 16:32). . . . It is important for the One who sends to be 'known' (15:21), 'believed' (5:24; 12:44) and 'honored' (5:23) in the One who is sent." *TD*3, 153.

[92] Regarding Jesus' acting by virtue of the Father's "perpetually operative love", see Balthasar, *TD*3, 110; *TD*2, 87; *GL*1, 147, 614, and 616; and *GL*7, 262 and 283. Balthasar's remarks on the incarnate Son being accompanied by the Father recognize the *generative* nature of this paternal accompaniment: "The accompaniment has a hardly imaginable intimacy which is expressed in the Son's prayer-life and, moving from this, in his whole existence. . . . The Father's [accompanying] love . . . becomes [in the Son] its answering coactuation or realization", thereby showing its *generative* power. *The von Balthasar Reader*, ed. Medard Kehl and Werner Löser, trans. Robert J. Daly and Fred Lawrence (Edinburgh: T&T Clark, 1985), 176.

[93] Hoffmann, "Atonement and the Sacred Heart", 172 (emphasis is the author's).

[94] Ibid., 173 (emphasis is author's).

excruciating absence, it is because the Father, with all *his* love, remains always united to Jesus and unceasingly moves and sustains him in his task of taking upon himself the desolation of sinners to the point of dying as their vicarious representative. And therefore, what Jesus experiences as God-forsakenness is the opposite of what in reality is taking place. On the Cross, sin is countered by the mutual love of the Father and the Son incarnate in such a way that the "unholy distance" between God and sinners is transformed from within by the "holy intimacy" between Father and Son. Hence Jesus' cry of God-forsakenness bespeaks paradoxically his unparalleled union with the forgiving Father.

Balthasar unequivocally affirms this view: if "the Father allows the Son to endure dereliction among sinners", nonetheless all the while the incarnate Son is " 'not only *moved by* the Father's love but also *borne and enveloped by* it.' In this . . . *their common work of love* for the world, Father and Son are closer together than ever."[95] Balthasar suggests that this state of God-forsakenness, when the Father conceals himself, "is rather like a photographic negative in its relation to the positive reality of a presence and a union that can never be disturbed".[96] Consequently, when the Son says of the Father, "He has not left me alone" (Jn 8:29), he is thinking also of his atoning Passion, when even in the most

---

[95] Balthasar, *TD4*, 348–49. Inner citation is from P. Althaus, *Die christliche Wahrheit*, 471–72. See *TD4*, 336.

[96] Balthasar, *Engagement with God: The Drama of Christian Discipleship*, trans. R. John Halliburton (San Francisco: Ignatius Press, 2008), 44. See also *TD4*, 336n8, where Balthasar quotes V. Taylor, *St. Mark*, 2nd ed. (1966), 594: "The depths of the saying [Christ's cry of dereliction on the Cross] are too deep to be plumbed, but the least inadequate interpretations are those that find in it a sense of desolation in which Jesus felt the horror of sin so deeply that for a time the closeness of his communion with the Father was obscured. Glover writes: 'I have sometimes thought there never was an utterance that reveals more amazingly the distance between feeling and fact'."

profound forsakenness, the Father will remain always with him. This will be true even when Jesus no longer experiences it. He knows that, in this dereliction, when the Father himself is manifest as the forsaken God, he will be in absolute unity with him.[97] For this work of love cannot but originate in the Father, who moves the Son to act willingly as his definitive image and collaborator in suffering through the estrangement wrought by sin. Indeed "through it all, the Son's relationship with the Father who generates him remains intact; in fact, everything serves to reveal this eternal relationship."[98] In short, the Son's bearing away the sin

---

[97] See Balthasar, *TD5*, 263, and *GL7*, 234 and 249–50. In this light we should understand Benedict XVI's words about "the suffering Father, who, as Father, shares inwardly the sufferings of the Son". He adds that "the Father supports the cross and the crucified, bends lovingly over him and the two are, as it were, together on the cross. . . . It is not a matter of a cruel justice, not a matter of the Father's fanaticism, but rather of . . . the true overcoming of evil that ultimately can be realized only in the suffering of love." From an interview by Jacques Servais, "The Christian Faith Is Not an Idea but a Life", *Inside the Vatican* 24.4 (April 2016): 34; translated by Robert Moynihan from the Italian edition of *L'Osservatore Romano*, March 17, 2016. Also see Benedict's *Jesus of Nazareth*, vol. 1, 38.

[98] Balthasar, *TD5*, 264. If we ask after the possibility of the Father's self-distancing from Jesus during the Passion while he nonetheless remains at work in his Son, Balthasar answers that the condition for this paradoxical unity "must lie within the eternal Trinity, in the absolute distance/distinction between the Hypostasis who surrenders the Godhead and the Hypostasis who receives it". *TD4*, 333. The Father, in giving the Son autonomy [*Selbst-ständigkeit*], gives the Son the distance [*Abständigkeit*] that is necessary in order to maintain the personal distinction of the Other in the exchange of self-giving love between them (see *TD5*, 94; *TD2*, 257.) "In God," says Balthasar, "begetting is the definitive, irrevocable leaving-free [*Freilassung*] the Begotten." *TD5*, 83. And the Begetter's modality of leaving-free entails both his *withdrawing from* and *remaining in* the Begotten. It is a kind of *withdrawal* inasmuch as the generating Father "detaches himself [*Sich-lösen*] from the One on whom he bestows this gift". *TD5*, 93. Indeed, the Father's power to let the Other be [*Sein-lassen-Können*] is expressed precisely as the power to separate himself from his own [*Sich-vom-Eigenen-abscheiden-Können*]. See *TD5*, 83 and 85. At the same time, the Father's leaving-free the Son is a *remaining in* the Son insofar as the Begotten One, while receiving himself in such a way that

of the world is in the first place the work of God in his
Paternity.[99]

Thus, the Father and the Son incarnate are jointly involved in this redemptive work: sin as opposition to the extension of their paternal-filial relationship in the economy
of grace is countered by their willingness to endure mutual
forsakenness as an expression of their unswerving love for
us—"while we were enemies" (Rom 5:10).

Of course, the role of the Holy Spirit is indispensable here
too. As the "bond of love", the Holy Spirit maintains the
unity between the Father and the crucified Son in their common work of reconciling the world to God. "If the Spirit is
the 'Go-Between' of Father and Son, then he is supremely
so on the Cross, when he both reveals and makes the most
extreme 'separation' of Father and Son to be the epiphany
of their supreme unity."[100]

---

he subsists in himself, is yet the hypostatic locus in whom the Begetter ceaselessly expresses his Paternity. This means that the Son's "receiving himself
(in which he receives the divine substance) can never be cut off from the
paternal act of generative love". *TD5*, 92. For an extensive treatment of this
paradox, see Turek, *Towards a Theology of God the Father*, 123–42. See also
ITC, "Theology, Christology, Anthropology", 216.

[99] Of course the work of the Triune God *ad extra* is the common work of the
three divine Persons, who operate by one and the same nature. Nonetheless,
"each divine person performs the common work according to his unique
personal property." *CCC* 258. Hence, because our four guides agree that
the Father's act of generation *ad intra* is an act of love, they are critical of
the tendency among some theologians to let the Father's personal modality
of divine love dissolve into an undifferentiated Godhead when operating *ad
extra*. See John Paul II, *The Trinity's Embrace*, 90, 183, and 309; Ratzinger,
"Understanding the Concept of Person in Theology", *Communio* 17.3 (Fall
1990): 444; and Balthasar, *YCY*, 144 and 158–59.

[100] Balthasar, *Epilogue*, 121. (I have slightly edited the translation.) Space pre-
vents us from elaborating on the role of the Holy Spirit in the Cross event.
For more on this, see Balthasar, *GL7*, 404; *TD3*, 151, 186–201, 520–23, and
533; *TD4*, 257; *TD5*, 262. See also Hoffmann, "Atonement and the Sacred
Heart", 177–78.

The God-forsaken Son reveals
the forsaken God, the Father

Thus far in this chapter we have focused primarily on atonement as a work of annihilating sin by transforming it from within through the power of filial love. Going forward we will extend the scope of our discussion of the Son's mission of atonement to include its twin dimension: its revelatory nature and purpose. We are justified in doing so since Scripture itself shows that God's redemptive action is not simply executed but also takes the form of revelation. Both God's *work* and God's *word* form an integral unity. In the New Testament, this unity is strikingly conveyed in the Letter to the Colossians, with the concept of the "mystery of God" (μυστηρίου τοῦ Θεοῦ; *mystēriou tou Theou*) which is Christ (Col 2:2). Here both aspects are held together: the "mystery of God" is that which is both *actually done* and *made known* at the same time.[101] To be sure, we have already argued that the process of atonement as pictured in the Bible is revelatory of the living and loving God. Yet now we will explore this facet in a methodical and in-depth way with our gaze fixed on Christ, the "mystery of God" made visible.[102]

First of all we need to acknowledge that Jesus Christ

---

[101] See Hoffmann, "Atonement and the Sacred Heart", 189; and R. Schulte in *Mysterium Salutis*, vol. 4/2 (Einsiedeln, Switzerland: Benziger Verlag, 1967), 76.

[102] Because of space constraints we cannot include a discussion of the patristic literature where the foundation is laid for our elaboration of Christ's revelation of the Father. It must suffice to point back to Athanasius, who teaches that the Son, through his redemptive incarnation, "repaired the image of God in humanity by reuniting it with his own divine *imaging* of the Father. . . . Through his incarnation, the Son repairs our human participation in his *imaging* of the Father from within his human constitution." Indeed, through his Passion and death, the Son communicates the efficacy of his divine *imaging* of the Father to his human nature as he bears sin's consequences for us. Anatolios, *Retrieving Nicaea*, 107–8, emphasis added.

defines his mission as doing the will of him who sent him
(Jn 4:34; 6:38; 10:18), performing his Father's works (4:34;
9:4; 10:37; 14:10), speaking his Father's words (3:34; 7:16;
12:49–50; 14:10, 24)—professing, moreover, that he can
only do what he sees the Father doing (5:19). Plainly, "according to Jesus Christ's own portrayal of himself . . . [he
presents] himself consistently as the definitive 'interpretation' (Jn 1:18) of God the Father."[103]

Our next step is to discern a twofoldness in the person of
Jesus as he performs his mission. Jesus is simultaneously the
expression of the Father (*receptive* to paternal action) and his
own filial manner of expressing himself (*actively* imaging and
thereby interpreting the action of the Father). While Jesus
knows that the Father works in him, he is equally aware
that what is required of him is a total self-investment in the
work he is sent to carry out: "*he* does his Father's works
(Jn 10:37), *he* gives himself up in love for the many and
for each individual (Gal 2:20); *he* gives himself away in his
Eucharist."[104] This twofold structure of Jesus' *persona* can
be sufficiently explained only if we grant that the Father
gives over to the incarnate Son an "area" for collaborative
activity, in which "area" Jesus is left free or "let be" vis-à-
vis the Father's work. This is indicated by the words of the
Johannine Jesus: "The Father who dwells in me is doing his
works. Believe . . . because of the works themselves . . . the
works that I do" (Jn 14:10–12).

Yet if earlier we gleaned from this Johannine passage that

---

[103] Balthasar, *TD*3, 506. "The task given him by the Father, that is, that of
expressing God's Fatherhood through his life and death in and for the world,
totally occupies his self-consciousness." Ibid., 172. See *GL*1, 135, 154, 189,
195, and 611–13; *TD*2, 91; *TD*3, 172; *Does Jesus Know Us*, 73; *Unless You
Become Like This Child* (San Francisco: Ignatius Press, 1991), 10; and "God
Is His Own Exegete", *Communio* 4.4 (Winter 1986): 280–87. See also *CCC*
516.

[104] Balthasar, *TD*3, 519 (emphasis Balthasar's).

the Son's work is *derivative*, now we must realize that it is also *imitative*. Filial work *mirrors* or *images* paternal work. Indeed, Jesus constantly points back to the Father as the original model on whom he patterns his life. The Gospels bear this out in numerous texts, perhaps most notably in John 5:19–20 (RSVCE): "Truly, truly, I say to you, the Son can do nothing of his own accord, but only what he sees the Father doing; for whatever he does, that the Son does likewise. For the Father loves the Son, and shows him all that he himself is doing." It is by virtue of the Father "showing" the Son everything he does that the Son "does likewise", and thus in his turn "shows" us the Father (Jn 14:9). The loving Father presents himself to Jesus as the model that finds expression in all his Son's actions. And Jesus, in seeing the loving Father, is moved to dispose of himself in imitation of his paternal Origin.

In view of these biblically founded observations and in order to make this interpersonal dynamic between the Father and the Son more intelligible, we may adopt some insights from personalist philosophy and consider the relationship between parent and child to be an *imago Trinitatis*—a distant creaturely echo of the Son's being shown, and thereby likewise showing, the Father's self-donation.[105] The first insight

[105] See Balthasar, "Movement Toward God" in *Explorations in Theology*, vol. 3, *Creator Spiritus*, trans. Brian McNeil (San Francisco: Ignatius Press, 1993), 15–55. Balthasar's use of the insights of modern personalist philosophy is intended only to serve as an articulation of biblical revelation. What cannot be overly stressed is that the primary reality is the I-Thou relation eternally in God that surpasses our apprehension at every point. The human person and its I-Thou relation are the faint reflections of it. Still, if anyone should object that we are making too great a leap here, consider that the mystery of the human person is rooted in Christ, and that the mystery of Christ is inseparable from his identity as Child of God and of man. It is precisely as the one who ushers in the kingdom of the Father in virtue of his twofold filial identity, that Jesus sets a child before his disciples and assures them that they must regard the disposition of children as the condition for entering the

to note is that every human being on coming into the world must first be loved in order to be able to love. A little child cannot at the outset take the initiative in acting out of love; for the child comes to self-awareness and self-love (preconditions for the giving of self) only through an encounter with a "Thou", whose love he needs first to receive. It is the parent's initiative of self-giving, a "work" of parental love expressed in a manner as simple as smiling at the little child, that induces the child to give himself reciprocally, to smile back at his parent as an answer of love to love. The child's mirroring response is evoked and engendered in the face of the parent's self-donation. Hence, parental love is manifest in the child's return of love, for the child's self-giving points back to (and thus reveals) the love he has first been shown.

With this *imago Trinitatis* in mind, let us observe that the capacity to give himself in love that Jesus demonstrates is "to the end" (Jn 13:1), indicating a self-giving that has attained its most perfect and definitive expression. Now, in the condition of a human life, the finality of a self-donation that gathers up and gives over the totality of the person is most fittingly expressed in a self-sacrificial death (Jn 15:13). Yet inasmuch as it is a *filial* self-donation, it is an action reflective of *paternal* love. "As the Father has loved me, so I have loved you" (Jn 15:9, RSVCE). Assuredly, then, the Son's self-sacrificial death makes known the boundlessness of God's fatherly love through his own filial capacity to love unreservedly.[106] Hence an adequate understanding of Jesus'

---

kingdom (Mk 10:15). The Johannine Gospel identifies this filial disposition with being begotten "from above" (Jn 3:3).

[106] See Balthasar, *GL7*, 283; and *The Christian State of Life*. See also John Paul II, "The Spirt Is the Source of Communion" (General Audience, July 29, 1998), in *The Trinity's Embrace*, 90. Luis Cardinal Ladaria affirms something similar: "If the Son reveals the Father's love, it is not wrong to think that the Son shows in his self-giving to us the Father's infinite capacity for

representation of the Father must grasp that it is in his obedient "imaging love" that the Father's original self-donation
"appears". This enables Balthasar to assert that even "the
Son's suffering love becomes the inverted mirror-image of
the Father's love."[107]

On this matter, too, Ratzinger's stance is congruent with
Balthasar's. He affirms that Jesus' whole human existence,
including his suffering love as the sin-bearing Son, is in
the service of his "interpretation" of the Father.[108] In fact,
Ratzinger maintains that the Son's work of revelation reaches
its acme only when his work of atonement is accomplished:

> He who sees Christ truly sees the Father. . . . "The sur-
> render to death makes the love of the Father visible. . . .
> The Crucified One is 'the image of the invisible God'
> (Col 1:15)." . . . Therefore he who sees Christ, the Cru-
> cified One, sees the Father, and the entire Trinitarian mys-
> tery. For we must add, when one sees the Father in Christ,
> *then* in him the veil of the temple is truly rent, and the in-
> terior of God is laid bare.[109]

Ratzinger (Benedict XVI) reiterates this view in the first
volume of *Jesus of Nazareth*:

---

self-giving. The self-giving of the Son is founded on the abyss of the love of
the Father which is infinite capacity of donation and love." *The Living and
True God: The Mystery of the Trinity* (Miami: Convivium Press, 2010), 350.

[107] Balthasar, *Prayer*, 86. See *TD3*, 157, 224, 340, and 511; *GL7*, 376–77.
Also see Turek, *Towards a Theology of God the Father*, 63–64.

[108] Benedict describes the mission of Jesus as "the concrete realization of
the Father's action". *Jesus of Nazareth*, vol. 1, 208. "By the way he acts, then,
Jesus himself becomes 'the revelation of the one he called his Father.' . . .
[Jesus] bases his conduct on the Father's. . . . Jesus justifies his own conduct
by relating it to, and identifying it with, the Father's." Ibid., 207–8.

[109] Ratzinger, "Jesus Christ today", *Communio* 17.1 (Spring 1990): 80–81,
with inner citations from C. Schönborn's work, *Die Christus-Ikone* (Schaff-
hausen, Switzerland: Novalis Verlag, 1984), 96–97.

"When you have lifted up the Son of man, *then* you will know that I am he" (Jn 8:28). On the Cross, his Sonship, his oneness with the Father, becomes visible. . . . On the Cross, Jesus is exalted to the very "height" of the God who is love. It is *there* that he can be "known," that the "I am he" can be recognized. . . . What we find here is not metaphysical speculation, but the self-revelation of God's reality in the midst of history.[110]

For Benedict, it is "on the Cross"—when enacting his passion of love "to the end" (εἰς τέλος, Jn 13:1)—that Jesus reaches the "height" of his exegesis of God's love as Father.

A further aspect, which we noted previously, emerges in volume 2 of *Jesus of Nazareth*, where Benedict pinpoints the inmost essence of Jesus' suffering. Jesus' cry on the Cross (Mk 15:34; Mt 27:46) indicates, says Benedict, that Jesus is enduring "for us" the experience of estrangement from the One who sent him. "He is taking upon himself" the state of all those "who *suffer from God's concealment*" and who cry out "*at God's absence.*"[111]

Now if, as Benedict holds, the Son's "surrender to death makes the love of the Father visible",[112] and if "death's spiritual content" is "distance from God",[113] then we suggest what comes to visibility regarding *the Father's* love is *his* willingness to endure sin-wrought distance from his beloved as a modality of his generative power, that is, the form that paternal love takes in producing its answering filial image unto

[110] Benedict XVI, *Jesus of Nazareth*, vol. 1, 349 (emphasis added). See also 6–7 and 137.

[111] Benedict XVI, *Jesus of Nazareth*, vol. 2, 214 (emphasis added). "In this last prayer of Jesus, as in the scene on the Mount of Olives, what appears as the innermost heart of his Passion is not any physical pain but *radical loneliness*"—suffering the Father's apparent absence. Ratzinger, *Introduction to Christianity*, 298.

[112] Ratzinger, "Jesus Christ today", *Communio* 17.1 (Spring 1990): 80.

[113] Ratzinger, *Eschatology*, 81 and 93.

the forgiveness-atonement of sin. Hence the Crucified One, precisely in suffering "distance from God", unveils the suffering love in the Heart of the Father, such that "through the suffering Son, [we] recognize the true God."[114]

John Paul II, for his part, fully agrees with the others that "the Paschal Mystery is Christ at the summit of the revelation of the inscrutable mystery of God. It is precisely *then* that the words pronounced in the Upper Room are completely fulfilled: 'He who has seen me has seen the Father' (Jn 14:9)."[115]

More yet, as we noted in the previous chapter, John Paul II stands firmly with those who see the *suffering Father* in his crucified Son.[116]

> 39. It is not possible to grasp the evil of sin in all its sad reality without "searching the depths of God." [If the world is to be convinced concerning sin, it will] have to mean revealing suffering. Revealing the pain . . . on account of sin [which Scripture, notwithstanding certain anthropomorphic formulations] seems to glimpse in the "depths of God" and in a certain sense in the very heart of the ineffable Trinity. The Church, taking her inspiration from Revelation, believes and professes that sin is an offense against God. What corresponds, in the inscrutable intimacy of the Father, the Word and the Holy Spirit, to this "offense," this rejection of the Spirit who is love and gift? . . . [I]n the "depths of God" there is a Father's love that, faced with man's sin, in the language of the Bible reacts so deeply. . . . This inscrutable and indescribable fatherly

---

[114] Benedict XVI, *Jesus of Nazareth*, vol. 2, 224. This squares with his insistence that God the loving Father suffers in the face of sin. See our discussion in chap. 1.

[115] John Paul II, encyclical letter *Dives in misericordia* (November 30, 1980), no. 8 (emphasis added).

[116] It warrants repeating that this stance is not to be mistaken for "patripassianism", which is a brand of modalism.

"pain" will bring about above all the wonderful economy
of redemptive love in Jesus Christ . . . in whose humanity
the "suffering" of God is concretized. . . .[117]

41. If sin caused suffering, now the pain of God in Christ
crucified acquires through the Holy Spirit its full human expression. . . . In Christ there suffers a God who has been rejected by his own creature: "They do not believe in me!";
but at the same time, from the depth of this suffering . . .
in the depth of the mystery of the Cross, [divine] love is
at work, that love which brings man back again to share in
the life that is God himself.[118]

In what does God's "fatherly 'pain'" consist? John Paul II
situates this pain in the face of sin, understood as the rejection of God's love.[119] This suggests that the pain of God that
is "concretized" in his crucified Son involves sin-wrought
estrangement. This suggestion is supported by John Paul's
teaching on the essence of the human suffering of Christ on
the Cross. As we saw above, the pope maintains that "the
most acute pain for the soul of Jesus"—that pain which reveals God's "fatherly 'pain'"—consists in suffering separation on account of sin. "He no longer feels the presence of
the Father. . . . [T]he Father is silent now. . . . This sense
of the absence of, and abandonment by, God was the most
acute pain for the soul of Jesus."[120]

Taken altogether, these texts of John Paul II uphold the
notion that Jesus' expiatory suffering of separation brings to

[117] Hoffmann concurs: "The 'consequences' of sin extend to the Heart of
God." "Atonement and the Sacred Heart", 165.

[118] John Paul II, *Dominum et vivificantem*, nos. 39–41.

[119] Cf. Hos 1:2, 9; 4:10; 8:3; 11:1–11; Is 1:2, 4; 63:16; 64:7; Jer 31:9;
Deut 32:6, 18; Mal 2:10; see also Jon D. Levenson, *The Love of God: Divine
Gift, Human Gratitude, and Mutual Faithfulness in Judaism* (Princeton: Prince-
ton University Press, 2016), 101.

[120] John Paul II, General Audience (November 30, 1988), nos. 4–6. Translated by Adrian Walker.

completion the historical revelation of the *passio caritatis* of the almighty Father.[121] Far from being incapacitating, the Father's suffering love is *effective* (at work) in Jesus as the divine archetype and generative source of his bearing sin in filial fashion, unto sin's atonement.

At this point we can say that if the Father directs Jesus to expiate sin by bearing the God-forsaken state of sinners, it is only because the Father, on his side, is first to allow himself to endure being forsaken (Hos 11:1–8; Is 1:2; 30:9). It is this resolutely passionate love shown by the Father that serves Jesus as the model that he imitates in allowing himself to be forsaken on the Cross. For such a paternal love is worthy of nothing less and engenders nothing other than a return of filial love in kind. And so it is that the crucified Son as "the God-forsaken" images and thus reveals "the forsaken-God", his Father.

Given the positions of our recent popes, we can hardly regard as idiosyncratic Balthasar's assertion that the climax of the Son's revelation of the Father is presented in the figure of the Forsaken One.

> "This is what the Father is like." . . . The high point of Jesus' interpretation of God is the time . . . that the Son on the Cross is forsaken by the Father. . . . Here, certainly, Jesus is the man who takes away the sin of the world, and God can only turn his face away from the monstrous proportions of this sin [*an allusion to God's wrath*]. But is this God who has turned his face away not also a forsaken God? [*an allusion to God's paternal love-suffering*] "He who has seen me has seen the Father" (Jn 14:9)— he who has seen my forsakenness has seen also the Father's

---

[121] See John Paul II, *Crossing the Threshold*, 65–66. Significantly, when Paul asserts in 1 Tim 2:4 that God "*wills* everyone to be saved", the Greek term *thelo* usually designates a strong desire of the heart, a passion (*passio*).

forsakenness. So far does Jesus' transparency go, allowing
the Father to shine through him.[122]

Noteworthy here is that Balthasar brings together, albeit
allusively, wrath and love-suffering as two aspects of the Father's passionate involvement in the Cross event. If up to
now we have concentrated on the latter aspect, the Father's
suffering love, next we shift our focus to the former, the
Father's wrath at work in the Cross event.

Divine wrath at work in the Cross event

Anger at sin is an ineradicable feature of the biblical God.
As we noted in chapter 1, God's wrath in the face of sin
is not an independent power of destruction separate from
or set in opposition to God's love. Rather, God's wrath is
the form that God's love takes when it encounters whatever is opposed to and hardened against the designs of his
love.[123] It is always exercised in the service of these designs. God's wrath coincides with his zeal to carry out the

---

[122] Balthasar, *YCY*, 103-4. Elsewhere Balthasar says: "The highest interpretation of the Father, takes place . . . in the last stage of the earthly existence of Jesus—in the Passion." "God Is His Own Exegete", 283. See also
GL7, 85-86; *TD3*, 225; and Turek, *Towards a Theology of God the Father*, 43-
45. Cardinal Ladaria agrees with our four guides that the Cross event is the
summit of the revelation of the eternal Trinity and, in the first place, of God
the Father; see his discussion in *The Living and True God*, 99-103, 111-16,
and 429-32.

[123] See Johannes Fichtner, "Der Zorn Gottes im AT", in Gerhard Kittel
and Gerhard Friedrich, eds., *Theologisches Wörterbuch zum Neuen Testament*,
vol. 5 (Stuttgart: W. Kohlhammer Verlag, 1958), 404 and 408-10; Hellmut Bandt, "Zorn Gottes IV: Dogmatisch", in *Die Religion in Geschichte und
Gegenwart: Handwörterbuch für Theologie und Religionswissenschaft*, 3rd ed., vol.
4 (Tübingen, Germany: J. C. B. Mohr, 1960); and Martin Bieler: "The wrath
of God is nothing other than an aspect of God's love." "God and the Cross",
Communio 42.1 (Spring 2015): 72.

work of his love against sin: producing living images of his own paternal "Heart" while overcoming sin in all its consequences. This side of the eschaton, divine wrath serves his beloved's salvation.[124] This carries over into the New Testament, where "God's 'anger' becomes the burning and 'consuming fire' (Heb 12:29) of his unshakable love, which must annihilate, cauterize and excise (Heb 4:12) all that is not love."[125]

We find support for this understanding in the Gospels, which portray Jesus as displaying anger at the obstacles that impede the working of divine love (Mk 3:5; 4:10-12; 9:25; Mt 11:20-24; 15:7; 12:34; and Lk 14:21). This support is reinforced by the earnestness and boldness with which our four guides interpret Jesus as the definitive revealer of the Father. Undoubtedly the works and words of Jesus derive from one who loves with a fully human nature. Nevertheless, these are truly understood only "if they are seen and expounded as expressing the nature of divine love".[126] Accordingly, those Gospel texts which speak of Jesus' anger can be read as revelations of "the divine attitude".[127] This

---

[124] "God's anger only 'turns' or 'stands still' (2 Macc 7:38) when sin is overcome in all its consequences, when the sinner is finally 'cleansed' and 'healed' from sin, and forgiveness is fully achieved." Hoffmann, "Atonement and the Sacred Heart", 151. See Jer 31:31-34; Ezek 36:24-26, 33; also Joseph Scharbert, "Vergebung", in Heinrich Fries, ed., *Handbuch Theologischer Grundbegriffe*, vol. 2 (Munich: Kösel-Verlag, 1963), 741-42; and Walther Eichrodt, *Theology of the Old Testament*, vol. 1, (Louisville, Ky.: Westminster John Knox Press, 1961), 160.

[125] Balthasar, *TD*3, 119. For Balthasar, God's anger expresses a "free self-involvement that is controlled by love and righteousness". *TD*4, 344. It contributes to implementing his loving will against man's ego-driven resistance. See *GL*7, 205 and 300; *TD*5, 266; also Nichols, *Balthasar for Thomists*, 88.

[126] Balthasar, *Prayer*, 184.

[127] See Balthasar, *TD*4, 340-45; and *Theo-Logic: Theological Logical Theory*, vol. 3, *The Truth of God*, trans. Adrian J. Walker (San Francisco: Ignatius Press, 2004), 139.

reading is endorsed by the International Theological Commission, which regards Jesus' anger (Mk 3:5) as "a manifestation of a certain way of behavior on *God's* part".[128]

Indeed, we can look back (albeit briefly) to the mission of the prophet in the Old Testament, where certain features throw light on and substantiate this reading. Discernible there is "a fellowship in *attitude* and *destiny*" between God and the prophet, which is brought about by the Spirit of God. To begin with, the Spirit communicates to the prophet God's *pathos* of love toward his people. "It is not only the knowledge of God's designs in history that is communicated to him, but also the *pathos* of God's heart: wrath, compassion, sorrow . . . (Hos 6:4; 11:8; Is 6:8; Jer 6:11)."[129] The prophet, for his part, is to be "sym-pathetically open, by divine design, to God's *pathos*".[130] In this way, the prophet is empowered both to endure (to appropriate receptively) and to reproduce (to manifest actively) the modalities of God's love in its exposure and opposition to sin. Precisely for this reason, the prophet is also drawn into a fellowship in destiny with God. Insofar as the prophet expresses God's disposition toward a sinful people, he himself becomes exposed to their hostility toward God (cf. 1 Sam 8:8; 1 Kgs 19:14; Ps 69:8, 10; Jer 15:15). Surely it is possible to recognize these features of the prophetic mission in that of Jesus Christ, even if in him we encounter someone greater than a prophet (Mt 12:41). From this Old Testament vantage point, there are grounds for regarding the crucified Christ as both the con-

---

[128] ITC, "Theology, Christology, Anthropology", 226, no. 2. (emphasis added). The ITC continues: "In other places [of the NT] it is stated explicitly that God gets angry (Rom 1:18; 3:5; 9:22; Jn 3:36; Rev 15:1)."

[129] Von Rad, *Old Testament Theology*, vol. 2, 63; cited by Balthasar in *GL6*, 234.

[130] Balthasar, *TD4*, 344.

summate revelation of the Father's anger and, just so far, the voluntary brunt-bearer of animosity against the Father so as to reveal sin for what it is (Mt 21:37–39).

In an effort to refine our sketch of a biblical and Trinitarian understanding of divine anger (as to its essence and motive as well as its definitive revelation and agency in the Cross event), we turn to the work of Martin Bieler in his book *Befreiung der Freiheit*. Here Bieler distinguishes "true anger" from sheer vengeance. Sheer vengeance is ego-driven and lacks the motivation of love for another, whereas "true anger" works to remove the hindrances to the attainment of good, even the good of one's enemies, who are to be regarded as creatures of God and whom God wills to be converted and saved. "True anger" is motivated by love. "Indeed, anger *is* love in its whole impetus."[131] "True anger", therefore, "is not primarily an urge to inflict injury, but rather distinguished by an urge to remove the hindrances that disunite man from the good."[132]

Bieler notes that for Saint Thomas the characteristic manifestation of anger (the irascible power) is not a lashing out

---

[131] Martin Bieler, *Befreiung der Freiheit. Zur Theologie der stellvertretenden Sühne* (Freiburg im Breisgau, Germany: Verlag Herder, 1996), 171. Quoted in Kryst, *Interpreting the Death of Jesus*, 395. Balthasar agrees: "The wrath of God and his love, in the final analysis, are but one. Consult St. Thérèse of Lisieux on this point, and she will confirm it for you." *To the Heart*, 33. Clement of Alexandria says the same in *Paedagogus*: "Even the passionate rising of anger—if one wishes to call [God's] reprimands true anger—comes from his love for man." *Christ the Educator*, trans. Simon P. Wood (Washington, D.C.: Catholic University of America, 1954), 67.

[132] Bieler, *Befreiung*, 170–71. Bieler refers to Aquinas' *De Veritate* q. 25, a. 2: "The irascible power [anger] is in a certain way ordered to the concupiscible as its defender"; quoted in Kryst, *Interpreting the Death of Jesus*, 396n117. Yet in Aquinas' view anger, properly speaking, is never attributed to God: *ST* I, q. 19, a. 11; II-II, q. 162, a. 3, etc. All the same, Aquinas concedes that it is possible to speak of God hating sin and sinners, and so of being placated in the context of a work of atonement (III, q. 49, a. 4, obj. 2, resp. 2).

but rather an assumption and bearing of all the difficulties on the way to accomplishing the good goal. Notably, Thomas holds that the highest concrete expression of the power of wrath (*vis irascibilis*, the irascible power) for a human being is the readiness for martyrdom in the face of opposition to the gospel. "Truly the principal act of the irascible is to overcome even death on account of Christ."[133] If this is true, and if martyrdom is the highest form of imitation of Christ, then how are we to think of Christ's own exemplary act of overcoming mankind's opposition to God?[134] It would seem that Christ, in assuming and bearing the sin of the world, and thereby accomplishing the Father's will to save (Jn 3:17; 19:30; 1 Tim 2:4), is the pre-eminent concrete expression of the irascible power (anger) in his humanity. And if, moreover, with Saint Irenaeus we regard Christ as "the Visible of the Father"—for the humanity of Christ serves as the language in which he expresses what God the Father is like (Jn 1:18; 14:9–11)—can we say then that the crucified Christ is the highest human expression of divine wrath, that is, of divine love in its work of eliminating sin? In this perspective, "wrath is wholly dedicated to the good of another, as Aquinas insists it must be, even as it works determinedly against the evil that the other does."[135]

But now if the crucified Son is the highest human expression of divine wrath engaged in the work of eliminating sin, what is the *manner* or *way* in which Christ manifests anger? Balthasar's observation may shed light here. "The instruc-

---

[133] Thomas Aquinas, *Commentary on the IV Book of the Sentences* d. 49, q. 5, a. 5, qca. 1, co.; quoted in Kryst, *Interpreting the Death of Jesus*, 396n120. The original Latin reads: "Irascibilis vero actus potissimus est etiam mortem propter Christum superare."

[134] This question is raised by Kryst, *Interpreting the Death of Jesus*, 396–97.

[135] Ibid., 398.

tion of Jesus, which expresses the behavior of God, newly and ultimately, moves toward a refusal to hit back, toward an ultimate defenselessness."[136] What is provocative here is that the crucified Son manifests divine wrath in a disposition of *defenselessness* to the end of *overcoming* sin for the sake of those who are yet enemies. Indeed, whatever violence is on display during Christ's Passion is due not to divine wrath, but to the fury of the demonic powers against God, and to those men who are in some way under its influence. As Balthasar notes:

> In the suffering of the living Jesus, there is a readiness to . . . let the whole power of sin surge over him. He takes the blows, and the hate they express, upon himself and, as it were, amortizes it through his own suffering. The impotence of suffering (and the active readiness to undergo that impotence) outlasts every power of hammering sin. Sin's impatience . . . [against God] is finally exhausted in comparison to the patience of the Son of God. His patience undergirds sin and lifts it off its hinges.[137]

Thus the Son's patience is the final filial iteration of divine love's all-powerful "powerlessness". On the side of *sonship* we find "true anger" in the form of defenseless self-surrender with the will to save enemies. On the side of *sin* we find the contrary: violent aggression against the meek and innocent Son.

[136] Balthasar, "Crucifixus Etiam pro Nobis", *Internationale katholische Zeitschrift "Communio"* 9 (1980): 28–29; cited in Kryst, *Interpreting the Death of Jesus*, 398. Also see Balthasar, *GL7*, 321 and 437–38.

[137] Balthasar, "On Vicarious Representation", in *Explorations in Theology*, vol. 4, *Spirit and Institution*, trans. Edward T. Oakes (San Francisco: Ignatius Press, 1995), 421. Also, "The quality of the loving obedience of the Son of God toward the Father" as he delivers himself into the hands of sinners "is beyond all comparison with the quality of hate spending its fury on him." *The von Balthasar Reader*, 153. See Aquinas, *ST* III, q. 48, a. 2, ad 2.

This view that the Son's defenselessness before sinners is a form of true anger against sin finds support in Saint Thomas who says, "The irascible power tends toward overcoming contraries and winning out over them."[138] Now, the work of atonement achieved by Jesus Christ involves filial love overcoming its contrary—sin. Atonement, in this reading, remember, is the assertion of sonship against sin. Sonship takes its contrary (sin) upon itself in order to transform sin into its contrary (sonship), thereby annihilating it.

In this Trinitarian perspective, divine wrath is purified of violent aims separated from love.[139] The Father's anger (his paternal work of love against sin) takes the form of concealing his presence from his sin-bearing Son, thereby plunging the Son into the most acute experience of spiritual dereliction so as to enable him to collaborate in wiping sin away. The Son's anger (his filial work of love against sin) takes a dual form according to his role as mediator between the Father and human beings. As the vicarious representative of *sinners*, Jesus resolutely assumes and bears sin as separation from the Father—thereby annihilating *the* great obstacle to the final goal of our creation, namely, our sharing in divine

---

[138] Aquinas, *ST* I, q. 81, a. 2.

[139] Speech about divine wrath is fairly common in Balthasar's Theodramatic theory, yet it is relatively rare for him to describe the Father's wrath with violent images (for instance, the Father "striking" the Son; the Father "unloading" or "outpouring" his wrath on the Son). For these instances, see *TD*4, 345–49. These images can be unduly misleading, and they undercut the main thrust of his theological efforts, since for Balthasar the Son suffers the Father's wrath inasmuch as he suffers being forsaken [*verlassen*] by the Father. Indeed, by his own admission, Balthasar wants to guard against "interpreting the suffering of Christ as a punitive raging of divine anger against the innocent victim (as the Reformers tended to do)". *GL*7, 204. Notable too is that in *TD*5, 267, Balthasar rules out the notion that the Father "strikes" the sin-bearing Son in anger. For their part, Hoffmann, John Paul II, and Benedict XVI consistently avoid using violent images of divine wrath.

filiation. On the other side, as *the Father's* representative before sinners, Jesus engages in combat without lashing out but by confronting and bearing the brunt of men's opposition to God; it is a form of combat that is paradoxical, since it unites humiliation and glory, surrender and conquest. Thus, both the Father and the Son incarnate distinctly yet inseparably display nonviolent anger in their zeal to overcome evil by means of love.[140]

It merits emphasizing that in the Cross event there is no interruption or gap between "the powerlessness of being slain and the power of conquest", since God in Christ conquers by total self-surrender.[141] God in Christ liberates man from the forces of sin (1 Cor 15:24–26) only because Christ yields himself willingly to these forces. It is precisely by handing himself over, by letting sin do its worst, that he overcomes sin. He actively combats and conquers these forces not from outside, but by way of suffering sin's effects all the way through, since it is only thus that he annihilates sin from within.[142] Moreover, this way in which Christ exhibits anger against sin—combining action with passion, combat with surrender—reveals how God can freely involve himself for our sake with impassible passion, namely, in such a way that his intimate contact with our estranged condition is totally real, but serves not to change God in his eternal nature, but to change us.

Pope Benedict thinks along similar lines. He envisions

---

[140] Norbert Hoffmann, *Sühne: Zur Theologie der Stellvertretung* (Einsiedeln, Switzerland: Johannes Verlag, 1981), 31; and Balthasar, *Engagement with God*, 44–45. This is why, for Balthasar, the death of Jesus is "the most radical expression of the *loving* purpose of the Father", a love that wholly subsumes anger. Ibid., 59.

[141] Balthasar, *TD*2, 180. See *GL*7, 321.

[142] See Balthasar, *Engagement with God*, 27–28.

Jesus' "*combat* with the 'strong man' (cf. Lk 11:22)" in terms of "tak[ing] upon himself all the sin of the world and then suffer[ing] it through to the end—omitting nothing in [his identification] with the fallen".[143] As the true human image of divine wrath engaged in the work of eliminating sin, the crucified Son manifests anger in a way that coincides with wholly selfless and unprotected love. Jesus is the revealer of the *pathos* of God, but not as one against whom the Father's rage is violently vented; rather as one who himself exhibits God's wrath directly in combating Satan by suffering through the godlessness of sin—for love of us and for our salvation.

This last phrase spurs us to extend reflection on this theme a bit further. Earlier we noted that for Pope Benedict, the Cross event is the height of God's self-revelation.[144] At the same time and inseparably, the Cross event is the highest and purest form of God's anger made manifest. (We are assuming, again, that "true anger" is a modality of love that works to remove the hindrances to the attainment of good, even the good of one's enemies.) Indeed, the hallmark of the God who is love, according to Benedict, is love for sinners while they were still enemies. Benedict makes this point repeatedly in *Jesus of Nazareth*. Jesus, he says, shows us "the essence of God the Father through *love of enemies*".[145] Truly the Father "is this love".[146] It then becomes clear that the figure of Jesus, who dies praying for his enemies as he bears their sin, is the mirror in which we come to see God's fatherly anger

---

[143] Benedict XVI, *Jesus of Nazareth*, vol. 1, 20.

[144] See ibid., 136.

[145] Benedict XVI, *Jesus of Nazareth*, vol. 1, 137. Also see John Paul II, "The Son of God Brings the Fullness of Salvation" (General Audience, February 18, 1998), in *The Trinity's Embrace*, 29.

[146] Benedict XVI, *Jesus of Nazareth*, vol. 1, 136.

in its "for us" character.[147] For Ratzinger (Benedict), "This is the vengeance of God: he himself suffers for us, in the person of his Son."[148]

While remaining faithful to the theology of Pope Benedict, we can apply much of his catechesis on God's exercise of omnipotence to the subject of God's anger.

> [We are] to learn to know that God's thought is different from our own, that God's ways are different from ours (cf. Is 55:8) and that his omnipotence [for our purposes, his anger] is also different. . . . His [anger] is not expressed in violence, it is not expressed in the destruction of every adverse power as we might like; rather it is expressed in love, in mercy, in forgiveness, in accepting our freedom and in the tireless call for conversion of heart, in an attitude only seemingly weak—God seems weak if we think of Jesus Christ who prays, who lets himself be killed. This apparently weak attitude consists of patience, meekness and love, it shows that this is the real way to be powerful! This is God's power! And this power will win! . . .
>
> This is the true, authentic and perfect divine power: to respond to evil not with evil but with good, to insults with forgiveness, to homicidal hatred with life-giving love. Thus evil is truly vanquished because it is cleansed by God's love; thus death is defeated once and for all because it is transformed into a gift of life. . . .
>
> Therefore, when we say "I believe in God the Father almighty", we express our faith in the power of the love of God who, in his Son who died and was raised, triumphs over hatred, evil and sin and unfolds before us the path to eternal life, as children who want to dwell for ever in their "Father's House". Saying "I believe in one God the

[147] See Ibid., 136–37.
[148] Joseph Ratzinger, Homily at the Mass *Pro Eligendo Romano Pontifice* (April 18, 2005).

Father almighty", in his power, in his way of being Father,
is always an act of faith, of conversion, of the transformation of our thought, of the whole of our affection, of the
whole of our way of life.[149]

Significantly, the recognition in Christ of the Father's way
of exercising power and manifesting anger in the work of
eliminating sin is, for Benedict, a vital catalyst for the "transformation of our thought, of the whole of our affection, of
the whole of our way of life"—of our thought and affec-
tions, because the perception that God's almighty anger is a
function of his love of enemies (Rom 5:8, 10) should incite
repentance and spur us sinners to surrender ourselves into
God's hands; of our entire way of life, because beholding
God's true way of being powerful means seeing that it con-
tradicts the violent aggression unleashed against God's Son
and thus calls for the rectification of our conduct toward
sinners—those with whom Christ identified himself.[150]

As for John Paul II, when he discusses the optimal conditions that conduce to our conversion from sin, his key
moves are wholly aligned with those of Benedict, Balthasar,
and Hoffmann. Beholding the Pierced One, we are enlightened by the Spirit to perceive not only the whole truth about
the evil of sin, but also, at the same time, the true face of
the Father, who is rich in mercy (Eph 2:4).[151] Indeed, the
simultaneity of this twofold revelation indicates that every
modality of divine love (for us)—including wrath—may

[149] Benedict XVI, General Audience (January 30, 2013). Balthasar says much
the same: The Triune God "is above the need to dominate, let alone use violence". *TD*4, 331. See also *Love Alone Is Credible*, trans. D. C. Schindler (San
Francisco: Ignatius Press, 2004), 85.

[150] See Benedict XVI, *Jesus of Nazareth*, vol. 2, 199.

[151] See John Paul II, *Dominum et vivificantem*, no. 39, and *Dives in misericordia*,
nos. 7–8.

be subsumed into the attribute of mercy. This is shown, for instance, where John Paul II explains that if "for our sake [the Father] made him to be sin" (2 Cor 5:21, RSVCE), this means that Jesus, for our sake, suffered "rejection *by the Father*".[152] And this means, further, that Jesus experienced the Father's merciful love in its mode as wrath.[153] When, therefore, we behold God's Son crucified, we are meant to be convicted of sin precisely while perceiving that Jesus both endured and reflected in filial fashion God's "true anger" in its work of conquering sin (cf. Jn 19:37; Zech 12:10).

It is surely noteworthy that all four of our guides consider beholding "the Pierced One" by the light of the Spirit to be paradigmatic of the process whereby repentance leads to atonement. So too does the *Catechism*: "Conversion is first of all a work of the grace of God who makes our hearts return to him (cf. Lam 5:21). . . . It is in discovering the greatness of God's love that our heart is shaken by the horror and weight of sin and begins to fear offending God by sin and being separated from him. The human heart is converted by looking upon him whom our sins have pierced (cf. Jn 19:37; Zech 12:10)."[154]

To acknowledge this is not to downplay the prophetic language of decision that reverberates throughout the New Testament. Quite the opposite, as Balthasar insists:

> The supreme threat—coming from God the Father, who as it were gives sinners his supreme love, God the Son— is a threat not to abuse this supreme gift, because, behind it, there is no greater love to call upon and to turn to (Heb 6:4–8; 10:26–31). And once again, the Spirit of Love cannot teach the Cross to the world in any other way than by

---

[152] John Paul II, *Salvifici doloris*, no. 18 (italics are the pope's).
[153] See John Paul II, General Audience (November 30, 1988), nos. 4–6.
[154] *CCC* 1432.

disclosing the full depths of the guilt that the world bears, a guilt that comes to light on the Cross and is the only thing that makes the Cross intelligible.[155]

Thus, we can take seriously the gospel references to divine wrath and judgment without jeopardizing the revelation that God is love (1 Jn 4:8–10). Clearly the work of divine wrath, or judgment, in the Cross event shows that sin is scarcely trivialized when the Holy Trinity goes to such dumbfounding lengths to annihilate it. Yet rather than manifesting a disposition equally ready to condemn as to forgive, this work of divine wrath, or judgment, stems wholly from love (1 Jn 4:8–10).[156]

Concluding remarks

We have suggested that the Father's forgiving love is co-extensive with his generative love (*ad extra*), which has as its inherent aim to produce a reciprocal, mirroring love—filial love—in the form of atonement. Atonement, on its side, is the form that filial love takes when asserting itself against the consequences of sin. Sin is expiated "once for all" (Heb 7:27) when Jesus, who is God's Son incarnate (Jn 1:1, 18; 1 Jn 4:8–10; Gal 4:4), lets the Father's love exercise its full effect in him as the definitive sin-bearer. In so doing, Jesus transforms the unholy distance between God and

[155] Balthasar, *Love Alone*, 93.

[156] The Cross event "constitutes a 'superabundance' of justice. . . . Nevertheless, this justice . . . springs completely from love: from the love of the Father and the Son" for sinful humanity. John Paul II, *Dives in misericordia*, no. 4. "Even the Old Testament teaches that . . . love is 'greater' than justice. . . . In the final analysis, justice serves love. The primacy and superiority of love vis-a-vis justice—this is a mark of the whole of revelation." Ibid., no. 7. See Balthasar, *TD*4, 239, 338, and 343; *MP*, 58; and *YCY*, 78–79.

sinners into material for the expression of his holy intimacy with the Father. Father and Son are jointly involved here: sin as opposition to the extension of their paternal-filial relationship in the economy of grace is countered by their shared willingness in love to transform the estrangement wrought by sin into its opposite, thereby annihilating it.

In our next chapter, we will argue that God leaves room for our participation in Christ's work of atonement. This claim will require illuminating the role played by the Holy Spirit, who is sent to prolong the mission of the Son into the realm of our personal, historical existence (Gal 4:6). At the same time, we will continue to highlight the patrogenetic character of the process of eliminating sin by showing that atonement is the result of God's empowering converted sinners to take action against sin as his sons in the Son, Christ Jesus.

3

Toward a Spiritual Theology
of Atonement

Straightaway we must assert that a doctrine of redemption
that restricts it to an objective work accomplished by the
crucified Son fails to do justice to the full scope and aim of
the Holy Trinity's involvement with us. (The "objective"
dimension of redemption refers to what the Holy Trinity
did for us antecedent to our personal consent, in advance
of our personal cooperation—while we were yet sinners;
Rom 5:8; Eph 2:5). For the totality of the Trinity's work is
accomplished when this objective redemption has reached
its subjective goal, when it is personally appropriated by
human beings. (The "subjective" dimension of redemption
refers to the "space" God leaves for our personal freedom
to accept Christ's work of redemption, to lay hold of it in
faith.)

Christ's "representation" enables us to
collaborate as sons in the Son

Much of what would need to be said under this heading
has already been introduced in the previous chapter: God
has eternally "made room" for the world in the "place"
that belongs to the Son within the Trinity. "The world",
as Balthasar says, "can only be created within the Father's
generation of the Son; [and therefore] only in the Son can

155

the world be 'recapitulated'."[1] Since humanity is created in the generated Son, then our God-given "place", the ultimate ground of our existence, is in him. And not only our *ground*, but our *goal* as well. Every human being is ordered to fulfillment in Christ, to be "born of God" in and through Christ (Jn 1:13; 1 Jn 3:9; 5:4).[2] As Saint Paul teaches, we are created and called "to be conformed to the image of his Son" (Rom 8:29), into whose "image" we are to be "changed" by his Spirit (2 Cor 3:18). Likewise, the Church Fathers teach that "through the incarnation, Jesus Christ's divine 'sonship by nature' opens up to offer the possibility for us to enjoy a 'sonship by grace'."[3] Our quartet of theologians concurs, of course, even as they accentuate the atoning purpose of the Cross event as integral to the *telos* of the Son's mission. "In Jesus' mission unto death", states Balthasar, "the entire (strict) judgment of God [upon the totality of sin in human history] is expressed and reaches its end", and precisely this event of redemption through judgment "creates the necessary condition for the Spirit of God to be infused in our hearts that we might be incorporated

[1] Balthasar, *TD*3, 326. We noted previously that this insight was taught convincingly by the Church Fathers, with Athanasius among the most influential proponents. See his *Orations against the Arians*, II.2.

[2] See *CCC* 50–52; Vatican Council II, Pastoral Constitution on the Church in the Modern World *Gaudium et spes* (December 7, 1965), no. 22; John Paul II, encyclical letter *Redemptoris mater* (March 25, 1987), no. 7, and General Audience (April 10, 1986). See also Balthasar *TD*2, 266–68, 330; *GL*7, 310–11, 393–94, and 405–9.

[3] Anatolios, *Retrieving Nicaea: The Development and Meaning of Trinitarian Doctrine* (Ada, Mich.: Baker Academic, 2018), 84. Anatolios sums up the thought of Alexander of Alexandria, for whom "salvation consists in our being incorporated by grace into the natural filiation of the Son to the Father." Ibid., 85–86. Indeed, throughout his book Anatolios shows that iterations of this teaching are widespread in patristic literature.

into the new and definitive covenant, becoming [God's filial beloved] in Christ."[4]

All this suggests that the Son, Christ Jesus, is a uniquely open and inclusive reality, not only inasmuch as all creation subsists in him (Col 1:16; 2 Cor 5:17), but also because, as the Crucified, he draws all things to himself (Jn 12:31–33). Indeed, not only Christ's sonship but also his mission unto death is eminently "shareable", made available for our participation.[5] In the words of the *Catechism*: "From the beginning, Jesus associated his disciples with his own life . . . and gave them a share in his mission, joy, and sufferings."[6]

For his part, Balthasar likes to regard the historical mission of the Son as a kind of stage or acting area upon which human beings are called to play a role (mission or vocation) in conformity to the prototypical mission of the Son. Ratzinger asserts the same basic idea in this way: "Christ, whom Scripture calls the final Adam, that is, the definitive human being, appears in the testimonies of faith as the all-encompassing [all-inclusive] space in which the 'we' of human beings gathers on the way to the Father. He is not only an example that is followed, but he is the integrating space in which the 'we' of human beings gathers itself toward the

---

[4] Balthasar, *TD4*, 250; see also 239.

[5] "This absolutely unique Man . . . is unique precisely because he is God [the Son]. And for this and no other reason, he can give a share in his once-for-all Cross to his fellow human beings, with whom he is in deeper solidarity than any man could ever be with another. He can give them, in other words, a share in his [Passion and] death." Balthasar, *MP*, 224. See *GL7*, 427; *The Threefold Garland*, trans. Erasmo Leiva-Merikakis (San Francisco: Ignatius Press, 1982), 96; and *Prayer*, trans. Graham Harrison (San Francisco: Ignatius Press, 1986), 58.

[6] *CCC* 787; see also 765; cf. Mk 1:16–20; 3:13–19; Mt 13:10–17; Lk 10:17–20; 22:28–30.

'You' of God."[7] Notice that this "integrating space" is not static but dynamic; we are gathered "in Christ" as those "*on the way* to the Father", that is to say, as those who share in *the mission* of Christ.[8] As expected, the *Catechism* endorses these insights and gives them a simple yet profound formulation: "Christ enables us to live in him all that he himself lives, and he lives it in us."[9] This inclusive capacity of Christ does not necessarily lead to mystical delights and consolations, since there is no moment of Christ's mission when he is more given away, more inclusive, than his atoning Passion and death.[10]

Now, this must mean that Christ's work of "representation" (representative atonement as in Gal 3:13; 2 Cor 5:21; 1 Pet 2:24; 3:18) is something more than simple "substitution". On the Cross, Christ's "exchange of place" with us sinners is not a mere "taking our place" as if Christ *dis*placed us. Rather it is an *em*placement of us, a re-establishment of us as sons, or children, of God (Gal 4:4–7; Eph 1:3–7; Mk 10:45; Jn 10:10). Christ's "representation" is a work that enables us to be freely acting persons who, in our turn, cooperate as filial partners with God.[11] To deny this would be

---

[7] Joseph Ratzinger, "Understanding the Concept of Person in Theology" in *Communio* 17.3 (Fall 1990): 452–53. See also Benedict XVI, *Jesus of Nazareth*, vol. 2 *Holy Week*, trans. Philip J. Whitmore, (San Francisco: Ignatius Press, 2011), 236.

[8] To affirm this is to recognize that Christ's coming from the Father wholly coincides with his returning to the Father.

[9] *CCC* 521.

[10] To be sure, this inclusive capacity of Christ does not operate like an automatic mechanism but belongs to Christ's personal and free self-giving.

[11] Christ, insists Balthasar, "could not reconcile us with God in a merely mechanical way; rather, on the basis of an act that was unique to him, he enabled us to make our own reconciliation." *MIC*, 158; see *TD*3, 119–20. See also Norbert Hoffmann, "Atonement and the Spirituality of the Sacred Heart", in *Faith in Christ and the Worship of Christ* (San Francisco: Ignatius Press, 1986),

to let our status as free persons be absorbed into and virtually nullified by Christ, who would then be the "only partner" with the Father. It would be to undercut "the glorious freedom of the children of God", which, according to Saint Paul, is realized only by way of our suffering with Christ so that we may also be glorified with him (Rom 8:14–17, 21).[12]

Precisely here, in the wake of our Christ-centered reflections, we must be careful not to overlook the generative power of the Father's love at work in the mission of the Son[13]—and hence in our mission too. We must understand that our participation in Christ's sonship and mission of atonement stems ultimately from the Father, inasmuch as atonement is the result of God's empowering converted sinners to act as his sons (1 Jn 3:9; 4:7). To shed some light on this claim, let us recall that the lover's work of engendering an imaging response in the beloved involves showing or making known the subjectivity of the lover. The meaning and goal of this self-showing is to draw the beloved into the inner attitude of the lover and to move the other to behave in a corresponding manner. But "no one has ever seen God" (Jn 1:18). Jesus, God's only Son, is sent to make him known fully and finally. And as the definitive revealer of the

---

162 and 174. "The unique mediation of the Redeemer does not exclude but rather gives rise to a manifold cooperation which is but a sharing in this one source." Vatican Council II, Dogmatic Constitution on the Church *Lumen gentium* (November 21, 1964), no. 62.

[12] See Hoffmann, "Atonement and the Sacred Heart", 173; Balthasar *GL*7, 305–6 and 310–11; *TD*4, 351; and *The Christian and Anxiety*, trans. Dennis D. Martin (San Francisco: Ignatius Press, 2000), 104. Cf. Aquinas, *ST* III, q. 49, a. 3, ad 2 and 3.

[13] Regarding Jesus' acting by virtue of the Father's "perpetually operative love", see Balthasar, *TD*3, 110; *TD*2, 87; *GL*1, 147, 614, and 616; and *GL*7, 262, 283, and 401.

Father, Jesus shares in the generative power and aim of the Father's self-revelation in the world. He not only manifests the Father's love in his own life but also thereby invites and empowers others to do the same: "As the Father has loved me, so I have loved you; abide in my love" (Jn 15:9, RSVCE).[14] And this means, further, that Jesus' power to elicit from human freedom a self-donation that corresponds to God's initiative of love should be seen as originating from the paternal font of the Holy Trinity: from the Father's un-begotten and archetypal manner of loving divinely, the generative power of which is made manifest in Christ's own self-giving-over on behalf of, and into the hands of, sinners.[15] Otherwise said: it is because the Son's representation of the Father's love underlies the Son's self-giving "to the end" (Jn 13:1) that human freedom, confronted with the figure of the Pierced One, can be moved to repent and drawn to love likewise and thus to participate in his glorification of the Father by way of atonement.[16] Therefore, when God sends his Son, this mission in its totality aims to accomplish God's all-embracing purpose: to beget us (by grace) in a way that elevates us to the dignity of his filial collaborators such that we are enabled to take action against sin.[17]

This should put to rest any suspicion that Christ's repre-

[14] It is precisely by virtue of the Son's "representation of God the Father as he is in himself (Jn 1:18)" through this final work of filial love (Jn 14:9–11) that human beings are confronted with "the unconditional necessity for accepting this truth of love, seeing its magnificence and responding to it through complete devotedness to one's brethren" (1 Jn 4:11). Hans Urs von Balthasar, *Dare We Hope "That All Men Be Saved"?*, trans. David Kipp and Lothar Krauth (San Francisco: Ignatius Press, 1988), 41 (hereafter *DWH*). See also *TD*3, 518.

[15] See Balthasar, *TD*4, 450.

[16] See Benedict XVI, *Jesus of Nazareth*, vol. 2, 236.

[17] See Norbert Hoffmann, "Atonement and the Spirituality of the Sacred Heart", 172–73; and *CCC* 2008–9, 2021–22.

sentative atonement is an automatic process that overrides our free cooperation. At the same time, it should satisfy those who object to a doctrine of redemption that "infantilizes" human beings by depriving us of our freedom and denying us the dignity of bearing our own guilt. The Holy Trinity exercises its power against sin in such a way that human freedom is not merely bypassed or overridden by a one-sided forgiveness. To the contrary. "The unconditional forgiveness of God is only really present for a sinner when he [in turn] hands himself over to God unconditionally, which means he is repentant, in order to assume and reflect the attitude of God."[18]

But let there be no mistake: we must remain steadfast in affirming the gravity of human freedom that can really and definitively reject God in his self-communication. On no account can we see this divine work of empowering as an *over*powering of human freedom. Otherwise, the end result (human freedom *dis*empowered) could not serve as an appropriate creaturely image of the gracious freedom out of which God acts. Instead, since the goal of God's self-communication is to bring to consummation a covenant of mutual love with his human partner, it must be that God allows human persons a genuinely free self-disposing vis-à-vis his advances of love and hence permits the grave risk that this involves.[19]

Given the popularized misrepresentation of Balthasar's position on this matter (as presuming hell to be empty and

[18] Hans Urs von Balthasar, "Crucifixus etiam pro nobis", *Communio* 9 (1980): 27.

[19] See Balthasar, *GL7*, 402; and *Does Jesus Know Us—Do We Know Him?*, trans. Graham Harrison (San Francisco: Ignatius Press, 1983), 40; and *CCC* 2021–22. The Church has formally condemned the position that maintains the absolute efficacy and irresistibility of divine grace. See Clement XI's *Unigenitus Dei Filius*, *DH* 2410 and 2430.

claiming certain knowledge that it will remain so), an extended quote in his own words is warranted:

> [A] sinner might so identify himself with his No to God that trinitarian love would be unable to loosen the resultant snarl, with the result that the fiery torrent of eternal *love* . . . would remain a torrent of eternal *wrath*. Hence the words, "it is a terrible thing to fall into the hands of the living God" (Heb 10:31). These words apply, not to just any sinners, but to those who resist the triune work of atonement with full consciousness and realization. "For it is impossible to restore again to repentance those who have once been enlightened, who have tasted the heavenly gift, and have become partakers of the Holy Spirit . . ." (Heb 6:4ff.); a person such as this has "spurned the Son of God, and profaned the blood of the covenant by which he was sanctified, and outraged the Spirit of grace" (10:29). *Scripture prohibits us from saying that this deliberate No is impossible.* . . . For this [definitive No] to take place, a creature must be able to identify itself with its refusal.[20]

Elsewhere, Balthasar takes an equally strong stand: "Once God has given his Son, he has nothing more to give; thus

---

[20] Balthasar, *TD*4, 350 (emphasis added). A helpful explanation of the final statement in this passage is given by Josef Pieper: "Eternal punishment applies only to 'deadly' sin in the strict sense. . . . To qualify as truly 'deadly,' this decision against God must go all the way to the roots. . . . It must be a decision so radical that its only analogue at the opposite pole would be the decision of a martyr or blood-witness. . . . The sinner must be willing not only to persevere in sin all the way through this earthly life, but he must also want to persevere in his sin 'into eternity,' (*in aeternum*). It belongs to the nature of this act to intend something definitive and thus to be 'irreparable'." *The Concept of Sin*, trans. Edward T. Oakes (South Bend: St. Augustine's Press, 2001), 89–90. John Paul II teaches that "only unrepentant attachment to evil" can separate one from the saving love of Christ. "The End of History Began with Christ's Coming" (General Audience, April 22, 1998), in *The Trinity's Embrace: Our Salvation History: Catechesis on Salvation History* (Boston: Pauline Books & Media, 2002), 44.

the guilty person cannot hope for any further grace of conversion. He has 'spurned the Son of God, and profaned the
blood of the covenant by which he was sanctified, and out-
raged the Spirit of grace' (Heb 10:29). The Letter of Jude
and 2 Peter are profoundly and awfully aware of this possibility."[21]

And one more quote, for good measure: "There is no
mention of an individual and subjective certainty of salvation. Man can avert his gaze from God, he can neglect to
give his life the 'splendor' of Christ's manifest glory; by doing so he will show that his contemplation of the glory was
not serious enough to be enduring."[22]

The Holy Spirit and our sonship

Thus far we have argued that God prolongs the mission of
Christ's atonement into the realm of our personal, historical
existence. Now we move on to discuss *how* this takes place.
At this point, we turn our attention to the third divine Person of the Trinity, the Holy Spirit, whom so far we have
more or less neglected.

Already in the fourth century A.D., Saint Athanasius develops a theology of salvation in an explicitly Trinitarian
direction and according to an emphatically "patrogenetic"

---

[21] Balthasar, *TD4*, 182.

[22] Balthasar, *Prayer*, 50. In addition, see *TD5*, 285–90 and 297; and *GL7*,
233–34, 291–92, and 417; see also *Does Jesus Know Us*, 81; *Engagement with
God: The Drama of Christian Discipleship*, trans. R. John Halliburton (San Francisco: Ignatius Press, 2008), 31; *Love Alone Is Credible*, trans. D. C. Schindler
(San Francisco: Ignatius Press, 2004), 77; *MP*, 177; "Crucifixus etiam pro
nobis", 34; *Epilogue*, trans. Edward T. Oakes (San Francisco: Ignatius Press,
2004), 118–19; and *DWH*, 16–28, 41–42, and 182. The sheer number of
these references invites the question as to what precisely is behind the misrepresentation of Balthasar's thought.

structure. What he says about the Spirit's role is seen ultimately in relation to the initiating love of God the Father. In
his words: "The love of God for humanity is such that by
grace he becomes Father of those in relation to whom he had
previously only been Maker. He becomes their Father when
created human beings receive 'into their hearts the Spirit of
the Son, crying out, "Abba, Father"' (Gal 4:6). . . . Being
creatures by nature, they would not become 'sons' except
by receiving the Spirit of the natural and true Son."[23]

Many centuries later, our four theologians situate their reflections in this patristic current, even as they reverse direction by moving from the Spirit to the Son (Christ, crucified
and risen) and finally to the Father. To start with, we are
"sons" of God by the Holy Spirit, that is, by a communication of the Spirit of *the* Son, Jesus Christ (Gal 4:6–7; Rom
8:10–17). Through his Spirit, the crucified and risen Christ
unites us to himself in a personal way and draws us into his
filial life.[24] This happens in such a way that we are not raised
to a place "alongside" the Son but are divinized "in" the
Son (Col 1:28). And since it is through the Spirit that we
share in Christ's divine sonship, then it is also through the
Spirit that we stand in relation to the Father as his children
(Rom 5:1; 8:9–11; 2 Cor 3:4; Gal 4:4–6; 2:19f.).[25] Here are
Balthasar's comments on the key Pauline texts:

[23] Athanasius, *Orations against the Arians*, II.59, quoted in Anatolios, *Retrieving Nicaea*, 125.

[24] See *CCC* 690 and 737. As Balthasar explains, it belongs to "the dispensation of the Holy Spirit to draw us into the redemption that has been objec-
tively accomplished, so that we may participate in it from within, understanding it and living it (Col 1:10)." *GL7*, 426. See also Hoffmann "Atonement
and the Sacred Heart", 177.

[25] See Balthasar, *Prayer*, 70; *GL7*, 422; and *TD4*, 242; John Paul II, "The
Spirit Accompanied Jesus' Public Life" (General Audience, June 3, 1998) and
"The Holy Spirit Sanctifies Us" (General Audience, July 22, 1998) in *The
Trinity's Embrace*, 68 and 86. See also R. Schulte in *Mysterium Salutis*, vol. 5
(Einsiedeln, Switzerland: Benziger Verlag, 1967), 145.

[It is] the "Spirit of Sonship, who makes us cry out: 'Abba, beloved Father!'" (Rom 8:15). And when Paul continues: "This Spirit confirms to our spirit that we are children of God" (8:16), then this . . . dialogue is not between our spirit and the *Pneuma*, but between our spirit, borne by the *Pneuma*, and the Father, a dialogue in which the *Pneuma* cannot be other than the *Pneuma* of the Son, in whom we have come to share in sonship: "because we now are sons, God sent the Spirit of his Son into our hearts, who cries out: 'Abba, beloved Father!'" (Gal 4:6).[26]

Furthermore, if through the Spirit we are sons of God, even so we are sons in *this* world—a world that in its concrete, historical condition is marked by sin. And as we have shown throughout this study, to assert sonship in the face of sin means atonement: bearing the baneful effects of sin (from within and from without) as the suffering of filial love. It means to accept that the Father's power to forgive takes the form of begetting sons capable of transforming sin-wrought estrangement into filial love's pain. Such pain is actually "salutary pain", which urges being expressed through "good fruits as evidence of repentance" (Lk 3:8; Mt 3:8).[27]

Truly, then, our yes to sonship in Christ—made effective by the Spirit—is a yes to co-atonement in Christ.[28]

The universal call to holiness: A call to the vicarious bearing of the guilt of all

But now, are we empowered by the Spirit of Sonship to atone for our own sins exclusively, or also those of others?

[26] Balthasar, *GL*7, 405; see also 407. Additionally, see Benedict XVI, *Jesus of Nazareth*, vol. 2, 162.

[27] See Hoffmann, "Atonement and the Sacred Heart", 180; and *CCC* 1431, 1428, 1433, and 1989.

[28] See Hoffmann, "Atonement and the Sacred Heart", 197, 199, and 205.

Before answering this question regarding the scope of our co-atonement in Christ, we should first look back to Christ himself and ask whether he gave himself up to suffering and death for the salvation of all or only for the "elect". The Church has given a formal and definitive answer to this question. In the Council of Trent's *Decree on Justification*, we find a clear affirmation that Christ died for the sins of *all* human beings (cf. 1 Jn 2:2; 2 Cor 5:14–15).[29] Additionally, the Council of Quiercy (858) teaches: "There is not, never has been, and never will be a single human being for whom Christ did not suffer."[30] We can also put forward papal condemnations of positions that deny that Christ died for all. For instance, there is Pope Innocent X's Constitution *Cum occasione* (1653), in which he condemns the view that "Christ died only to save the predestined"; indeed, he describes this view as "impious, blasphemous, disgraceful, derogatory of the divine piety, and heretical".[31]

Let's press on, however, to ask another (closely related) question. Did Christ suffer and die for *love* of all, including his betrayer, his accusers, and the "bad thief" who was crucified alongside him? May we say that Christ *prayed* for the salvation of all as he died bearing the sin of the world (cf. Lk 23:34)? Admittedly, some important figures in the theological tradition have answered negatively. They have opined that Christ on the Cross limited his saving love to the "elect" and stopped short of praying for anyone who would not accept him.[32]

---

[29] *DH* 1522.

[30] The Council of Quiercy (853): DS 624; cited in *CCC* 605.

[31] *DH* 2005. Sixty years later, in 1713, Clement XI added his own condemnation of the claim that Christ died exclusively for the "elect" rather than for all human beings, *Unigenitus Dei Filius, DH* 2432. See ITC, "Select Questions on the Theology of God the Redeemer [1995]", *Communio* 24.1 (Spring 1997): 207.

[32] Augustine denies that God desires the salvation of each and every hu-

Such a view, however, is regarded as short-sighted by
many others in the Church, including our group of popes
and theologians, and it is their position that is endorsed in
the *Catechism*. The latter affirms that Jesus Christ loved all
men when he offered his life in atonement for their sins. In
fact the *Catechism* sees that the universal scope of Christ's
love for sinners should be traced back to the loving Father's
desire that all men be saved.[33]

Since the patrogenetic structure of the process of redemption is a major theme of this book, we will pause briefly
to showcase the emphasis that the *Catechism* places on *the
Father's* "universal redeeming love". In the section entitled
"Jesus Died Crucified", the *Catechism* develops a line of in-
struction that leaves no doubt as to the nonrestrictive scope
of the Father's redeeming love for human beings: "By giving up his own Son for our sins, God manifests that his
plan for us is one of benevolent love, prior to any merit on
our part: 'In this is love, not that we loved God but that
he loved us and sent his Son to be the expiation for our
sins' (1 Jn 4:10). God 'shows his love for us in that while
we were yet sinners Christ died for us' (Rom 5:8)."[34] As if

---

man being; see *On the Predestination of the Saints* in *Four Anti-Pelagian Writings*
(Washington, D.C.: Catholic University of America, 1992). Aquinas, for his
part, thinks that "Our Lord did not pray for all those who crucified him, as
neither did he for all those who would not believe in him, but for those only
who were predestined to obtain eternal life through him." *ST* III, q. 21, a. 4,
ad 2.

[33] See *CCC* 607, 609, 616, and 601; also John Paul II, *Redemptoris mater*,
no. 7, where according to the pontiff, Ephesians 1:3–7 reveals the eternal
design of God the Father, whose plan of man's salvation in Christ is universal
in scope; it is a plan of love "which concerns all men and women . . . all
are eternally included in the divine plan of salvation." And see his apostolic
letter *Mulieris dignitatem* (August 15, 1988), no. 9, and his General Audiences
(April 10 and May 28, 1986). Also, Trent's *Decree on Justification*, *DH* 1522.
[34] *CCC* 604.

anticipating a too-narrow interpretation of the words "our" and "us" in these New Testament texts and the enveloping commentary, the *Catechism* immediately adds: "At the end of the parable of the lost sheep Jesus recalled that *God's love excludes no one*: '*So it is not the will of your Father who is in heaven that one of these little ones should perish*' (Mt 18:14). He affirms that he came 'to give his life as a ransom for many'; this last term is *not restrictive*, but contrasts *the whole of humanity* with the unique person of the redeemer who hands himself over to save us (Mt 20:28; cf. Rom 5:18–19)."[35] With unmistakable consistency, from paragraph no. 50 through no. 618 and beyond, the *Catechism* interprets the biblical testimony as refraining from placing restrictions on God's love for sinners. Instead, it avows the universal scope of "the Father's plan of divine salvation" in sending his Son as atonement for the sins of all, for the sake of all, for love of all.[36]

Of further interest is an essay by Matthew Levering on the extent of the atonement according to Roman Catholicism. Following the *Catechism*'s lead and persuaded by the wisdom of saints such as Francis de Sales, Levering arrives at this conclusion:

> It does not seem consistent with the biblical testimony to God or to Christ if we suppose that . . . Christ, on the cross, really is praying only for those whom he knows to be elect and does not superabundantly love those whom he knows will not repent. . . . God loves sinners and does not show himself to be a God whose love for sinners is limited or constricted. . . . God truly and superabundantly loves even those who do not love him and never will love him.[37]

[35] Ibid., no. 605 (emphasis added).

[36] Ibid., no. 606. See especially nos. 607–18. See also Vatican Council II, *Gaudium et spes*, nos. 92–93.

[37] Matthew Levering, "The Roman Catholic View", in *Five Views on the*

Needless to say, Levering's stance accords with the position maintained throughout this study.

If, then, the scope of God's redeeming love for human beings is universal and superabundant, then we who are "children of God" by virtue of receiving the Spirit of Sonship are called upon to follow suit.[38] Pertinent here is Saint Paul's exhortation to the Ephesians: "So be imitators of God, as beloved children, and live in love, as Christ loved us and handed himself over for us as a sacrificial offering to God" (Eph 5:1). Christ's atoning sacrifice for the sake of the whole world is what makes possible, summons forth, and provides the standard for a response of love in our lives. By loving after this pattern, we act as "imitators of God", according to the example set before us in Christ. And the standard of love that Christ exemplifies is a sacrificial love that extends itself to others without exception.[39]

Moreover, in this light we are to see that what Saint Paul said to the Corinthians holds good for all who are in Christ: "When ridiculed, we bless; when persecuted, we endure;

Extent of the Atonement (Grand Rapids, Mich.: Zondervan Academic, 2019), 83–84. Levering respectfully disagrees with Aquinas' opinion that Christ on the Cross did not pray for anyone whom he knew would refuse to repent. Levering also raises the difficult theological problem of predestination, particularly in regard to the interplay between divine freedom and human freedom. For an account of this interplay that represents the theology of our four guides, see Turek, "Dare We Hope 'That All Men Be Saved'?: On Balthasar's Trinitarian Grounds for Christian Hope", *Logos: A Journal of Catholic Thought and Culture* 1, no. 3 (1997): 92–121.

[38] See *CCC* 735.

[39] See Heinrich Schlier, *Der Brief an der Epheser* (Dusseldorf: Patmos-Verlag, 1971), 231; Benedict XVI, encyclical letter *Deus caritas est* (December 25, 2005), no. 11; and Balthasar, *Dare We Hope?*, 106–11 and 214–18, where we encounter the testimony of saints and mystics who offer themselves unreservedly as representative sacrifices for sinners: Catherine of Siena, Teresa of Avila, Mary Magdalen dei Pazzi, Marie de l'Incarnation, Marie de Vallées, and more.

when slandered, we respond gently" (1 Cor 4:12–13). By doing so, our aim is not merely to defuse an external situation rife with conflict or to protect the soul's equanimity under these circumstances. Far more is involved. By doing so, we live in love as Christ loved all sinners in his Passion and thus, animated by his Spirit, we participate in his mission of *vicarious* atonement. Indeed, we are enabled to bear guilt for anyone, since the extent of our love as Christians is determined by the extent of Christ's love.[40]

Building upon such biblical foundations, Balthasar develops a doctrine of discipleship—and simultaneously, of atonement—that advocates the universality and prodigality of the Christian's love ("not limited in any way, e.g., to members of the Church alone"), since this is a love that derives from and reflects God's universal redeeming love at work in the Cross event.[41] In fact, a hallmark of Balthasar's doctrine of discipleship is his staunch conviction that the universal call to holiness inevitably entails a call to the vicarious bearing of the guilt of all.

> Discipleship brings with it the gift of participation in the Cross and Resurrection of Christ. . . . This participation is bound to extend itself . . . to the *pro nobis* [for us] of

[40] See *CCC* 739. Our reflections are further illuminated by St. Paul's teaching in his Letter to the Romans: "We who are strong ought to put up with [βαστάζειν, *bastazein*, 'to bear'] the failings of the weak and not to please ourselves; let each of us please our neighbor for the good, for building up. For Christ did not please himself; but, as it is written, 'The insults of those who insult you fall upon me'" (Rom 15:1–3). According to the NT scholar Heinrich Schlier, the term βαστάζειν [*bastazein*, "to bear"] does not mean merely "putting up with" in the sense of tolerating another's faults but actually taking these faults upon oneself in love, bearing them in atonement. See Heinrich Schlier, *Der Romerbrief* (Freiburg, Germany: Herder, 1977), 419–20. See also Galatians 6:2, where Paul summons us to bear [βαστάζετε] each other's burdens; and Balthasar's commentary in *GL*7, 447–48.

[41] Balthasar, *GL*7, 443; see also 208, 312–13, 399, and 444.

Christ's Paschal Mystery. We have to speak of this with reticence as does the NT itself. . . . Is it not disconcerting to hear Paul say, unabashed, that he is crucified together with Christ (Gal 2:19)? He is quite aware, of course, of the vast gulf between Christ's crucifixion and his own (1 Cor 1:13) and wants to know and preach nothing but the Cross of Christ (1 Cor 2:2). There is a closeness *and* a distance here, as is shown by the phrase "I complete what is lacking in Christ's afflictions" (Col 1:24). *The sufferings of the God-man are all-sufficient, but within those sufferings a place has been left for the disciples* . . . (Jn 16:1–4; Mt 10:24f.). "Through grace" a fellowship of suffering and resurrection is created, and this fellowship only has meaning if the *pro nobis* is extended to the participants. The metaphor of the vine brings us as close as we can get to uttering its meaning: those who live in Christ, from the root and stem of Christ, will bear fruit.[42]

Disciples become branches of the vine and so are able to bear fruit (Jn 15:4–5). The image of the vine indicates that it is Christ himself who truly bears fruit in our hearts; we, as "branches", have this ability to bear fruit only in Christ, "out of him and through him, working in unity with him: 'without me, you can do nothing' (Jn 15:5)."[43] And what we can do in Christ is to leap beyond the limits we normally place on charity. The way of discipleship is certainly not the way of a sensible philanthropy.[44] As we learn from the saints, the Spirit may lead a person to experience the

[42] Balthasar, *TD*4, 387–88 (emphasis added). See also *Engagement with God*, 35–40.

[43] Balthasar, *GL*7, 419–20; see also 465. See also Aquinas, *ST* III, q. 1, a. 2, ad 2.

[44] "I am not just to love my neighbors as myself; I am to love them as Jesus loves them . . . and that must mean that [Jesus himself] goes on loving them in and through me." Thérèse of Lisieux, *The Story of a Soul*, trans. Ronald Knox (Glasgow: William Collins Sons, 1979), 266.

mystery of Christ's representative atonement in a deeper way than most, on behalf of sinners. Someone who is spiritually awake may be moved by grace to bear willingly in his soul the indifference and inner darkness of others who are asleep. Someone who is mature in charity may be inspired to practice renunciation on behalf of those who are lacking in charity, and hence in more danger.[45] Such a call and opportunity can be extended even to me. It is a call to live my filial existence in earnest.

> Whoever refuses to shut his eyes to the abyss of hatred, despair, and depravity that can be seen in the life of men on earth, and thus who refuses to close himself off from reality, will find it difficult to contrive his own escape from this damnation through a purely individualistic conception of salvation, and to abandon everyone else to the grinding wheels of hell. Just as God so loved the world that he handed over his Son for its sake, so too the one whom God has loved will want to save himself in conjunction with those who have been created with him, and he will not reject the share of penitential suffering that has been given him for the sake of the whole.[46]

Truly, if we wish to take seriously the universal call to holiness, we must accept it as "a call in grace to share in the distribution of grace and, therefore, a call to the vicarious bearing of the guilt of all".[47] We may even say that this universal call is a summons to become universalized, mystically "catholic", insofar as we bear sin in Christ, the universal Redeemer, as members of his Body.[48]

[45] See Balthasar, *TD*4, 350–51.

[46] Balthasar, *Love Alone*, 97.

[47] Balthasar, *Christian State of Life* (San Francisco: Ignatius Press, 1983), 417. See also *GL*7, 419–20.

[48] Catholicism "insists that the just person, to the extent that he shares in the holiness of the Redeemer, also receives a portion in the task of bearing a

Certainly, there is no question of usurping the uniqueness of Christ's Passion and death. Christ died "once for all" (*ephapax*). *Once*, because the death of God's only-begotten Son carries an infinite efficacy that no mere man could duplicate.[49] *For all* because, being the Son in whom, through whom, and for whom all creation exists, his death has a breadth and depth that no mere man could match.

All the same, the movement of God's universal redeeming love "continues beyond Christ's body on the Cross . . . [in] the form and work of his Mystical Body."[50] The Church as Christ's Body (σῶμα, *sōma*, Eph 1:23) and fullness (πλήρωμα, *plērōma*, Eph 1:23; 4:13) is to carry forward the work of vicarious atonement already achieved—with Christ and in dependence on him. Christ's Paschal event has more than the negative result of bearing away sin. Positively, there flows from it the gift of the Holy Spirit, who prolongs and completes the mission of the Son in us. By the will of the Father and the working of the Holy Spirit, we are incorporated into the Body of Christ (Eph 1:23) such that the suffering of Christians borne in filial love "completes" that of Christ (Col 1:24), the Atoner. Even so, in no way can the atoning suffering of Christians be viewed as something independent of or added to Christ's vicarious atonement (as if the latter were deficient and so needed

---

guilt not his own, thereby sharing in the very work of redemption". Balthasar, *The Theology of Karl Barth*, trans. Edward T. Oakes (San Francisco: Ignatius Press, 1992), 375.

[49] See Hoffmann, "Atonement and the Sacred Heart", 186; Balthasar *GL7*, 217, 395, 401, and 445; and *TD4*, 239.

[50] Heinrich Schlier, "Die Kirche als das Geheimnis Christi nach dem Epheserbrief", in *Der Zeit der Kirche: Exegetische Aufsätze und Vorträge* (Freiburg, Germany: Herder, 1956), 303. Quoted in Hoffmann, "Atonement and the Sacred Heart", 181. See also Balthasar, *GL7*, 390–91 and 395.

augmentation), but only as "the making effective" of Christ's atoning work in its "for us" (*pro nobis*) character. Said differently, Christ's vicarious substitution for sinners reaches its denouement when converted sinners become co-atoning sons. This is what it means to say that in us, Christ's atonement "blossoms".[51]

Support for these stances is everywhere evident in the writings of John Paul II, particularly in his apostolic letter *Salvifici doloris* (On the Christian Meaning of Human Suffering). Here the pontiff wastes no time in stressing the universal scope of Christ's mission of redemptive love-suffering, a mission that is open to the participation of all. "The Redeemer", he says, "suffered in place of man and for man. Every man has *his own share in the Redemption*. Each one is *called to share in that suffering* through which the Redemption was accomplished. . . . Thus each man, in his suffering, can also become a sharer in the redemptive suffering of Christ."[52]

Discernible in these words is a new iteration of the classic redemptive theme of the "wondrous exchange": Christ became the Redeemer of man so that man could become a redeemer in Christ and with Christ. The discovery of this "wondrous exchange" provokes the startling observation that "it seems to be part of the very essence of Christ's redemptive suffering that this suffering requires to be unceasingly completed." Nevertheless, there is no warrant for concluding from this that the atonement accomplished by Christ was not complete.

No. It only means that the Redemption of the world, accomplished through expiatory love, remains always open

---

[51] See Hoffmann, "Atonement and the Sacred Heart", 185 and 187.

[52] John Paul II, apostolic letter *Salvifici doloris* (On the Christian Meaning of Suffering) (February 11, 1984), no. 19. In *Redemptoris mater*, no. 7, John Paul II underscores the universal scope of God's saving will. See also *CCC* 618.

to all love expressed in human suffering. In this dimension of love, the Redemption which has already been completely accomplished is, in a certain sense, constantly being accomplished. Christ achieved the Redemption
completely and to the very limits but at the same time
he did not bring it to a close. [Rather] Christ opened
himself from the beginning to every human suffering and
constantly does so. Thus . . . this Redemption . . . lives
on and in its own special way develops in the history of
man.[53]

If these remarks underscore that Christ's mission of redemptive love-suffering is open to the participation of all,
John Paul II is equally clear that the locus in which this
redemption "lives on and develops in history" is the mystery of the Church as the Mystical Body of Christ. As the
pope explains, "The mystery of the Church is expressed in
this: that already in the act of Baptism, which brings about
a configuration with Christ, and then through his Sacrifice
—sacramentally through the Eucharist—the Church is continually being built up spiritually as the Body of Christ. In
this Body . . . Christ has in a sense opened his own redemptive suffering to all human suffering." In this Body, the redeemed are to bring redemption to its fullness through their
own grace-enabled collaboration. Their existence in Christ
is a *pro*-existence, a being-*for*-others, so much so that "*whoever suffers in union with Christ* . . . completes by his suffering
'what is lacking in Christ's afflictions' (Col 1:24)."[54] This
suffering in union with Christ is, in fact, the authentically
Christian form of solidarity with all humanity (Gal 6:2; Eph
5:1f.; Rom 15:1–3).

When next we turn to the teaching of Benedict XVI, we

[53] John Paul II, *Salvifici doloris*, no. 24.
[54] Ibid., no. 24.

find these positions not only confirmed but further developed.

They are confirmed, for instance, at Fatima on May 13, 2010, when Benedict assures the faithful that if their sufferings are united to Christ, they can "become—according to his design—a means of redemption for the whole world". Benedict crystallizes the core message of this chapter by declaring: "You will be redeemers with the Redeemer, just as you are sons in the Son."[55]

These positions are further developed, for instance, in his second papal encyclical, *Spe salvi*, where Benedict does not mince words in finding fault with an overly individualistic view of salvation, which unduly restricts the scope of the Christian's mission of atonement.

> How could the idea have developed that Jesus' message is narrowly individualistic and aimed only at each person singly? How did we arrive at this interpretation of the "salvation of the soul" as a flight from responsibility for the whole? . . .
>
> [But] no one lives alone. No one sins alone. No one is saved alone. . . . So my prayer for another is not something extraneous to that person . . . not even after death. In the interconnectedness of being . . . my prayer for the other can play a small part in his purification. . . . In this way we clarify an important element of the Christian concept of hope. Our hope is always essentially hope for others; only thus is it truly hope for me too. As Christians we should never limit ourselves to asking: how can I save myself? We should also ask: what can I do in order that others may be saved . . . ? Then I will have done my utmost for my own personal salvation as well.[56]

[55] Benedict XVI, Homily at Shrine of Our Lady of Fatima (May 13, 2010).

[56] Benedict XVI, encyclical letter *Spe salvi* (November 30, 2007), nos. 16 and 48; see also no. 25. See also *Milestones: Memoirs 1927–1977* (San Francisco: Ignatius Press, 1998), 98.

We have here a vision of Christian hope that proves its seriousness insofar as members of Christ's Mystical Body work for the salvation of others. This work includes not only overt missionary outreach to nonbelievers, but also the covert substitution of Christ's members on behalf of nonbelievers. In fact, Saint Thérèse of Lisieux sees the latter as a vital ingredient in making missionary outreach effective (more on her later).

Then in *Jesus of Nazareth*, Pope Benedict contributes a distinctive perspective regarding our foregoing themes by placing them within the framework of Christian worship. In doing so, he unites the existential with the liturgical dimensions of atonement.

First, he presses us to ask ourselves, "What does Christ's atoning passion and death mean for me?" The answer emerges insofar as we see the unity of Christian existence and Christian worship in reference to the twelfth chapter of the Letter to the Romans: "I appeal to you therefore, brethren, by the mercies of God, to present your bodies as a living sacrifice, holy and acceptable to God, which is your spiritual ['god-like'] worship" (Rom 12:1, RSVCE). To worship God in this manner, explains Benedict, means to offer one's whole existence to God such that one's whole person becomes "god-like".[57] This, of course, means nothing less than to imitate the Son in his humanity by virtue of his Spirit outpoured in our hearts. Yet this existential form of true worship should be recognized as inseparably related to the liturgical-ecclesiastical form, and vice versa. In Benedict's view, if "true *worship*" is the human being "who has become a total answer to God", then "true *priesthood* is the ministry of word and sacrament that transforms people into an offering to God." Certainly "we may identify the central

---

[57] See Benedict XVI, *Jesus of Nazareth*, vol. 2, 236.

focus of Christian worship as the celebration of the Eucharist, the constantly renewed participation in the priestly
mystery of Jesus Christ." Yet precisely the eucharistic Christ
directs us who receive him to imitate his own willingness
to give himself as a sacrificial offering (Eph 5:1–2). In true
Christian worship, therefore, there should be no other difference between the celebration of the Eucharist and our
everyday existence, except that between the source and its
living fruit.

Moreover, since the Mass sacramentally makes present
Christ's definitive self-offering in expiation for the sins of
the whole world (1 Jn 2:2), we must always keep in mind
the full scope of Christian worship, whether liturgical or
existential in form: "It is always a matter of drawing every individual person, indeed, the whole of the world, into
Christ's love in such a way that everyone together with
him becomes an offering that is 'acceptable, sanctified by
the Holy Spirit' (Rom 15:16)."[58] Indeed, since this mystery
of God's merciful love for all is manifested and actualized
principally in the liturgy of the Eucharist, it is fitting that
the Church's liturgical prayers can be offered for all, that is
to say, insofar as the breadth of her charity comprehends
the reach of God's mercy.[59] "Lord accept the offering of
your Church; and may what each individual offers up to
the honor of your name lead to the salvation of all. For this
we pray to you through Christ our Lord" (Week I, Tuesday,
Offertory Prayer). "Lord, may this sacrifice that has made

[58] Ibid., 238.
[59] "In the Eucharistic liturgy and in the daily prayers of her faithful, the
Church implores the mercy of God, who does not want 'any to perish, but
all to come to repentance' (2 Pet 3:9)." *CCC* 1037. The Fatima Prayer is also
relevant here: "Forgive us our sins, and save us from the fires of hell. Lead
all souls to heaven, especially those in most need of Thy mercy."

our peace with you, advance the peace and salvation of all the world" (Eucharistic Prayer III).

Lastly, Benedict turns his attention to martyrdom, which he sees as a paramount instance of true Christian worship. He points to the Letter to the Philippians, in which Paul offers a theological reflection in anticipation of his own martyrdom: "Even if I am to be poured as a libation upon the sacrificial offering of your faith, I am glad and rejoice with you all" (Phil 2:17, RSVCE). Benedict notes that "Paul views his expected martyrdom as liturgy and as sacrificial event. Once again, this is no mere allegory or figurative way of speaking. No, in martyrdom he is drawn fully into . . . the liturgy of the Cross."[60] In both the sacrifice of the Mass and that of martyrdom, we are to recognize the cruciform witness of a love more than human, pouring itself out on behalf even of enemies. At issue here is sacrificial love, which ought not to be reduced to an example of nobility and a memorial of courage in the face of death. Nor should it be mistaken for an unwillingness to betray one's convictions or most sacred cause. The acid test of Christian martyrdom, which witnesses most truly to Christ in his Passion, finds in the martyr's heart the willingness to surrender his life for the forgiveness of sins, including the sins of his persecutors.

Together, Christian life and death are a breathtaking vocation to "become bread" blessed, broken, and given away for others. In precisely this way, we who receive the Eucharist are summoned and enabled to worship God truly. And we know with surety that this true worship is possible, for we see it enacted in the lives of the saints.[61]

[60] Benedict XVI, *Jesus of Nazareth*, vol. 2, 239.
[61] See ibid., 240.

The witness of saints as
vicarious atoners in the Atoner

Already in the patristic era, biblical texts were understood as indicating that God does indeed inspire his children to exchange places willingly with those who are resisting God's merciful love, for the vicarious atonement of their sins. Origen, for instance, compares Romans 9:3 (where *Saint Paul* expresses his willingness to be cut off from Christ for the sake of others' salvation) with Exodus 32:32 (where *Moses* expresses his willingness to be blotted out of God's book of life if thereby the sins of the people will be forgiven). "Indeed Origen goes beyond that to compare Paul's offer to be accursed with what is said in Galatians 3:13, where *Christ* becomes a curse for our sake. Saint Gregory of Nazianzus (*Orations* 2:55) says the same: Saint Paul is here emulating *Christ.*"[62] Inspired by Christ's example, Paul is willing to "lose" God, to relinquish possession of God, so that his fellow Jews would possess Christ through faith (Rom 9:1–3). Such an outlandish and breathtaking self-sacrifice can be entirely sane and sober only in connection with the dying cry of Christ, "My God, why have you forsaken me?"— the cry of the Son who was made "to be sin" for the salvation of all.

In a poignant passage, Balthasar reflects on similar scenarios. "What sorts of things do we not find in the hidden, shadowy corners of Christian history? What limits are reached in the imploring prayers of Christian mothers for their sons and daughters who have gone astray? What limits to the offering up of self by martyrs for their ene-

[62] Balthasar, *DWH*, 206.

mies, or even by simple priests for those hardened in serious sin?"[63]

In recent times, the Church has been gifted with the personal testimony of two women saints—Saint Thérèse of Lisieux and Saint Teresa of Calcutta—who interpreted their sudden plunge into spiritual darkness as a sharing in Christ's mission of vicarious atonement.

Thérèse of Lisieux taught a way of spiritual childhood that finds its maturation in a willing participation in the way of atonement as modeled by Christ. Just as Christ in his Passion made no distinction between himself and sinners, but took upon himself their state of God-forsakenness, so Thérèse desired to exchange places with unbelievers (who, in her mind, typified modern sinners). This desire grew during her brief life as a Carmelite, despite the fact that, as a young girl, she could not conceive how anyone could live meaningfully in the absence of God. Freely appropriating this desire, she prayed that God would enable her to offer herself for the conversion of unbelievers. Her prayer was answered on Easter, 1896, when she coughed up blood for the first time—a sign of her tuberculosis. From then until her death, over a period of eighteen months, Thérèse was plunged into a state of spiritual darkness in which she experienced God's (apparent) absence. Significantly, she understood her experience not as a purgative phase through which the soul passes in the course of *ascending* to God (for the sake of one's own salvation), but as a way of identifying with unbelievers, a way of *descending* with Christ in *his* exchange of place with sinners (for the sake of others' salvation).

In her words:

---

[63] Ibid., 207. Even Aquinas does not sanction the notion that Christians should pray only for those whose salvation appears likely. See his *Commentary on the First Letter of Saint Paul to Timothy*, no. 62.

I told the good God that I was happy not to enjoy heaven on earth [the experience of his presence] in order that he may open heaven forever to poor unbelievers.

[The Lord] permitted my soul to be swamped by the thickest darkness, so that the thought of heaven, which had been so sweet to me, became nothing but a torment [seemed nothing but an illusion]. This trial was not just to last for a few days, or a few weeks; it was to last until the time determined by the good God. That time has not yet come.

When, exhausted by the darkness that surrounds me, I try to refresh my heart with the memory of the luminous country to which I aspire, my torment grows twice as great. Borrowing sinners' voices the darkness seems to mock me, saying: "You dream of light . . . you dream of eternally possessing the Creator . . . you believe that one day you will emerge from the fog which surrounds you. Keep going, then, proceed! Look forward to death—but it will not give you what you are hoping for [the possession of God]—but only an even deeper night, the night of nothingness, the darkness of extinction."

I offer these very great pains to obtain the light of faith for poor unbelievers.[64]

And in our own time, we have the remarkable witness of Mother Teresa of Calcutta. To one of her spiritual directors, she wrote about "this terrible sense of loss . . . this loneliness and this continual longing for God. . . . The place

[64] Thérèse of Lisieux, *Story of a Soul*, bk. 3, chap. 32. Balthasar observes that Thérèse "loses the feeling and triumphant sense of faith but never faith itself". *Two Sisters in the Spirit: Thérèse of Lisieux and Elizabeth of the Trinity*, trans. Donald Nichols and Anne Englund Nash (San Francisco: Ignatius Press, 1998), 341. Further, he regards Christ's agony on the Mount of Olives as pre-eminently St. Thérèse's mystery; see ibid., 356.

of God in my soul is blank. There is no God in me. I feel—He is not there."[65] At first, this feeling of having "lost" God took Mother Teresa off guard, since she had had intense experiences of intimacy with him. But under the guidance of spiritual directors, she came to understand that her communion with God was actually growing deeper. She was becoming more closely configured to Christ crucified, who willingly relinquished the felt presence of his Father in order to regain souls for heaven. In Mother Teresa's words:

> Lord, my God, who am I that You should forsake me? The child of your love—now become the one You have thrown away unwanted—unloved. I call, I cling—and there is No One to answer—No One on Whom I can cling—no, No One—Alone. The darkness is so dark—and I am alone. Unwanted, forsaken. . . . Where is my faith? . . . There is nothing but emptiness and darkness. . . . I dare not utter the words and thoughts that crowd in my heart and make me suffer untold agony. . . . When I try to raise my thoughts to Heaven there is such convicting emptiness that those very thoughts return like sharp knives and hurt my very soul. . . . I am told that God loves me—and yet the reality of darkness and coldness and emptiness is so great that nothing touches my soul. Before the work started, there was so much union—love—faith—trust—prayer. Did I make the mistake in surrendering blindly to the call of the Sacred Heart? . . . When You asked to imprint Your Passion on my heart—is this the answer? If this brings You glory—if souls are brought to You—if my suffering satiates Your thirst—here I am Lord, with joy I

[65] Teresa of Calcutta, *Come Be My Light: The Private Writings of the Saint of Calcutta* (New York: Image, 2009), 210.

accept all to the end of life—and will smile at Your Hidden Face—always.[66]

It seems to us that these spiritual experiences gain clarity when illumined by the theology and spirituality of atonement set forth in this study. Saints Thérèse and Teresa have given voice to a profound experience of being plunged into the pain of God's (seeming) absence, a filial love-suffering undergone "in Christ" and "for others". If the Father summons these saints to endure feeling abandoned in their identification with sinners, nonetheless they remain unceasingly inspired by the Holy Spirit to follow Christ "to the end" of his work of atonement. For this very reason, these words of Saint John apply outstandingly to them: "No one has ever seen God. Yet, if we love one another [including the 'ungodly'] God remains in us, and his love is brought to perfection in us" (1 Jn 4:12; cf. Rom 4:5; 5:6).

Returning again to the thought of Ratzinger, we encounter his daring words of recognition that to answer the call to sanctity may involve partaking, in the most radical way conceivable, in Christ's vicarious bearing of sin.

For the saints, "Hell" is not so much a threat to be hurled at other people but a challenge to oneself. It is a challenge to suffer in the dark night of faith, to experience communion with Christ in solidarity with his descent into the Night. . . . One serves the salvation of the world by leaving one's own salvation behind for the sake of others. In such piety . . . one shares in the suffering of [sin's dreadful] night by the side of the One who came to transform our night by his suffering.[67]

[66] Ibid., 187–88.

[67] Joseph Ratzinger, *Eschatology: Death and Eternal Life*, trans. Michael Waldstein (Washington, D.C.: Catholic University of America, 1988), 217–18.

What the saints experience in such cases is not a mystical state impervious to suffering but a sharing in the drama of Christ's own experience of the world's bitter distance from God.

In his capacity as prefect of the Congregation for the Doctrine of the Faith, Ratzinger finds an opportunity to anchor this line of reflection in the Church Fathers. In his 1989 *Letter to the Bishops of the Catholic Church on Some Aspects of Christian Meditation*, he states: "The Fathers insisted on the fact that the soul's union with God . . . can even be achieved through experiences of affliction or desolation. . . . These are not necessarily a sign that [God] has abandoned a soul. Rather . . . they may be an authentic participation in the state of abandonment experienced on the Cross by our Lord, who always remains the model and mediator of prayer." For Ratzinger, Christian love surely shows that its living source is the ever-greater God when it is willing to "leave behind" God's felt closeness in order to serve God's love for the world. *Such* love is a credible (because *in*credible, staggering) witness to the God and Father of our Lord Jesus Christ.

Implied here is a conception of "mysticism" as an ecclesial process in which members of Christ's Body grow in their participative understanding of the mysteries of their Head. Since we are to regard the Holy Trinity as the central mystery that illumines all others, we may consider the Trinitarian *perichoresis* (the mutual interpenetration and indwelling of the divine persons) as the ultimate ground, or condition for the possibility, of the saints' penetration and participative understanding of Christ's work of atonement. For if Christ during his historical mission attests to his being "in the Father" and the Father's being "in him", ultimately it is because from all eternity the Father and the Son mutually penetrate and experience from within each other's manner of being divine in the life of the Trinity. And when Christ declares that "No one knows the Son except the Father, and no one knows the Father except the Son" (Mt 11:27; cf. Lk 10:22), this intimate knowledge of each other's personal manner of existence rests upon the mystery of their mutual *perichoresis*, in which each is given access to the inner reality of the other. Accordingly, this pattern of *perichoresis* is graciously extended in analogous fashion (*mutatis mutandis*) to include all those in whom Christ abides (cf. Jn 15:5). If the saints can enter into the inner reality of Christ's filial mission and consciousness, it is because such is the primordial pattern or structure of the Trinitarian life itself. Participation in the Trinitarian *perichoresis* is implied in the biblical datum that we are created to partake in the divine nature (cf. 2 Pet 1:4). To partake in the divine nature, a nature constituted in terms of mutual interpenetration and indwelling, is to receive a share in this capacity vis-à-vis Christ (cf. Gal 2:20; Jn 17:23). All the same, we must admit that even the most profound instances of sharing in Christ's Passion "are at best approaches, distant allusions to the inaccessible mystery of the Cross—so unique is the Son of God, so unique is his abandonment by the Father."[68]

The foregoing qualification should guide us in understanding Balthasar's own perspective on where the call to share in Christ's Passion may lead.

> God distributes his gifts as he will. From the treasury of Christian grace, he can select individual pieces which he earmarks for this or that person in particular. As the Curé of Torcy explains to his young friend in Bernanos' novel

---

[68] Balthasar, *MP*, 79.

The Diary of a Country Priest, in Christ's following we all have our special place. Our place can be on the Mount of Olives or at any one of the Stations of the Cross. In such a place, however, it is possible that the Christian, in some special way which somehow is suited to his calling, will be led into situations where he feels himself abandoned by God. God can bring about such situations as he will; they differ in intensity as in the length of time they last and the frequency with which they recur. They may be situations which could be described as mystical (in the narrower sense of that term), like the dark night of St. John of the Cross. On the other hand, they may be brought about by external events, as, for example, by the cruelty of concentration camps or the gas chambers, or by the torture chambers of so many a modern totalitarian state. On this subject of the fearsomeness of God's grace we can add . . . that no Christians may acquire it by themselves. . . . The most a Christian could do would be to be allowed to ask God that if it should so please him, he might vicariously experience some of the darkness of his fellow men. But God alone can decide this.[69]

As a final word we should note that Balthasar recognizes a "rule" that governs this "representative" experience of God-estrangement. The suffering of this spiritual night is grounded in that soul's prior renunciation of sin and in its intimacy with God. God leads a soul into the experience of God-abandonment only *after* it has known God's redeeming embrace. Balthasar is clear and firm about this: "In God there is no darkness, and in guilt there is no light. The Son of God became like us in all things except sin, and this 'except' is the prerequisite that enabled him to take each and every sin upon himself and to atone for it completely. Whoever

[69] Balthasar, *Engagement with God*, 100–101.

deviates a hairsbreadth from that rule entangles everything. A Christian can share burdens and be in solidarity precisely in the measure that he has separated himself from sin."[70]

The "excommunicate person" and our mission of co-atonement

Besides the existential witness of Thérèse of Lisieux and Teresa of Calcutta, there is yet another source from which we can draw to illustrate the theology and spirituality of atonement presented in this study. It is the pastoral application that Ratzinger makes in regard to the problem of "the excommunicate person".[71]

In reflecting on the purpose of excommunication, Ratzinger observes that its primary aim is to induce repentance and lead to the restoration of full communion with the Lord's Church. The suffering of separation that the excommunicate person endures may be likened to an ecclesiastical state of "exile". The spiritual distance suffered by the excommunicate is meant to serve as a condition for the graced recalibration of love for God, in such a way that it contributes to the restoration of communion. And yet if the excommunicate is to be led through this state of "exile" toward reconciliation with the Lord and his Church, the latter must go in advance of the excommunicate and accompany him on the journey homeward, albeit in a hidden spiritual manner. Thus, for Ratzinger, if the excommunicate person opens his heart to the hidden springs of grace, and thereby suffers in repentant love the sin-wrought distance indicated by his ecclesiastical penalty, in reality he is already

[70] Balthasar, *The Christian and Anxiety*, 114.
[71] See Joseph Ratzinger, *Behold the Pierced One: An Approach to a Spiritual Christology* (San Francisco: Ignatius Press, 1986), 94–98.

united to his Redeemer. He is indeed enveloped by the love-suffering of the Son who bears the sins of all.[72] And due to the all-embracing inclusivity of Christ's redemptive mediation, those who are members of his Mystical Body may be invited to participate lovingly in Christ's expiatory solidarity with those suffering this sort of "exile". In Ratzinger's words:

> [T]he "ex-communicate" is supported by the love of the living Body of Christ, by the sufferings of the saints, who unite with his suffering and his spiritual hunger, and both parties are enveloped by the suffering, the hunger, the thirst of Jesus Christ, who bears and endures us all. On the other hand, the suffering of the excommunicate person, his stretching out for communion (the communion of the sacrament and of the living members of Christ) is the bond which unites him to the saving love of Christ. . . . Here too, therefore, the "healing of love" takes place, which is the ultimate aim of Christ's Cross, of the sacrament and of the Church. We can understand how, paradoxically, the impossibility of sacramental communion, experienced in a sense of remoteness from God, in the pain of yearning which fosters the growth of love, can lead to spiritual progress [indeed to atonement and reconciliation].[73]

It is not difficult to detect in these reflections the biblical and Trinitarian pattern of forgiveness-atonement that elucidates them. More remarkable still is Ratzinger's subsequent suggestion that the faithful fast from the Eucharist on Good

---

[72] "Only love gives the power to forgive, that is, to accompany the other on the road of the suffering that transforms. . . . The cross of Christ means that he precedes us and that he accompanies us on the painful way of our healing and salvation." Joseph Ratzinger, *To Look on Christ: Exercises in Faith, Hope and Charity* (New York: Crossroad, 1991), 88–89.

[73] Ratzinger, *Behold the Pierced One*, 96.

Friday as an act of spiritual solidarity with the excommunicate (among other intentions). To be sure, he is quick to
note that this practice dates back to apostolic times. Yet it
is not the ancient origin of the practice that proves most
persuasive to his mind; rather, he is attracted to this spiritual fast mainly because he sees it as "a particularly profound
way of sharing in the Lord's Passion". For by voluntarily renouncing being fed by the eucharistic presence of the Lord
on Good Friday, the faithful are spiritually identifying with
the Lord himself, who willingly renounced the felt presence
of the Father (upon whom his soul "fed", Jn 4:34) in bearing the sin of the world. Paradoxically, voluntarily to suffer
a sense of remoteness from the Lord becomes a means to
draw close to him on the very day the Church commem-
orates his atoning Passion and death. This alone suffices to
explain Ratzinger's description of this practice as "a part of
the Church's spirituality of communion".[74]

Furthermore, this spirituality of communion with the
Lord embraces the "for us" (*pro nobis*) character of the
Lord's Passion: just as Christ, for our sake, willingly suffered an acute sense of the Father's absence, so those who
voluntarily fast from the Eucharist on Good Friday should
do so for the sake of sinners—even especially for excommunicate persons. Such a fast, he advises,

> could also be an act of solidarity with all those who yearn
> for the sacrament but cannot receive it. It seems to me that
> the problem of the divorced and remarried, as well as that
> of intercommunion (e.g., in mixed marriages), would be

[74] "The ancient Church had a highly expressive practice of this kind. Since
apostolic times, the fast from the Eucharist on Good Friday was a part of the
Church's spirituality of communion. This renunciation of communion on
one of the most sacred days of the Church's year was a particularly profound
way of sharing in the Lord's Passion." Ibid., 97.

far less acute against the background of voluntary spiritual fasting, which would visibly express the fact that we all need that "healing of love" which the Lord performed in the ultimate loneliness of the Cross.[75]

We should remember, of course, that the purpose of such "an act of solidarity" extends beyond a gesture of simple accompaniment. The faithful are not to be mirroring the state of the excommunicate person *per se* but that of their crucified Lord, whose work of atonement entailed his identification with sinners in their plight. (Here we must be mindful of the "rule" that was stated above: "a Christian can share burdens and be in solidarity precisely in the measure that he has separated himself from sin."[76]) If the faithful voluntarily suffer spiritual hunger on Good Friday for the sake of those who remain at a distance from full ecclesial and sacramental communion, their spiritual sacrifice aims to advance or contribute to the process of restoring excommunicate persons to the people of God (without, of course, bypassing the freedom of these persons in response to the offer of God's grace).

Whether or not one agrees with Ratzinger's suggestion to fast voluntarily from the Eucharist on Good Friday, there are simply no grounds for misconstruing Ratzinger's stance in terms of a solidarity with excommunicate persons as indicating a protest against the ecclesiastical penalty itself. Instead, he discerns a positive spiritual aim behind it. For our purposes, his suggestion gives us a practical application that accords with and substantiates the biblical, Trinitarian, and spiritual theology of atonement developed in this study.

[75] Ibid., 98.
[76] Balthasar, *The Christian and Anxiety*, 114.

Mary under the Cross

What of Mary, the Mother of God, who stood at the foot of her Son's Cross as he willingly bore the sin of the world? May we speak of a co-atoning role in her regard, and if so, in what sense and with what qualifications and clarifications?

From the outset we should note that our quartet of theologians all endeavor to understand Mary's role in light of the mystery of the Church, and more specifically, with regard to the Church as the Body of Christ.[77] First of all they illuminate the Body of Christ against the backdrop of Gen 2:24, "the two of them become one body." The Church is the Body of Christ, in a way analogous to how Adam and Eve become one body "in a unity of love that does not abolish dialogical reciprocity" (Eph 5:30–32).[78] To be sure, Christ is the eternal Son of God, consubstantial with the Father, whereas the members of his Body the Church, including Mary, are creatures made *ex nihilo*. So if between Adam and Eve the dignity of their persons is equal, we must readily admit that "between Christ and the New Eve —whether she be Mary or the Church—there is no parity: Mary is nothing but a servant, though full of grace":[79] and the Church is nothing but the recipient of grace in Christ, though this includes "every spiritual blessing in the heavens" (Eph 1:3). All the same, Mary is the epitome of this ecclesial mystery: the receptive handmaid enabled by grace

[77] See Vatican Council II, *Lumen gentium*, nos. 64–65; John Paul II, *Redemptoris mater*, no. 5; and Joseph Ratzinger and Hans Urs von Balthasar, *Mary: The Church at the Source*, trans. Adrian J. Walker (San Francisco: Ignatius Press, 2005).

[78] Ratzinger, *Mary*, 26.

[79] Hans Urs von Balthasar, *To the Heart of the Mystery of Redemption*, trans. Anne Englund Nash (San Francisco: Ignatius Press, 2010), 52.

"speaks her fiat and, in so doing, becomes bride and thus body".[80] Hence Mary may be designated "the Church at its source". "At the moment that she pronounces her yes, Mary is the Church in person, and as a person. She is the personal concretization of the Church."[81]

Now, if Paul can say that he, by his suffering, fills up what is lacking in the afflictions of Christ for the sake of his Body the Church (Col 1:24), how much more can we say that Mary, who is "the Church in person", has a sphere of co-suffering reserved for her within the all-sufficient suffering of Christ?[82] Obviously we must not think that Mary could "co-redeem" on the same level as Christ. For it is impossible that she who is redeemed in advance (in being immaculately conceived) could have redeemed herself. Indeed, whatever the ecclesial Body of Christ "adds" to the afflictions of Christ is *derived from* Christ's Cross. "It is through grace from the Head", says Balthasar, "that the Body can collaborate; it is an effect of the fullness of Christ that a place is reserved for us in the redemptive work."[83] So let us avoid any misunderstanding: the Marian and ecclesial "collaboration" with Christ "is always response, consent—never the first action. The latter, in the domain of grace, belongs to God alone."[84] And indeed the response is itself a grace that is given along with the divine call or command.

Moreover, at the heart of the Marian response is *faith*. In his encyclical *Redemptoris mater*, John Paul II sees faith as the key to unlocking the question of Mary's role in relation

[80] Ratzinger, *Mary*, 27.
[81] Ibid., 30.
[82] See Balthasar, *Threefold Garland*, 81.
[83] Balthasar, *To the Heart*, 58.
[84] Ibid., 59. Likewise, Balthasar says of Mary: "She works with God only in the sense that she lets him work in her." *Threefold Garland*, 32–33.

to her sin-bearing Son. This key is given us in Luke's infancy narrative, through the words of Elizabeth addressed to Mary: "Blessed are you who believed" (Lk 1:45).[85] The pontiff depicts the inner shape of Mary's faith in conformity with *Dei verbum's* description of faith as a free act by which a person entrusts his whole self to God (cf. *Dei verbum*, no. 5). "This description of faith", says John Paul II, "found perfect realization in Mary." From her first to her final appearance in the Gospels, "Mary entrusted herself to God tely."[86] Indeed, the entire trajectory of Mary's role in the Gospels can be traced along the lines of a perpetual act of faith, which assents in obedience to whatever God asks of her.[87] Intimated here is that the Mother assumes the filial attitude of her Child: to be an unreserved answer to whatever the Father disposes. Or what amounts to the same: the Mother willingly shares her flesh with her Child, because the Child has already shared his Spirit of Sonship (of obedience) with her.

Now, assuredly this description of faith resonates with a dramatic quality, which the pontiff amplifies throughout his encyclical. "To believe", he continues, "means 'to abandon oneself' to the truth of the word of the living God, knowing and humbly recognizing 'how unsearchable are his judgments and how inscrutable his ways' (Rom 11:33)."[88] Applied to Mary, who finds herself at the center of those "inscrutable ways", her obedience of faith consists essentially in her abandoning herself without reserve.

Notably, John Paul II makes a point of stressing that

[85] See John Paul II, *Redemptoris mater*, nos. 12 and 19.

[86] Ibid., no. 13.

[87] See Balthasar, *To the Heart*, 57.

[88] John Paul II, *Redemptoris mater*, no. 14.

Mary's faith does not exclude lack of understanding.[89] When the child Jesus returns to Mary and Joseph after being "lost" for three days, Luke tells us that Mary still does "not understand" (Lk 2:48–50). Some years later, after her Son leaves home to undertake his public ministry, Jesus seemingly rebuffs his mother on several occasions: "Who is my mother?" (Mt 12:48); "Rather, blessed are those who hear the word of God and observe it" (Lk 11:28); "Woman, behold, your son" (indicating the disciple at her side) (Jn 19:26). Nowhere are we told how much of all this Mary "understands" during her years of solitude. What is clear to our guides, however, is that Mary's faith, along with the darkness that it includes, reaches its apex when she stands beneath the Cross.[90] Precisely there Mary's faith is plunged into "total darkness".[91] For under the Cross, the word of promise at the Annunciation "seems to be definitively proved wrong", namely, the promise spoken by the angel Gabriel: "The Lord God will give him the throne of David his father, and he will rule over the house of Jacob forever, and of his kingdom there will be no end" (Lk 1:32–33).[92]

Despite the "darkness" of her faith, Mary does not despair of the power of God's goodness in the face of his non-intervention, indeed his seeming absence. She has to let it happen and can only offer to God this letting-it-be-done. She must leave the burden to him, inasmuch as vicarious atonement "once for all" is truly *the Son's* business qua son. If this is the case, we may venture to call her spiritual condition the Marian form of love-suffering. It can be

---

[89] Ibid., no. 17. See also Ratzinger, *Mary*, 76.

[90] See John Paul II, *Redemptoris mater*, no. 18.

[91] Ratzinger, *Mary*, 51.

[92] Ibid., 50; and John Paul II, *Redemptoris mater*, no. 18.

distinguished from that of God the Father, for its expression does not entail concealing herself from her Son. Yet if, as Ratzinger insists, "the Father suffers in allowing the Son to suffer", then Mary's love-suffering (symbolized by her sword-pierced heart) is the closest creaturely reflection of the "Heart" of God the Father vis-à-vis his crucified Son.[93]

Yet it is not comparisons of Mary to God the Father that draw the attention of our theologians so much as comparisons of Mary to Christ, the Son. The pivotal move they make is to discern a *sacrificial* character in Mary's faith as she stands beneath the Cross. For instance, John Paul II regards Mary's act of faith—first voiced in her fiat at the Annunciation—as implied in the Psalm text (40:6–8) "*Sacrifice* and *offering* you did not desire, but a body you prepared for me; *holocausts* and *sin-offerings* you took no delight in. . . . Behold, I come to do your will" (Heb 10:5–7).[94] This is the very same text that the Letter to the Hebrews "interprets as expressing the Son's yes to his Incarnation and Cross".[95] Even more suggestively, our group of theologians portrays this sacrificial character of Mary's faith as a *kenosis*, inasmuch as her obedience of faith involves "a letting go, a releasing",[96] a relinquishing of what (whom!) she loves more than herself. It is in surrendering her beloved Son that her faith "enters into its utmost kenosis".[97] Yet precisely in this way, Mary's faith becomes a perfect participation in Christ's kenosis unto death (Phil 2:5–8). In the

[93] Ratzinger, *Behold the Pierced One*, 58. Also see Ratzinger's remarks on "God's compassionate suffering" in *Mary*, 77–79. "She [Mary standing under the Cross] is the *compassio* of God, displayed in a human being who has let herself be drawn wholly into God's mystery." Ibid., 78.

[94] See John Paul II, *Redemptoris mater*, no. 13.

[95] Ratzinger, *Mary*, 49.

[96] Ibid., 49.

[97] Ibid., 50.

words of John Paul II: "At the foot of the Cross, Mary shares through faith in the shocking mystery of [Christ's] self-emptying. This is perhaps the deepest 'kenosis' of faith in human history."[98] For just as Christ's kenosis led him to relinquish willingly the felt presence of his Father, so Mary is asked to relinquish willingly her Son, to let go of him, to suffer his absence, in order that he be able to complete his mission. If her first major step in faith was to utter her fiat and thereby to receive and accept the miraculous gift of her Son, thereafter she must learn to relinquish the Son she has borne. She must complete the yes to God's will that first made her a mother, only now on Golgotha her yes must be offered in view of God's will to make her sinless Son "to be sin" (2 Cor 5:21). Precisely by inwardly surrendering her Son to perform his atoning work—that is, by consenting in faith to the necessity of his suffering these things (cf. Lk 24:26)—"the Mother shares in the death of her Son, in his redeeming death."[99]

With an insightful shift of perspective, Balthasar highlights the deliberate self-withdrawal that takes place on Golgotha—the Father from his Son, the Son from his mother—in reference to Jesus' last words to Mary in John 19:26, "Woman, behold, your son." With these words, Jesus "*withdraws* from her his sonship in order to substitute another for it. And it is precisely in this way that the perfect *union* between the two is accomplished: just as the Father *abandons* his Son, so the Son *separates* himself from his mother. *This*

---

[98] John Paul II, *Redemptoris mater*, no. 18.

[99] Ibid., no. 18. Also see "We Must Love Mary as Christ Loved Her" (General Audience, April 29, 1998), in *The Trinity's Embrace*, 47. Mary "cooperated by her obedience, faith, hope and burning charity in the Savior's work of restoring supernatural life to souls." Vatican Council II, *Lumen gentium*, no. 61. See *CCC* 618.

form of union was necessary so that Mary might know from experience the mystery of the redemption."[100]

Furthermore, this form of union was necessary if Mary, who is "the Church in person",[101] is to offer a simultaneous consent—itself sacrificial in character—to Christ's atoning sacrifice. For the notion of sacrifice calls to mind above all *renunciation*: the renunciation of an object (someone or something) very dear to me, or of something of myself (even my very life). Christ, for his part, renounces his earthly life in expiation for the sins of the whole world (1 Jn 2:2). Even more profoundly, he renounces his sense of intimacy with the Father. Regarding the Church, however, if we ask what she is renouncing (what you and I are renouncing) in the holy sacrifice of the Mass, what can we say? How does the Church renounce something or someone in the sacrifice of the Mass? Balthasar believes that the answer lies in the role of Mary as "the Church in person" under the Cross. Her "loving consent to the immolation of the Victim" (*Lumen gentium*, no. 58) is, at the same time, her self-renunciation —the sacrifice of her maternal heart. She let what she held dearest be returned to the bosom of the Father while she let herself be emptied out, despoiled of her true treasure. And though her renunciation adds nothing to the infinite value

[100] Balthasar, *To the Heart*, 56; (emphasis added). Without wishing to bedim or obscure Balthasar's insight but only to expand the scope of our vision, we would add that Mary, by accepting the "replacement" of her Son with John, does not lose Jesus any more than Mary Magdalene loses him through allowing him to ascend to the Father in order to send the Holy Spirit. For John is a figure of the Church, the Mystical Body of Christ, to which she relates as mother in the order of grace. By the acceptance of her motherhood in relation to the Church, Mary's motherhood in relation to Jesus comes to its fullest perfection, since, as Jesus says: "For this I was born, and for this I came into the world" (Jn 18:37). None of this is to deny Mary's painful passage through darkness to arrive at this point.

[101] Ratzinger, *Mary*, 30.

of her Son's sacrifice, nonetheless, no greater sacrifice offered by a human person can be conceived.[102] Hence, these words of Balthasar apply pre-eminently to her:

> The distance between the "Head" and the "Body" must be maintained under all circumstances, so that Christ as the Head is the sole Redeemer of all, even of his "proleptically redeemed" mother; but at the same time, the one Redeemer takes up the "Body" of the Church into his redemptive activity, and this becomes yet more fruitful the more a member conforms itself to the selflessness that is Christ's disposition, and the less he exercises reserve in putting his existence at the service of universal redemption.[103]

What of Mary's immaculate conception?[104] How does it enhance her participation in Christ's work of atonement? Let us recall a "rule" that governs all who are called to share in Christ's work of vicarious expiation: "A Christian can share burdens and be in solidarity precisely in the measure that he has separated himself from sin."[105] Since Mary, by a unique grace, is preserved from original sin at her conception (indeed, she is pre-redeemed), she can share burdens in a measure beyond her fellow Christians. Mary has the spiritual liberty to offer an utterly selfless consent to her Son's redemptive work "to the end". Moreover, since she herself is sinless, the sorrow that she experiences as she beholds

---

[102] See Balthasar, *To the Heart*, 45–46; and *Does Jesus Know Us*, 51. According to *Lumen gentium*, no. 62, we are to understand Mary's co-atoning role in such a way "that it neither takes away nor adds anything to the dignity and efficaciousness of Christ the one Mediator".

[103] Balthasar, *GL7*, 465.

[104] See Pius XI, apostolic letter *Ineffabilis Deus* (December 8, 1854); Vatican Council II, *Lumen gentium*, no. 53; and John Paul II, *Redemptoris mater*, no. 10.

[105] Balthasar, *The Christian and Anxiety*, 114.

"the pierced one" cannot be contrition for her *own* sins (cf. Jn 19:37; Zech 12:10–11), but only for those of the world. Mary is the only human person who can suffer spiritually the effects of sin (as she witnesses these being borne by her Son) with a heart that bears them *entirely for others*. She stands at the foot of her Son's Cross, reflecting back to him a mirror image of *his* wholly innocent suffering in atonement for the sins of the world. To be sure, Christ's vicarious bearing of sin on behalf of the whole world makes possible, indeed is the very wellspring of, the grace that enables Mary to play this role: a role that is subordinate to Christ's, and dependent on his.[106] Nonetheless, from the Cross, Christ sees Mary as his unique human reflection (his feminine counterpart), who, while entirely derived from him (by creation and by grace), acquiesces to let go of him, and thus mirrors (albeit from an immeasurable distance) Christ's purely vicarious expiatory suffering. If the First Adam can say, "This one, at last, is bone of my bones and flesh of my flesh" (Gen 2:23), the New Adam can say of Mary, "Here at last is heart of my heart."

Forgive, as God forgave you in Christ

Thus far our reflections have led us to see that the totality of the Trinity's forgiving-atoning work is accomplished when the *objective* redemption has reached its *subjective* goal. In Christ and by the interior working of the Spirit of Sonship, the Father enables the sinner to be a son in a manner that is appropriate to a "convert": namely, by bearing the effects of sin with filial (God-engendered) love, thereby converting them into material for the expression of sonship. And given the sin-marred condition of human nature and

---

[106] See Vatican Council II, *Lumen gentium*, no. 60; John Paul II, *Redemptoris mater*, no. 22; and Balthasar, *GL*7, 218.

the world, every Christian must inevitably live out his identity as a beloved child of God by way of participating in Christ's work of atonement.

Moreover, as we have seen, the Christian is enabled by the Triune God to atone in a *representative* capacity. To love others "in Christ" and as Christ has loved us can take the form of *vicarious* atonement. Atoning for others is an appropriate response in the face of the most serious plight of our fellow human beings: alienation from God, sin-wrought distance from the Father.

Yet what remains to be discussed, if only briefly, is how the three factors that we identified as integral to the process of forgiveness-atonement are operative not only when believers stand in relation to God as sinners, but also when our neighbor's relation to us is like our relation to God: that is to say, when we have been wronged.[107]

Pope Benedict explores this question in his book *Jesus of Nazareth* in the chapter "The Lord's Prayer", where he comments on the second-to-last petition: "Forgive us our trespasses, as we forgive those who trespass against us." Benedict asserts straightaway that forgiveness is not a cheap gift. After all, "guilt is a reality, an objective force", and hence it has real effects, real consequences: it "causes damage that must be repaired".[108] A vow is broken, a reputation ruined, a body ravaged, a life taken. "For this reason," says Benedict,

---

[107] These ideas are given helpful expression by Romano Guardini: "We cannot enjoy the benefits of redemption unless we collaborate in the act of redemption. To collaborate in Christ's redeeming work is to love our neighbor. And this love becomes forgiveness as soon as our neighbor's relation to us is like our relation to God; i.e., when he has done us wrong." *Der Herr* (Mainz, Germany: Matthias Grünewald Verlag, 1937), 358, quoted in Hoffmann, "Atonement and the Sacred Heart", 201n317.

[108] Benedict XVI, *Jesus of Nazareth*, vol. 1, *From the Baptism in the Jordan to the Transfiguration*, trans. Adrian J. Walker (New York: Doubleday, 2007), 158.

"forgiveness must be more than a matter of ignoring, of merely trying to forget." The baneful effects of sin and guilt "must be worked through, healed, and thus overcome".[109]

Now this means that "forgiveness exacts a price"—and "*first* of all from the person who *forgives*."[110] This might surprise us. We might expect that the cost of forgiveness would rest entirely on the guilty person, on the trespasser. The guilty person should have to take the first step (so we think), should have to "pay up front" with some token of regret in order to be tendered forgiveness. But Benedict says otherwise. The cost of forgiveness is paid in the first place by the person who forgives. *This* person—the one wronged —takes the initiative in the process of forgiveness by willingly keeping his heart open and "suffering through" the evil done to him. Suffering of this kind we have called "love-suffering": not that the sufferer loves to suffer (that would be masochism) but that the lover is willing to suffer for the sake of love's continuance, in order that love endure. This capacity for love-suffering is what Saint Paul extols at the conclusion of his "hymn to love" in 1 Cor 13:7–8. Love "bears all things . . . endures all things. . . . Love never fails." "As a result," asserts Benedict, "he also involves the other, the trespasser, in this process of *transformation*."[111] For if the trespasser's heart is "pierced through" in seeing the inner meaning of such love-suffering (love that is not withdrawn despite being wounded), the trespasser can be moved to reproduce it on his side. This replication is demonstrated by his corresponding willingness to face up to and restore the

---

[109] Ibid., 158. Guardini affirms much the same: "God's forgiveness did not take place as 'mere forgiveness' but as atonement." *Der Herr*, 358, quoted in Hoffmann, "Atonement and the Sacred Heart", 201n317.

[110] Benedict XVI, *Jesus of Nazareth*, vol. 1, 158 (emphasis added).

[111] Ibid., 159 (emphasis added).

damaged relationship caused by his wrongdoing, to bear the consequences until they are "suffered through".

Thus "*both* parties" are involved in this process of forgiveness; it is a shared work of love-suffering that begins with the person who forgives. At this point, says Benedict, "we encounter the mystery of Christ's Cross"—"the great mystery of expiation"—which unveils the unity of forgiveness and love-suffering in the heart of God the Father.[112] Indeed, when Saint Paul extols Christian love that endures and bears all, he arguably means God's love for us, which we are to imitate and reproduce in our turn.[113]

Probably the attentive reader has already recognized in Benedict's commentary on this petition of the Lord's Prayer the presence of the three factors integral to the process of forgiveness-atonement. Two factors are found on the side of the one who forgives; this side (1) takes the initiative to restore the damaged relationship in such a way that he (2) reveals his affective involvement in the face of one who has trespassed against him. The third factor lies on the side of the trespasser, the one who atones; this side (3) reciprocally collaborates to restore the damaged relationship by way of mirroring the forgiver's love-suffering in bearing the effects of the trespass. As was the case with his pastoral reflections on the problem of "the excommunicate person", here too Benedict's biblical commentary substantiates the key notions and dynamic patterns spotlighted in this study.

A further aspect, not fully developed in Pope Benedict's brief remarks on this petition, regards the generative efficacy of the love-suffering exhibited by the one who forgives. We

[112] Ibid., 159.
[113] See John Paul II, *Crossing the Threshold of Hope* (Alfred A. Knopf, 1994), 66; and Balthasar, "Finding God in All Things", *MIC*, 462.

need be mindful in this regard of the biblical and Trinitarian theology presented in chapters 1 and 2, which maintains that God "fathers" a living image of his manner of loving; God engenders in his filial beloved a mirroring response of love. When this grace-engendered response of love is directed toward the Father as the one sinned against, it takes the form of *atonement*. When the grace-engendered response of love is directed toward those who have trespassed against us, it takes the form of *forgiveness* (Lk 6:36).[114] In fact, the two directions are intimately related since forgiving others is among the "good fruits as evidence of . . . repentance" (Lk 3:8; Mt 3:8), which can serve to atone (Mt 6:14–15). It is precisely in this light that we are to interpret Benedict's assertion that *God's forgiveness of us* in Christ "calls us first and foremost to thankfulness for that, and then, with him, to work through and *suffer through evil by means of love*."[115]

In all this, it is crucial to understand that our willingness to forgive does not give rise to God's willingness to forgive us. Rather, God's forgiving love is at the beginning of this cycle. God's love as forgiveness takes effect in us by engendering our willingness to mirror his mercy toward those who have done us wrong.[116] The relation between God's forgiveness and our forgiveness is presupposed in the proclamation of the Good News: "God [the Father] proves his love for us in that while we were still sinners Christ died for us. . . . [For] while we were enemies, we were reconciled to God [the Father] through the death of his Son" (Rom 5:8, 10; cf. Eph 2:4–5). If God proves his love in showing mercy when we were yet his enemies, then we prove that we are true

---

[114] The Christian who forgives not only imitates the forgiving Father but also shares in the generative purpose and efficacy of divine forgiveness.

[115] Benedict XVI, *Jesus of Nazareth*, vol. 1, 160 (emphasis added).

[116] See Benedict XVI, *Jesus of Nazareth*, vol. 1, 157.

children of the Father, begotten in his likeness by deifying grace, by our obedience to this command: "As the Lord has forgiven you, so must you also do" (Col 3:13).[117]

Toward a renewal of the spirituality of atonement

Perhaps never more than today has the seeming absence of God been so acute. We are living, after all, in a largely secular culture that insulates us against God's nearness. While many things have contributed to this trend toward secularization, John Paul II identifies "secular*ism*" as the most troubling cause. "Secular*ism*", as John Paul II defines it, "is a movement of ideas and behavior which advocates a humanism totally without God". In this respect it resembles sin at the level of objective intentionality inasmuch as it promotes the choice "to live as if God did not exist".[118] This movement as well as other secularizing influences cannot but lead to the gradual obscuring or weakening of the sense of God's presence. The resultant situation explains why Martin Buber famously identified the "eclipse of God" as the hallmark of our time, the distinctive mark of our secular age.

Yet in view of the theology and spirituality of atonement sketched in this study, we are primed to discern that these very circumstances can serve as the material for a profound sharing in Christ's mission of atonement, whereby every sort of desolation can be transformed into the expression

---

[117] John Chrysostom makes a similar point: "You cannot call the God of all kindness your Father if you preserve a cruel and inhuman heart, for in this case you no longer have in you the marks of the heavenly Father's kindness." *Hom. in illud "De angusta porta, et in orationem Dominicam"* (*Patrologia graeca* 51: 44B; hereafter *PG*) cited by John Paul II in "The Demanding Love of God the Father" (General Audience, April 7, 1999) in *The Trinity's Embrace*, 196.

[118] John Paul II, *Reconciliatio et paenitentia*, no. 18.

of intimate union with the forgiving Father. The Father, after all, sent his Son to establish the nearness of God in the midst of the dreadful experience of distance from God. Not even that "space" of human experience apparently most emptied of God is meant to be left vacant, God-forsaken. In the Cross event, the Son of God himself enters into that "space" in order to fill it with his filial love (both human and divine). Consequently, in whatever situation of desolation or distance from God we (or our neighbor) may be, Christ can enable us to convert these conditions into filial love's pain and, by bearing them in this manner, to atone with him and in him.

Here we may recall how Balthasar exhorts the Christian "not to shut his eyes to the abyss of hatred, despair, and depravity" that can be seen in this world marked by sin, but to accept "the share of penitential suffering that has been given him for the sake of the whole".[119] The "whole" includes the "secular world", certainly, but also the Church that lives and labors in the world. In point of fact we have grown painfully aware that evil and depravity penetrate into the hearts of even those ordained to the priesthood and raised to the episcopacy. "The Church", admits Balthasar, "has sins stretching over centuries for which a later generation will justly have to suffer even though it can do nothing about them."[120] The least we should do is resolve to be willing to bear what is given us to bear.

To be sure, this is not meant to encourage a kind of Christian "dolorism"—a morbid cult of sorrow and misery that seeks to sink into suffering as a work of self-perfectioning (or of self-loathing, as the case may be). Nor should this

---

[119] Balthasar, *Love Alone is Credible*, 97.
[120] Balthasar, *The Threefold Garland*, 89.

be misconstrued as doing "works" in the pejorative Pauline sense of the term. Rather, it is a matter of facing the conditions of sin in ourselves, in the Church, and in the world, and of willingly bearing sin's consequences. We can do so "in Christ" not only for ourselves, but also for others and especially for our enemies. We can do so even without being chosen by God to endure his seeming absence in the radical and drastic way experienced by Saints Thérèse and Teresa. For Christ himself commands us, without exception, to carry our cross every day (Lk 14:27; Mt 10:38; 16:24). Surely this implies very ordinary, even dull, burdens to bear. But if they are borne with faith and charity, even mundane troubles and trials can be transformed into situations that share in the fruitfulness of Christ's atoning work.[121] We ourselves are to echo the conviction of Saint Paul, who declared: Anything I suffer I offer up in union with Christ *for your* salvation (cf. 2 Cor 1:3–7).

Let us, then, recover and newly appreciate the Catholic expression: "I offer it up."[122]

Almsgiving as atonement

There is, moreover, another Catholic expression to complement "I offer it up": namely, "I give it away." Both carry

---

[121] See Balthasar, *To the Heart*, 58; and John Paul II, "Salvation is Mankind's Ultimate Destiny" (General Audience, August 11, 1999), in *The Trinity's Embrace*, 240.

[122] In the Catholic tradition of spirituality, the expression "I offer it up" recapitulates the offering of spiritual sacrifices to God for the atonement of sins. Of course, it can be repeated out of habit as a mere formula. But when said with full awareness of its meaning, it expresses participation in Jesus' own prayer in the Garden: "Not what I will but what you will" (Mk 14:36). See *CCC* 1473.

connotations of sacrifice. If the expression "I offer it up" bespeaks that aspect of filial love which is primarily receptive (albeit willingly, actively, collaboratively so)—as when I consent to bear the effects of sin as a work of expiation, then the expression "I give it away" accentuates the active aspect of filial love at work—as when I give my treasure for the good of others. Until now, our study has concentrated on the (primarily) receptive aspect of sacrifice that entails letting God beget us as his filial images and collaborators in suffering through the effects of sin. Yet here at this juncture we will pause to consider the second aspect: filial love expressed actively as giving up or giving away.[123] More specifically, we will consider the biblical motif of *almsgiving*. For a thorough study of when and how almsgiving was regarded as a sacrifice of atonement in Jewish Scriptures and rabbinic literature, see Gary Anderson's book *Charity: The Place of the Poor in the Biblical Tradition*.[124] For our purposes, we need cite only a few biblical passages to establish the fact, before presenting a line of reflection to show how this work of mercy complements the theology of atonement that we have developed thus far.

Straightaway let us consider the Book of Tobit, which was probably written early in the second century B.C. and bears a strong resemblance to the wisdom literature of that era. The book's literary setting, interestingly, is the pagan city of Nineveh, to which Israelites were exiled in the eighth century (722/721) B.C.; hence there was in Nineveh no altar

[123] When this twofold aspect is applied to Jesus Christ in his Passion, the first aspect gives prominence to his role as Victim, whereas the second puts the accent on his role as Priest.

[124] Gary Anderson, *Charity: The Place of the Poor in the Biblical Tradition* (New Haven: Yale University Press, 2013). See also Anthony Giambrone, *Sacramental Charity, Creditor Christology, and the Economy of Salvation in Luke's Gospel* (Tübingen: Mohr Siebeck, 2017); and Balthasar, *TD*3, 118.

to YHWH on which the exiles could offer ritually sacrifices of atonement.

In our first passage, Tobit advises his son, Tobias:

> Give alms from your possessions. Do not turn your face away from any of the poor, so that *God's face will not be turned away from you.* Give in proportion to what you own. If you have great wealth, give alms out of your abundance; if you have but little, do not be afraid to give alms even of that little. You will be storing up a goodly treasure for yourself against the day of adversity. *For almsgiving delivers from death and keeps one from entering into Darkness. Almsgiving is a worthy offering in the sight of the Most High and for all who practice it.* (Tob 4:7–11, emphasis added)

It is noteworthy that giving alms to the poor is likened to a sin-offering. This expression of charity, according to Tobit, results in deliverance from the most serious consequences of sin: from God's wrath (indicated by God's face being turned away) as well as from death and its darkness.

In our second passage, it is the archangel Raphael who exhorts Tobit to tell his fellow Jews in exile of the atoning efficacy of almsgiving. "It is better to give alms than to store up gold, *for almsgiving saves from death, and purges all sin*" (Tob 12:8–9, emphasis added). According to Raphael, it is Israel's sinfulness that accounts for their state of exile, which is why he describes their exile as a deathlike state (Sheol), that is, a state of separation from the living God. The exiles will not be delivered from this deathlike state until their sins have been atoned for. Raphael recommends almsgiving as a means by which they can collaborate with God in bringing about their restoration.[125] To be sure, the giving of alms that carries atoning efficacy must issue from

---

[125] See Anderson, *Charity*, 61.

a profound conversion of heart. "He [the Lord] will gather you from all the nations among whom you have been scattered. When you turn back to him with all your heart, and with all your soul do what is right before him, then he will . . . hide his face from you no longer" (Tob 13:5-6).[126]

Let us pause just a moment to acknowledge the presence of the theme of God's wrath in these passages, the mode that God's love takes in opposition to sin. As we have seen, God turns his "face" away from attitudes and actions that are contrary to authentic filial love. The touchstone of the latter is love that *mirrors* God's paternal love, since the proper work of divine fatherhood is to engender its living *image*. Attitudes and actions that misrepresent those of the heavenly Father cannot be condoned but rather must be discredited as false by God's withdrawing from association with counterfeit "sons".

Now, this raises the question as to why the hoarding of riches ("storing up gold" for oneself) is to be deemed "ungodly", as conduct that bespeaks a failure to know and mirror the true God, and therefore results in God turning his "face" away. Conversely, we must ask how almsgiving can be understood as conduct expressive of love in imitation *of God*—in a word, as expressive of sonship.

Remaining for the moment within the Old Testament, let us consider Exodus 34:6, when the Lord reveals himself to Moses as abounding in "steadfast love" (*rab-ḥesed*) toward Israel. The description of God's love in the original Hebrew text places the accent on God's fidelity toward his chosen people. Yet the accent shifts a bit when the Hebrew text is

---

[126] The Book of Tobit was likely influenced by the Book of Proverbs, which contains a verse that strongly resembles the exhortation given by Raphael to Tobit that is addressed to the people in exile. "Wealth is useless on a day of wrath, but charity [almsgiving] saves from death" (Prov 11:4).

translated into Greek during the third and second centuries B.C. *Ḥesed* is translated as ἐλεήμων and ἔλεος (*eleos*, doing mercy, an act of mercy), which supports the belief that doing acts of mercy is a fundamental way in which to imitate the Lord himself. And this permits one to regard almsgiving as an action that bespeaks authentic filial love engendered by the loving God.

Furthermore, let us look at a key passage in Hosea. Again it is the Lord who speaks: "It is loyalty (*ḥesed*) [toward me] that I desire, not [just] sacrifice" (Hos 6:6). In the original Hebrew, this text asserts that God prefers filial fidelity (by way of obedience to his "words") over mere ritual service. But when the Greek translator of this Hebrew text renders *ḥesed* (signifying loyalty to God) with *eleos* (the Greek word for doing mercy), the translation shifts the perspective from the vertical to the horizontal dimension. As Anderson explains: "Whereas the Hebrew had privileged loyalty to God over sacrifice, the Greek translation said, 'I desire mercy [toward the poor] not [just] sacrifice.' In other words, a Hebrew term that had denoted a *vertical* relationship between man and God . . . now had a *horizontal* set of referents (the merciful conduct of one man toward another)."[127]

But lest we sharply divide these two dimensions, we must remember that for the devout Jew, keeping those commandments that shape one's conduct toward one's neighbor is an opportunity to express in action one's filial devotion to the Lord himself. Such acts of *filial* love, as we have consistently maintained, are also revelatory of God, who has compassionate love for his people (cf. Ex 10:17–19; Deut 24:20–22). Once we appreciate this, we can draw out a significant theological implication from the Aramaic phrase *bar*

---

[127] Anderson, *Charity*, 144.

mitzveta. Bar is the Aramaic word for *son.* And according to Saul Lieberman, *mitsva* is the Aramaic term for *commandment.* Interestingly, *mitsva* is often understood as synonymous with *almsgiving* (in rabbinic literature to the present day). Hence, the Aramaic phrase *bar mitzveta* can mean not only "son of the commandment" or "commandment keeper", but also "a generous son", one whose sonship is attested by his almsgiving; or in other words, one who reflects God's fatherhood in light of his attribute of compassionate generosity.[128]

Now, if almsgiving is a touchstone of genuine filial love within the context of the covenant, then we can readily see why "storing up gold" for oneself denotes a failure to know and mirror the true God and therefore signals sin as estrangement from God. Here sin is recognizable as an exercise of (filial) freedom, which, instead of responding in kind to God's compassionate generosity, retreats into a calculating self-centeredness. We may say, therefore, that sonship (expressed in almsgiving) and sin (implied in the hoarding of riches) are contraries. This insight—that sonship and sin are contraries—is in accord with a key principle already identified and discussed in the theology of atonement developed by our four main guides. Furthermore, this insight allows us to infer that if atonement is a work of sonship that "cleanses" from sin by transforming sin into its opposite, then almsgiving can atone for sin inasmuch as it affirms filial love against its contrary. We intend to develop this inference below, once we cross the threshold to the New Testament. Yet what is clear even now is that in the second and first centuries before the coming of Jesus Christ, the belief that giving alms can serve to cleanse from sin, that almsgiving can

---

[128] See Ibid., 156; and Saul Lieberman, whom Anderson regards as the leading Talmudist of the twentieth century, "Two Lexicographical Notes", *Journal of Biblical Literature* 65 (1946): 69–72.

function as an atoning sacrifice, was not unknown among Jews.

When next we turn to Jesus himself, we find him speaking these words in Luke's Gospel: "But as to what is within, give alms, and behold, everything will be clean for you" (Lk 11:41). The cleansing to which Jesus refers is cleansing from sin. His directive undoubtedly alludes to the idea that almsgiving is comparable to a sacrifice with atoning efficacy.

But now in what respect can this means of atonement—by way of almsgiving—be seen as modeled by Jesus himself, the Atoner, and in a pre-eminent and unparalleled way? Can it be seen in him as a modality of sonship affirming itself against its negation in sin? And therefore can we say that in him it is conclusively revelatory of God's Trinitarian Fatherhood, the primal exemplar and generating source of filial love? If we can give an affirmative answer to these questions, we will simultaneously show how this means of atonement is essentially compatible with the Trinitarian theology of atonement explored in this study. As we proceed, we will remember the *Catechism*'s avowal that "the mystery of the Most Holy Trinity is the central mystery of Christian faith and life . . . the source of all the other mysteries of faith, the light that enlightens them" (no. 234). This (we repeat) warrants our earnest efforts to illuminate the mystery of atonement—now by means of almsgiving—chiefly against the backdrop of the Trinity.

Our first task is to understand in what sense Jesus, the Atoner, may be seen as the transcendent filial prototype of almsgiving: giving liberally to the poor out of one's wealth. The most obvious initial move is to turn to Saint Paul's Second Letter to the Corinthians: "For you know the gracious act of our Lord Jesus Christ, that for your sake he became poor although he was rich, so that by his poverty you might become rich" (2 Cor 8:9). The gracious act to which Paul refers encompasses the entire trajectory of Christ's mission, from the event of his Incarnation to his Paschal event. The trajectory of this gracious act in its entirety is described in a hymn that is embedded in one of Saint Paul's earliest epistles, his Letter to the Philippians.

> Have among yourselves the same attitude that is in Christ Jesus,
> Who, though he was in the form of God,
> did not regard equality with God something to be grasped.
> Rather, he *emptied* himself [ἐκένωσεν]
> taking the form of a slave,
> coming in human likeness;
> and found human in appearance,
> he humbled himself,
> becoming obedient to death, even death on a cross.
> *Because of this*, God greatly exalted him
> and bestowed on him the name
> that is above every name,
> that at the name of Jesus
> every knee should bend,
> of those in heaven and on the earth and under the earth,
> and every tongue confess that
> Jesus Christ is Lord,
> to the glory of God the Father. (Phil 2:5–11, emphasis added)

Paul introduces this hymn by exhorting us to have "the same attitude" that is in Christ Jesus: the attitude that willingly "empties" oneself, that is not grasping or possessive. In Christ's case, what he does not grasp or clutch to himself is the "wealth" of his divinity. In due time, we will consider implications to be drawn from this hymn for the atoning work of Christ's disciples. For the moment, though, let us draw implications from the "kenosis" of Christ for Trinitarian theology.

We can, with Saint Thomas, regard the historical mission of the Son as the graciously free extension or expression of his eternal generation from the Father.[129] And with Balthasar, Hoffmann, Ratzinger (Benedict XVI), and John Paul II, we can describe the attitude or inner disposition that marks the Son's entire mission as utterly selfless charity, indeed as self-renunciatory filial love. Now if this is the case, then a divine "supra-form" analogous to kenotic love denotes his eternal sonship. For since the Son as man lives historically the divine sonship he is in eternity, we may say that the Son's self-emptying unto death is grounded in and shaped by the filial way he loves divinely in the eternal Godhead.[130]

And yes, this has profound implications for Trinitarian theology. For although we cannot fully comprehend the mystery of God, whatever we can know is characterized by a threefold manner of giving, of handing over. After all, God is eternally "Father" only in giving the divinity. In begetting the Son as "God from God", there is nothing of

---

[129] "Thomas Aquinas . . . teaches that the Son's being sent, his mission (*missio*), into finite, passing time, is only the extension, the economic form, of his eternal procession (*processio*) from the Father." Balthasar, *MIC*, 56. "The Son's *missio* is his *processio* extended in 'economic' mode." Balthasar, *TD4*, 356. See Aquinas, *ST* I, q. 43, a. 2, ad 3.

[130] *CCC* 470 supports this inference: "Christ's human nature belongs, as his own, to the divine person of the Son of God, who assumed it. Everything that Christ is and does in this [human] nature derives from 'one of the Trinity.' The Son of God therefore communicates to his humanity his own personal mode of existence in the Trinity [that is to say, his filial way of being divine]. In his soul as in his body, Christ thus expresses humanly the divine ways of the Trinity."

what it means to be God that the Father keeps to himself.
The Father gives all that is his to the Son—the divinity in
its entirety ("Everything of yours is mine", Jn 17:10).

   According to Balthasar (who borrows insights from Saint
Gregory of Nyssa and Sergei Bulgakov),[131] we may char-
acterize the limitless generosity of the generating Father as
the "original *kenosis*" of absolute love. The word *kenosis* (in
its *verb* form: ἐκένωσεν, *ekénōsen*) is used in verse 7 of the
hymn to describe the event of the Incarnation in terms of
an act of self-emptying on the part of God *the Son*. But what
does it mean to speak of an act of kenosis on the part of
God *the Father*? We are to perceive that it is the Father who,
in the first place, does not grasp the divinity to himself,
but "empties" himself without remainder in generating the
consubstantial Son. Nor does the Father exist as the first
divine Person "before" this kenotic self-surrender, as if in
a prior disposition of conserving for himself the "wealth"
of the divinity. Rather, the Father "*is* this original movement of self-giving that holds nothing back".[132] The Father
only *possesses* the divinity *in giving it away* to the Son. He
is *wealthy* only in making himself *poor* for the sake of his
Beloved.[133]

   And as for the Son, the divinity he receives is originally

---

[131] See Balthasar's study of St. Gregory's doctrine of God, *Presence and
Thought: Essay on the Religious Philosophy of Gregory of Nyssa* (San Francisco:
Ignatius Press, 1995) and Anatolios' discussion of Gregory's Trinitarian theo-
logy in *Retrieving Nicaea*, 182–204. Balthasar acknowledges his dependence on
Bulgakov's work, *Le Verbe incarné: Agnus Dei* (Paris: Aubier, 1943) in *TD4*,
313–14.

[132] Balthasar, *TD4*, 323. See Ratzinger, "Understanding the Concept of Person in Theology", *Communio* 17.3 (Fall 1990): 444.

[133] See Hans Urs von Balthasar, *Theo-Logic: Theological Logical Theory*, vol.
2, *Truth of God* (San Francisco: Ignatius Press, 2004), 177–78; and Turek, *Towards a Theology of God the Father, Hans Urs von Balthasar's Theodramatic Approach* (New York: Peter Lang Publishing, 2001), 106.

shaped by the Father to the form and measure of "emptying" oneself for the sake of another.[134] Hence the Son does not consider equality with the Father something to be grabbed at, something to be tightly held onto (Phil 2:6). He, too, is God only in relinquishing all, in hoarding nothing of what he receives from the Father. We can, if we like, talk of God the Father and God the Son possessing their common God-head, the "wealth" of divinity; yet we can with equal truth talk of their dispossessing themselves of it out of love, for each other's sake. "They are God only in giving themselves to each other."[135]

And from this mutual gift-exchange there proceeds the Holy Spirit, who is the personified Gift of the divinity. Nor does the Holy Spirit clutch to himself the divinity he receives, but he lets himself be poured out (think of Pentecost, Acts 2:17) as the Giver of divine life to human souls. Thus each of the divine persons possesses the "wealth" of the divinity in giving it away.[136]

In a notable passage, Balthasar describes the Christian God as possessing divine life only in this movement of dispossession among the three Persons:

> Only in holding-onto-nothing-for-himself is God "Father" at all; he pours forth his substance and generates the Son; and only in the holding-on-to-nothing-for-himself of what has been received does the Son show himself to be of the

---

[134] Inasmuch as the divine essence, coinciding as it does with the Father's primordial self-disposing, proceeds from the Father as self-emptying love in favor of the Other, the Son "cannot, for his part, *be* and *possess* the absolute essence of God except in the mode of receiving this unity" of wealth and poverty; *TD4*, 325–26. See *TD3*, 518–19; and *TD2*, 258. See also Turek, *Towards a Theology of God the Father*, 109.

[135] Simon Tugwell, *The Beatitudes* (Springfield, Ill.: Templegate Publishers, 1986), 25.

[136] See Tugwell's entire discussion in *The Beatitudes*, 23–25.

same essence of the Father; and in this shared holding-onto-nothing-for-themselves are they one in the Spirit, who is, after all, the expression and personification of this holding-onto-nothing-for-himself of God. If the Second Person steps out of this circling life in order to offer the world what is the totality of God, his style of life will not be the grasping demeanor of a pantocrator but the opposite: the Son lays bare the heart of the Father as he becomes the servant of all and breathes out into the world his Spirit of service and of the last place. [137]

With this passage, Balthasar offers an explanation as to why, when the Son "empties" himself in his earthly mission to the extreme of death on a cross, his holding-onto-nothing-for-himself is "to the glory of God the Father"—since it is the Father's self-emptying that generates its perfect reflection in the Son (from all eternity within the Godhead), which the Son then "lays bare" in his mission as a man. In other words, it is the self-renunciation of the Father, who in generating "will not be God for himself alone but 'lets go' of his divinity" in favor of the Son (albeit without losing it) [138] —which the Son reflects in his historical mission when he, as it were, will not be begotten for himself alone but "lets go" of his divinity in taking the form of a slave in favor of humanity (without, of course, losing his divine status). [139] Thus the earthly life of Christ, from his conception to his

[137] Hans Urs von Balthasar, *Christian States of Life* (San Francisco: Ignatius Press, 1983), 186.

[138] "Inherent in the Father's love is an absolute renunciation: he will not be God for himself alone. He lets go of his divinity" in favor of the Son. Balthasar, *TD*4, 323–24. "It is precisely in this infinite surrender and self-renunciation, in this absolute preference of the Thou to the I, that the life of the Trinity consists." Hans Urs von Balthasar, *Word and Revelation* (New York: Herder and Herder, 1964), 33–34.

[139] Balthasar, *TD*4, 323–24. Certainly "we cannot say the Father gives over his substance in generating the Son in such a manner that, as he hands it over

death, follows a trajectory of kenosis meant wholly for the ultimate good of human beings and the glorification of God the Father.

Now, at the climax of Christ's kenosis, during the Passion, the evangelists (especially Mark and Matthew) describe a rapidly progressing renunciation. For us, the Son lets himself be stripped of his only "treasures". His disciples desert him and the Jewish leaders reject him in handing him over to the enemies of Israel. He gives away his mother to his beloved disciple. He inwardly consents to being stripped of his human dignity and finally of earthly life itself. His renunciation culminates in the "supreme spiritual despoilment" expressed in Christ's words: "My God, my God, why have you forsaken me?" (Mt 27:46). This cry from the Cross bespeaks the loss of the felt presence of God his Father.[140] In this sense, the Son relinquishes "possession" of the Father as he bears the full consequences of sin. *This* is the utmost spiritual poverty that he willingly endures so that we might become spiritually rich (cf. 2 Cor 8:9)—so that we might regain possession of God and receive "every spiritual blessing in the heavens" (Eph 1:3).[141]

Once again it must not be forgotten that the Son's radical renunciation derives from and images the Father's pattern of loving. Saint Paul, after all, portrays the Father as he who

---

to the Son, he does not retain it at the same time; otherwise he would really cease to be the divine substance (Fourth Lateran Synod, DS 805)." *TD4*, 326-24.

[140] Servais Pinckaers, *The Pursuit of Happiness God's Way: Living the Beatitudes*, trans. Mary Thomas Noble (Eugene, Ore.: Wipf & Stock, 2011), 48.

[141] See John Paul II, General Audience (November 30, 1988), nos. 4-6; Benedict XVI, *Jesus of Nazareth*, vol. 2, 205 and 214; Ratzinger, *Eschatology*, 93; *Introduction to Christianity*, 226; Balthasar, *TD4*, 338; Hoffmann, "Atonement and the Sacred Heart", 170.

did not hold back his own Son but gave him up for us all
(cf. Rom 8:32; Jn 3:16). As the primal Lover within the
Trinity, the Father is first to commit himself to the path of
self-sacrifice. By giving up his only Son, the Father gives up
all that his paternal Heart lives for (in a manner of speaking). It is this self-renunciatory love shown by the Father
—this sacrifice of his paternal Heart—that draws Christ to
Golgotha and moves him to filial imitation (cf. Jn 5:19–20).

Yet the Son's radical renunciation is not the last act in this
drama of redemption. "*Because of this*, God greatly exalted
him . . . [and now] every tongue [must] confess that Jesus
Christ is Lord" (Phil 2:9–11). Only in "letting go" of his
divine status does Christ "possess" his cosmic Lordship, is
he adored as equal with the Father (2:10–11). Only in relinquishing his sense of intimacy with the Father is Christ
exalted to the Father's side (2:9). Perhaps here in this hymn
we are meant to see the Son himself living out a spiritual
"law" that was central to his teaching: "Whoever seeks to
keep his life will lose it, but whoever loses it will save it"
(Lk 17:33).

This spiritual "law" holds true regarding the way to possess the supernatural life that God bestows (*his* very self and
a share in his divine beatitude). If we are to reach full stature
in Christ as sons, children of God, we must be ready to give
to others from the "wealth" of divine grace that we have
received. This is what Balthasar means when he says:

> With respect to God there can be no will-to-possession,
> since God himself has no desire to possess. . . . No man
> can be rich in God if he does not want to partake of God's
> poverty. [Everyone] will have to learn what it means "to
> possess as if one did not possess" (1 Cor 7:30), to be ready
> at all times to let what one holds dearest pass over to the

side of God and to let oneself be drawn along on this path [to sanctity].[142]

Indeed one of the surest signs that we are becoming more Godlike is that we show greater generosity in letting go of our wealth (of whatever kind). This is strikingly confirmed in Luke 6:27–36, where Jesus enjoins:

> But to you who hear I say, love your enemies, do good to those who hate you, bless those who curse you, pray for those who mistreat you. . . . Give to everyone who asks of you, and from the one who takes what is yours do not demand it back. . . . If you lend money to those from whom you expect repayment, what credit [is] that to you? Even sinners lend to sinners, and get back the same amount. But rather, love your enemies and do good to them, and lend expecting nothing back; then your reward will be great and you will be children of the Most High, for he himself is kind to the ungrateful and the wicked. Be merciful, just as [also] your Father is merciful.

In this single passage, a number of ideas pertinent to our discussion are clustered together: to give without self-interest is to love as a son, or child, in imitation of the merciful Father. Of special import here (in the New Testament) is that filial love in imitation of the heavenly Father should extend itself beyond one's family, friends, and compatriots. It should be expressed in the concrete form of "doing good", doing works of mercy, even to one's enemies and those who do evil. To appreciate the newness of the Christian concept of filial love and of the God who is its source and exemplar, we must realize that no religious authority within

---

[142] Balthasar, *The Threefold Garland*, 63. See also *GL7*, 271, 400, and 428–30.

Judaism had ever commanded the people to love their enemies. Leviticus 19:17–18 had commanded the Israelite not
to hate his kinsmen.[143] At most, the school of Hillel had
taught that "one should love the righteous and one should
not hate the sinner." Jesus, however, instructed: "You have
heard that it was said, 'You shall love your neighbor and hate
your enemy.' But *I* say to you, love your enemies, and pray
for those who persecute you" (Mt 5:43–44; cf. Lk 6:27).
Hence, while almsgiving had been endorsed in Judaism as a
work of charity shown to the poor, and moreover as a work
that had atoning value (Tob 4:7–11; 13:5–6), it is Jesus who
is first to insist vigorously that works of mercy toward evil-
doers is a vital criterion which proves filial love in the face
of sin to be genuine.[144]

So far we have seen that the way to possess the gifts that
God bestows entails the willingness to relinquish what we
have received. And undoubtedly the greatest gift that God
has to give is himself with the possibility of possessing God
in an everlasting way. Yet the attitude with which we should
possess God and the spiritual wealth that God gives must be
that of Christ himself, as Saint Paul insists (cf. Phil 2:5).

From this it follows that we ought not to be exclusively
preoccupied with *our own* possession of God, with *our own*
salvation. We should be capable of discerning the godliness
of those who, inspired by Christ's example, are willing to
"lose" God, to "let go" of God, for the sake of others'
salvation. This radical spiritual form of almsgiving can be

[143] Qumran had said: "I [the person praying] will not have mercy on all of
those who have abandoned the way." 1 QS 10:20f., cited by Christoph Cardinal Schönborn, *God Sent His Son: A Contemporary Christology* (San Francisco:
Ignatius Press, 2010), 59.

[144] See Balthasar, *TD*5, 278–79; *GL*7, 435–36; and Roch Kereszty, *Jesus
Christ: Fundamentals of Christology*, revised and updated edition (New York:
Alba House/A Communio Book, 2002), 14.

seen in the life and writings of the saints, as we discussed previously. Saint Paul is willing to relinquish his possession of God, so that his fellow Jews would possess Christ through faith (Rom 9:1-3). And Paul is not alone in this. Other saints too, such as Thérèse of Lisieux and Teresa of Calcutta, epitomize a willingness to empty themselves of spiritual wealth so that others can become rich from their poverty. The atoning efficacy of such spiritual almsgiving is not lost on Ratzinger, who affirms: "One serves the salvation of the world by leaving one's own salvation behind for the sake of others."[145] (Here we see clearly that spiritual almsgiving can coincide with atonement in the form of "nearness to God in the filial love-suffering of distance from God".)

Now, certainly "self-love will remain too" in the disposition of the heart, "but only 'on the margin' and unaccented."[146] In the teaching and example of Jesus Christ, the limits on the scope of love that were previously set are deliberately abolished by an unconditional directive to imitate God himself, who wills to bring home the very last of the lost sheep.

We have already discussed how Thérèse, from Easter of 1896 until her death eighteen months later, underwent a state of spiritual darkness in which she was despoiled of the felt confidence that God and his heaven really exist. Yet even before her plunge into this spiritual darkness, Thérèse had endeavored to reshape a notion of popular piety that was influencing the spirituality of her fellow Carmelite nuns. It was a notion of piety that saw spiritual growth as a matter of acquiring spiritual riches. One said so many prayers, did

---

[145] Ratzinger, *Eschatology*, 217-18.
[146] Balthasar, *GL7*, 438.

so many good works, and bore sufferings with faith in order to secure heaven for oneself. A shortcoming of this kind of piety, though, is that spiritual development can stall at the level of self-love. Good deeds are done, to be sure, but the main motive is to gain something for oneself. To amend this shortcoming, Thérèse put forward her practice of spiritual almsgiving. Instead of amassing spiritual wealth for oneself, hoarding the gifts of God's grace, Thérèse advised her sisters in Carmel: "Hold nothing back; distribute your goods as soon as you get them. . . . That is what I do in my spiritual life: as soon as I acquire something [e.g., merit for a virtuous act, an interior light or consolation], knowing that there are souls on the point of falling into hell, I give them my treasures."[147] It is surely significant that Thérèse intends her spiritual almsgiving to benefit "souls on the point of falling into hell", those who are dreadfully estranged from God. She willingly relinquishes her gifts from God so that the "godless" may benefit from her impoverishment.

There is a prayer attributed to Thérèse entitled "With Empty Hands: A Prayer to Christ Crucified", which reflects her practice of spiritual almsgiving:

> I come before You with empty hands, all the secret store of grace I fling into needy hearts, crying in the bitter night of

[147] *Story of a Soul*, cited in Balthasar, *Two Sisters in the Spirit*, 244–45. Thérèse explains her way of radical spiritual poverty to Abbé Bellière in a similar vein: "I know there are some saints who spent their life in the practice of astonishing mortifications to expiate their own sins, but what of it? 'There are many mansions in the house of my heavenly Father', Jesus has said, and it is because of this that I follow the way he is tracing out for me. I try to be no longer occupied with myself in anything, and I abandon myself to what Jesus sees fit to do in my soul, for I have not chosen an austere life to expiate my own sins but those of others." Letter to Abbé Bellière, June 21, 1897, in Letters of St. Therese of Lisieux, vol. 2, 1890–1897, trans. John Clarke (Washington, D.C.: Institute of Carmelite Studies Publications, 1988), 1134.

fear and loneliness. Spendthrift of Your love, I keep before me Your empty Hands—empty and riven with the great nails hollowing out rivers of mercy, until all Your substance was poured out. So I, my Jesus, with hands emptied for Your love, stand confident before Your Cross, love's crimson emblem. It is the empty who are filled: those who have made themselves spendthrifts for You alone, fill the last of Your brethren while they themselves are nourished by Your Love, more and more emptied that they may be filled with You.[148]

To others, Thérèse hands over every spiritual gift that God had given her—even as her empty hands made her capable of receiving always more from God. Here too we must note that Thérèse is imitating Christ crucified, the Atoner, whose mission of mercy entailed his unreserved self-outpouring. She assumes the fundamental posture of the Son before the Father: receiving all from him and giving all in turn. If the Son shows himself to be of the same essence of the Father—*God* from God—"in holding-on-to-nothing-for-himself of what has been received", so Thérèse and all who are born of God as "sons in the Son" show themselves to be truly Godlike in handing on to others the gifts that the Father bestows "in accord with the riches of his glory" (Eph 3:16).

As we bring to a close our consideration of almsgiving as a means of atonement, beyond question we have encountered yet another iteration of the three factors integral to the process of "cleansing" from sin. The consistency and

---

[148] Quoted by Benedict J. Groeschel in *Arise from Darkness* (San Francisco: Ignatius Press, 1995), 167. Fr. Groeschel attributes this prayer to Thérèse, though his source is a prayer card citing Sr. Teresa of the Trinity, "Meditations Based on the Writings of St. Thérèse of Lisieux" (Carmel of Terre Haute, Indiana). See Thérèse's "Act of Oblation to Merciful Love", June 9, 1895, in *Story of a Soul*, trans. John Clarke (Washington D.C.: Institute of Carmelite Studies Publications, 1976), 276–78.

coherence of these three features, evident from start to finish in our study, arguably indicates that the inner essence of atonement has this threefold shape. At minimum, it shows that these three factors are not simply an arbitrary selection from biblical and spiritual texts but may well be of decisive importance in discerning the deeper, Trinitarian dimensions of redemption. In support of this claim, we have just shown how atonement by means of almsgiving can be seen to arise out of the mystery of the eternal Trinity.

Concluding remarks

Throughout this chapter, we shed light on the nature and meaning of our participation in Christ's work of atonement against the horizon of the Holy Trinity. We argued that the interpersonal pattern of forgiveness-atonement is the form taken by the Father-son relationship when God enables "converts" to assert their sonship in a sinful world. We spotlighted the Holy Spirit, who divinizes us by drawing us into Christ's Filial life (Col 1:28; Rom 5:1; 8:9–11; 2 Cor 3:4; Gal 4:4–6; 2:19f.). By the working of the Holy Spirit in our hearts, we are empowered as "sons in the Son" to be and act as God's filial images in bearing sin away.

Moreover, we argued that Christians are enabled by the Triune God to atone in a *representative* capacity. To love others "in Christ" and as Christ has loved us can take the form of *vicarious* atonement. "The believer", says Hoffmann, "who knows that he *himself* has been redeemed by the Son and brought into filial nearness to the Father will look up to the wounded heart of Jesus, and in doing so he will 'be for others' in such a way that he will help to bear and endure *their* own sin (cf. Gal 6:2; Eph 5:1f.; Rom 15:1–3)."[149]

Naturally the atoning work of Christ is not deficient. Yet it is meant to be productive, effective, not simply of itself, independently of us, but in us and with us. "As the Father has loved me, so I have loved you; abide in my love" (Jn 15:9, RSVCE). *As the Father* lets himself be dependent on Christ's free cooperation in accomplishing the work of atonement —even as the Father engenders the cooperation he seeks, *so Christ* in turn lets himself be dependent on our personal and free cooperation in bringing his work of atonement to completion—even as Christ enables us, through the gift of his Spirit, to cooperate with him and in him.

These words must suffice to serve as our response to Benedict XVI's question (mentioned above): "What does Christ's atoning passion and death mean for me?" It means that we are liberated and equipped to fulfill Christ's new commandment to love all as he has loved us. And this commandment is a matter of ultimate importance, according to the parable of the Final Judgment in Matthew 25. For the criterion by which each of us will be judged lies in the extent to which we have lived out the disposition of love exhibited by Jesus as he identifies himself with the least of his brethren. In Jesus this disposition attains its acme with his Passion and death when, before the Father, he assumes a condition of non-distinction from sinners. Our main concern should be, therefore, to glorify God by emulating the unrestricted and unrelenting love that Jesus himself exemplifies.

---

[149] Hoffmann, "Atonement and the Sacred Heart", 200.

Conclusion

In the introduction to this book, we identified some reasons for the modern aversion to explaining the Cross event as a work of atonement: the trivialization of sin, the inability to grasp why God's merciful love does not one-sidedly effect forgiveness but calls for the atonement of sins, the failure to preserve the generative and exemplary character of God's love in the process of atonement, and faulty notions of divine wrath. We kept these reasons in mind as we presented our exposition of a biblical, Trinitarian, and spiritual theology of atonement. We can now bring our exposition to a close by reflecting briefly on how we undertook to overcome these aversions.

The central aim of our theology of atonement was to make understandable the biblical claim that God shows himself to be love *precisely in view of* God's sending his Son as atonement. "God is love. . . . In this is God's love . . . that he . . . sent his Son as expiation for our sins" (1 Jn 4:8–10). Guided by the insights of our quartet of theologians—John Paul II, Joseph Ratzinger (Benedict XVI), Hans Urs von Balthasar, and Norbert Hoffmann—we presented a coherent reading of Sacred Scripture by sketching the gradually emerging pattern of a "patrogenetic" process of atonement: a process that originates from and is engendered by God's own power to love. Beginning with the Old Testament, we identified three factors integral to this process. Two factors were found on God's side; the third factor on the side of God's covenant partner. On the side of God, (1) God takes the initiative to restore the damaged relationship in such a way that (2) God reveals his passionate involvement vis-à-vis his beloved-turned-sinner. This revelation of God's affective involvement serves to induce in his beloved a contrite love and, with God's Spirit working from within, draws the repentant beloved to reflect or represent God's steadfast passion of love in the face of sin-wrought estrangement. On his side, God's beloved (3) willingly collaborates to restore the damaged relationship by way of imaging in creaturely fashion God's suffering love in bearing the effects of sin. And so paradoxically, God's generative (fore-giving) love brings about a union between himself and his beloved that takes the form of a reciprocal willingness in love to suffer through and transform the separation wrought by sin, thereby enabling his beloved to efface sin and, simultaneously, to fulfill his vocation as the image of God's glory in this sin-marred world.

Then having crossed the threshold into the New Testament, we showed that this pattern of reciprocal love reaches its (utterly astonishing) acme in the Father's sending of his only-begotten Son, his divine Image, to atone for the sins of the whole world and, simultaneously, to make his glory known (Jn 1:1–18; Heb 1:3; 7:27; 2 Cor 4:4; Col 1:15; 1 Jn 2:2; 4:8–10). The Son's mission is accomplished when Jesus lets the Father's love work its full effect in him as the definitive sin-bearer (Jn 19:30). Precisely this dynamic of paternal-filial (archetypal-imaging) love is given consummate expression in Jesus' self-surrender unto death on a cross. Indeed, we are to look upon Jesus Christ as the true "pierced one" (Zech 12:10; Jn 19:37) whose (mirroring) manifestation of God's passion of love in the bearing of sin brings to fulfill-

ment not only Israel's but also humanity's vocation to glorify God's paternal love as God's filial image. This occurs in
such a way that Christ does not simply exclude our participation in his filial mission. Indeed the "for us" character of
the Son's mission only reaches fruition when we, with the
aid of the Holy Spirit outpoured into our hearts, consent to
being born of God into Christ's sonship and hence also to
our personal share in Christ's twofold work of expiating sin
and glorifying the Father. On this account Pope Benedict
assures us, "you will be redeemers with the Redeemer, just
as you are sons in the Son."[1]

One of the merits of this account of atonement, in our
judgment, is that it presents a compelling vision of atonement as a patrogenetic process, a vision that provides a (relatively rare) illumination of the wholly gratuitous, radically
forgiving, passionate and powerful nature of the love of God
the Father. One of its key claims is that the Father's forgiving love is co-extensive with his generative and exemplary
love, which has as its inherent aim to produce an answering, imaging love—filial love—in the form of atonement.
If the Father "leads" his beloved to bear in love the effects
of sin, this divine strategy is not simply vindictive but truly
restorative and (even) perfective of his beloved's vocation
to be the image of God's glory "east of Eden".

A closely related gain, arguably, is that it shows how the
Father's capacity to endure love-suffering in the face of sin
is no mere passivity but proves effective in working against
sin. We brought to light the efficacy of the Father's passion
of love to engender an imaging correspondence in his filial
beloved, whose suffering love in turn is effective in annihilating sin. John Paul II gave this insight poignant expression

---

[1] Benedict XVI, Homily at Shrine of Our Lady of Fatima (May 13, 2010).

in an encyclical in which he asserted that God's "paternal pain"—God's paternal love-suffering—"is at work" in the Cross event, "that love which brings man back again to share in the life that is in God himself".[2] For all four of our guides, God's love demonstrates its immutability and omnipotence paradoxically in showing its capacity to deal with sin effectively in enduring it without damage or diminishment. Indeed, the God who *is* love shows he can suffer sin with impassible passion—in such a way that far from being incapacitated or weakened, his suffering love is actively engaged against sin and in reality "reveals itself as stronger than sin. So that the 'gift' [of divine love] may prevail!"[3]

Additionally, with Ratzinger we can put forward two benefits that flow from this Christian concept of God for our contemporaries: on the one hand, it overcomes a one-sidedly rationalistic theology, whose notion of God brings to mind the unfeeling intelligence of "Alexa", and on the other, it challenges a banalization and debasement of the love of God into "a cheap conception of a merely 'nice' God". If a biblical—indeed an incarnational—theology is taken seriously, it can avoid these extremes while developing a "passional" theology and spirituality, since "the Paschal Mystery, being the mystery of suffering, is by its very nature a mystery of the heart."[4]

A further gain from this theology is the recognition that a merely juridical understanding of the relation of forgiveness

[2] John Paul II, encyclical letter *Dominum et vivificantem* (May 18, 1986), no. 41 (emphasis original).

[3] Ibid., no. 39.

[4] Joseph Ratzinger, "The Paschal Mystery as Core and Foundation of Devotion to the Sacred Heart", in *Towards a Civilization of Love*, ed. International Institute of the Heart of Jesus (San Francisco: Ignatius Press, 1985), 155.

and satisfaction cannot do justice to the profoundly interpersonal quality of the process by which sin is eliminated.
In fact, our study has brought to light that what is at stake
in the Christian doctrine of atonement is nothing less than
the Christian concept of God. To see into the heart of the
Cross event is to perceive it as a dramatic epiphany, shaped
in response to sin, of the mystery of the eternal Trinity. It
is to perceive that forgiveness and atonement are rooted in
the Trinity like fatherhood and sonship, active and receptive
generation.

Another of the virtues of this account is the prominence
given to the human mediations of divine love. For all our
concern to interpret the biblical data on atonement in light
of the mystery of the Holy Trinity, we consistently relied
on the life-testimonial of the prophets, the saints, and pre-
eminently the historical humanity of Jesus Christ. Perceiving Christ to be the keystone of God's relationship with
humanity, we unfolded christological images and patterns
in the experiences of both the prophets of Israel (in chapter
1) and the saints of the Church (in chapter 3).[5] By virtue of
their participation in the mission of Christ, these holy men
and women provided us with a vital resource in order to
understand the mystery of atonement "from within". Inasmuch as Christ draws the saints into the drama of his own
filial pattern of love vis-à-vis the Father for the sake of the
world, he grants them an experiential knowledge of the essential features of biblical revelation. No one has made this
claim more emphatically than Benedict XVI, regarding the
saints of the Church. "The saints are the true interpreters of

---

[5] See Benedict XVI, *Jesus of Nazareth*, vol. 2, *Holy Week*, trans. Philip J.
Whitmore, (San Francisco: Ignatius Press, 2011), 240; and Balthasar, "Theology and Sanctity" in *Explorations in Theology*, vol. 1, *The Word Made Flesh*,
trans. A.V. Littledale (San Francisco: Ignatius Press, 1989), 204.

Holy Scripture", he insists. "Interpretation of Scripture can never be a purely academic affair, and it cannot be relegated to the purely historical. Scripture is full of potential for the future, a potential that can only be opened up when someone 'lives through' and 'suffers through' the sacred text."[6] These considerations also support our use of primarily biblical and spiritual language about the mystery of atonement throughout our study. This language, we believe, is particularly helpful in providing readers with more accessible light by which to navigate their way into those depths of Christ's mission reserved for them.

A further gain from this approach is that it overcomes the split between theology and sanctity—or, just as truly, between contemplation and action. Beholding Christ as "the pierced one", we are to perceive his twofold role of representation: that he represents the Father whose love is "pierced" by our rejection of sonship by grace, and that he represents us sinners by being the definitive exemplar of filial love, whose suffering transforms sin into its opposite and thus bears sin away. If we see Christ as such in the light provided by the Holy Spirit, grace induces us to open our hearts to the "salutary pain" of contrition, which presses on to be actively expressed through "good fruits as evidence of . . . repentance" (Lk 3:8); in other words, through good works as evidence of filial love in opposing sin. This would include asserting our sonship against the manifold ways in which alienation

[6] Benedict XVI, *Jesus of Nazareth*, vol. 1, *From the Baptism in the Jordan to the Transfiguration*, trans. Adrian J. Walker (New York: Doubleday, 2007), 78. Some years earlier, Ratzinger had made this claim in a homily given on December 3, 1987: *Joseph Ratzinger/Benedict XVI: Selected Writings on Love*, trans. Michael J. Miller (San Francisco: Ignatius Press, 2020), 12. Balthasar, for his part, makes the same claim in his seminal essay "Theology and Sanctity" and his book *Two Sisters in the Spirit*.

from God impinges on us and the world at large. (We suggest that Saint Thérèse's "little way of spiritual childhood" should be understood in this light.) Atonement, then, would not be a task separable from an existence lived in ongoing contemplation of the living God who reveals himself in his crucified Son (cf. Eph 5:1; 1 Jn 4:8–12). Rather, atonement would be its proper fruit. Recognizing this would mean, in the first place, that our contemplation must remain centered on the mysteries of Christian revelation and secondly, that our "activism" (our being-for-others) would be genuinely Christian insofar as it derives from and is sustained by this contemplation.

No doubt the above-mentioned gain is owing to the way in which our four guides do theology: they exemplify an "iconic" theological method. In reading their works, one learns that contemplation of Christ, the "living icon of love" (Saint Maximus the Confessor), is the wellspring from which theological reflection derives its depth, vitality, and sustenance. Just as an icon, inasmuch as it faithfully represents the ancient patterns, is never a mere mechanical copy of its model but is always a new encounter with the face of Christ, so too theology, inasmuch as it ceaselessly returns to the sources of revelation, is never a static and sterile repetition of the tradition but is recast anew and given added depth of meaning from beholding the inexhaustible mystery of the human face of God. And just as an icon is simultaneously a product and a medium of prayer, so too a theology of this kind is a "prayed theology", "a theology *at* prayer" (Balthasar). In virtue of its contemplative orientation, it is able not only to enrich theological content but also to interpret and express the Christian mysteries in a manner that draws others to share in the mysteries themselves. It deliberately aims to enlighten, inspire, and shape Christian lives, precisely so that Christian lives can offer a credible and effective witness to Christ in the world. Such an approach to theology is especially suited to the work of priestly and diaconal formation, which has been my primary apostolate for twenty years. From what I have observed firsthand, the priest who can appropriate this contemplative orientation proves capable of applying his theological knowledge more intuitively and effectively in the work of forming disciples to play their part in the mission of the Church.

As our study comes to a close, some readers might wish that we would venture beyond Good Friday into the realm of speculation about Holy Saturday or extend our theological reflection to the Resurrection of Christ on Easter Sunday. Others might wish that we would press on to develop a doctrine of the eternal Trinity that would shed light on how the Son's being sent by the Father as the Atoner within salvation history corresponds to the Son's being generated by the Father as his Image and Beloved within the life of the Trinity. Such a task would involve showing how the atonement accomplished by the Son as man is the form that the Son's generation *ad intra* assumes when it is prolonged *ad extra* and enters the world's situation of sin. Though we have stopped short of exploring these subjects in this work, we have pursued them elsewhere: see Turek, *Towards a Theology of God the Father: Hans Urs von Balthasar's Theodramatic Approach* (New York: Peter Lang Publishing, 2001).

Despite these shortcomings (among many others), it is our hope that this account of atonement has effectively showcased a pivotal conviction of our four guides: that in the Cross event, the manifestation of "God's love for the world is so dazzling that it completely outshines the old 'chief commandment' with its anthropocentric formulation, as we see in the sentence which begins, then breaks off and reverses itself: 'In this is love: not that we loved God, but that he loved us and sent his Son to be the expiation of our sins' (1 Jn 4:10)."[7]

Ad majorem Dei gloriam.

---

[7] Balthasar, *GL*7, 455.

APPENDIX A

Formation of Missionary Disciples

(and a word in fairness to Balthasar)

I ask the reader to allow me this opportunity to present a brief *apologia* for one of our group of theologians, Hans Urs von Balthasar, whose reputation and theological legacy have been attacked in recent years for allegedly contributing to the declining numbers of those who take seriously Catholic faith, morals, and spiritual/sacramental practice. In my judgment, enough has been said already in this book to prove unfounded the facile misrepresentations of Balthasar as a heretic who blithely presumes hell to be empty of human souls and claims to know with certainty that it will remain so. If someone wishes to read a more thorough treatment of the issue, see Dr. Nicholas Healy's article, "Vatican II and the Catholicity of Salvation",[1] my article, "*Dare We Hope 'That All Men Be Saved'?*: On Balthasar's Trinitarian Grounds for Christian Hope",[2] Dr. Larry Chapp's blog,

[1] Nicholas J. Healy Jr., "Vatican II and the Catholicity of Salvation: A Response to Ralph Martin", *Communio* 42.1 (Spring 2015): 36–60. Healy's article provides numerous magisterial texts from Vatican Council II, John Paul II, and Benedict XVI on the universal scope of (i) predestination, (ii) the (objective) redemption worked by Christ, and (iii) "the real possibility [not presumption] of salvation in Christ for all mankind and the necessity of the Church for salvation" (John Paul II, encyclical letter *Redemptoris missio* [December 7, 1990], no. 9).

[2] Margaret M. Turek, "Dare We Hope 'That All Men Be Saved'?: On Balthasar's Trinitarian Grounds for Christian Hope", *Logos: A Journal of Catholic Thought and Culture* 1, no. 3 (1997): 92–121. Before submitting this article for publication, I emailed a draft to Christoph Cardinal Schönborn, O.P., who was appointed by John Paul II and (then-) Joseph Cardinal Ratzinger to serve as the primary editor of the *Catechism of the Catholic Church*. Cardinal

Gaudium et Spes 22, and Bishop Robert Barron's foreword to the second edition of Balthasar's much-discussed yet little-read *Dare We Hope*. Of concern to me here, however, is the claim that Balthasar's works are fostering spiritual presumption and complacency in readers as well as dulling, even disabling, missionary zeal.

For those who put in the time and effort to read attentively Balthasar's numerous works, there is no more recognizably Balthasarian theme than the "Theo-drama" involving the Holy Trinity (divine freedom) and human beings (human freedom in need of redemption and called to divinization). Essential to this Theo-drama is a *real interplay* between divine freedom and human freedom. On his side, God "leaves free" human beings over against his Fatherhood of grace. "Within the Trinity, God's all-powerful love is also powerlessness, not only giving the Son an equal, divine freedom but also giving the creature itself—the image of God—a genuine power of freedom and taking it utterly seriously."[3] On our side, Scripture prohibits us from undermining this seriousness by saying that a definitive No to God's deifying love is impossible.[4]

The seriousness with which Balthasar takes the role played by human freedom is best measured by his intense concern

---

Schönborn read the draft carefully, we discussed it together over the telephone, and he assured me that my article presented the correct understanding of the *Catechism*'s stance on the issue. Only then was the article published.

[3] Balthasar, *TD4*, 330–31.

[4] See Balthasar, *TD4*, 182 and 350; *TD5*, 285–90 and 297; and *GL7*, 233–34, 291–92, 402 and 417. See also Hans Urs von Balthasar, *Epilogue* (San Francisco: Ignatius Press, 2004) 118–19; *Engagement with God: The Drama of Christian Discipleship* (San Francisco: Ignatius Press, 2008), 31; *Love Alone is Credible* (San Francisco: Ignatius Press, 2004), 77; *Prayer* (San Francisco: Ignatius Press, 1986), 50; "Crucifixus etiam pro nobis", *Communio* 9 (1980): 34; *Does Jesus Know Us—Do We Know Him?* (San Francisco: Ignatius Press, 1983), 40 and 81; and *DWH*, 16–28, 41–42; and *MP*, 177.

and relentless efforts to form disciples of Christ who dare to desire sanctity. He always insisted that his entire theological project had but one fundamental aim: to equip Christians to respond to the universal call to holiness, for the greater glory of God and the sanctification of the world. Far from fostering complacency, Balthasar's writings (including his most scholarly) function as spiritual exercises for the purpose of priming believers to be effective and credible witnesses to Christ in our secular age. If Balthasar is vulnerable to fair criticism as a formator, it is due to his raising the bar of discipleship so very high—not to promoting a complacent and mediocre way of being Christian.

Like the French Catholic novelist Georges Bernanos (whose work resonates strongly with him), Balthasar regards mediocrity as a major obstacle to holiness and happiness.[5] By mediocrity, Bernanos and Balthasar do not mean being average in intelligence, creativity, or religious sensibility. Rather, the mediocre life is the superficial life: a life that refuses to take risks, to make commitments, to devote oneself wholeheartedly to a cause. True greatness, on the other hand, is the willingness to risk, the ability to commit, the readiness to place oneself at the disposal of the God and Father of Jesus Christ. The painful dilemma for the human heart in our "post-Christian" era is that it retains the desire for total commitment and self-sacrifice, but can see nothing truly worthy of such risk, such total self-giving.[6] Consequently,

[5] See Hans Urs von Balthasar, *Bernanos: An Ecclesial Existence* (San Francisco: Ignatius Press, 2011).

[6] In Bernanos' novel *A Bad Dream*, the character Philippe is a "post-Christian" man. At first, he toys with political ideologies, only to find them inadequate, mediocre. When he cannot find a "cause" worthy of his aspirations, he decides to commit suicide. But he wonders whether this is a cowardly act. Philippe reflects: "I'm probably not a coward but I now realize with horror that I shall never be certain. I shall never know whether, in another period of history, I might have been a saint or a hero. I merely state that the

Balthasar dedicates himself to the task of healing the eyes of our hearts so that we can see God (to paraphrase Saint Augustine): see the astounding love of God for the world made manifest in his crucified Son (Jn 3:16; 1 Jn 4:8–10), which alone is worthy of our answering self-donation.

This task undeniably guides Balthasar's charter for the formation of missionary disciples, *Engagement with God: The Drama of Christian Discipleship*. Here he addresses all the faithful who, in the years following the Second Vatican Council, should have become familiar with "the universal call to holiness". Yet insofar as the eyes of our hearts remain unhealed, we remain somewhat blind to the infinitely greater and more meaningful mission to which we are called. Thus here in his "program of mission to the world",[7] Balthasar straightaway directs our gaze to the figure of Christ crucified. In beholding him, the discerning eye seizes on "the whole essence" of the Christian faith: "that we should understand that the love which characterizes the life of the Trinity has been manifested in [Christ], and in him has been *abundantly* proved."[8] Abundantly, indeed. For Balthasar, the hallmark of the true God, that which renders the mission of Christ wholly credible as *God's* definitive engagement with the world, is love that radiates the quality of "excess", the "ever greater", the "yet more". *Deus semper major.* In the face of the recklessly self-forgetful character of God's passion of love, the only appropriate response is summed up in the Ignatian motto "*ad majorem Dei gloriam*" and in the Johannine exhortation "so

---

period I'm unlucky enough to be living in doesn't offer me the faintest hope of success in the experiment." Georges Bernanos, *A Bad Dream* (Providence: Cluny Media, 2020), 100.

[7] Hans Urs von Balthasar, *My Work: In Retrospect* (San Francisco: Ignatius Press, 1993), 52.

[8] Balthasar, *Engagement with God*, 48.

we ought to lay down our lives for our brothers" (1 Jn 3:16). The more the Christian grasps the lengths to which the Triune God involves himself for us, the greater grows his own ambition to live no longer for himself; at the same time, the less satisfied he is with spiritual mediocrity or complacency. In contemplating God's active involvement *pro nobis*, we are spurred to play our part in the action. "We suddenly realize that we have been created to take our part" in God's engagement with the world. And as our graced capacity to see God in Christ increases, so "we are drawn deeper into the springing source [of divine love] and simultaneously thrust out from the source into our own channels of activity."[9]

This means, to be sure, that the form and measure of God's action in Christ provides the model for Christian action. Balthasar, however, is acutely aware that something more is involved. If the action of missionary disciples is to be *effective* as a sign and an instrument of God's saving love, it is not enough to attempt to imitate God by standing in social solidarity with the poor, the stranger, and the oppressed. Neither the life of the Trinity nor the life of Christ is to be regarded as a mere paradigm to guide programs of social and political involvement. The crucial factor, for Balthasar, is that Christian action *participates in God's own life* of Trinitarian love. Christ, through his Incarnation and the bestowal of his Spirit, imparts to us a participation in the divine freedom of his sonship, by virtue of which we are made capable of taking part in his Trinitarian mission.[10]

Indeed the significant factor in being a Christian is that he does all with reference to and in dependence on the

[9] Ibid., 47–48. Indeed, "all our actions in the world should echo and correspond to this initial experience of God, who is made known in Christ Jesus; for the grace of God is prior to all our involvement, undertaken for God in the world, and for the needs of the world for his sake."

[10] See ibid., 27–29 and 38–40.

ultimate source of his actions, through loving first and above all things, the God who loves us in Christ in order that he may then, by means of and together with God's love, turn his attention to the needs of those who are the object of the love of God. Only if we start from this "Alpha" will our involvement lead us to the "Omega" of the man who is loved, only thus will we succeed in caring for him inwardly in order that he may find his true destiny, only thus will we achieve that solidarity with him which is only possible in God.[11]

Plainly, Balthasar's program of mission to the world performs a prophetic and critical function against a "secularization of salvation". All that it affirms about the Triune God's self-giving is pregnant with the insight that the transformation God intends to effect in human beings is nothing less than divinization. By rousing the Christian consciousness to a renewed awareness that man's full and final liberation coincides with his divinization, Balthasar enables us "to judge clearly how basically unsatisfying it is for man . . . to have as his ultimate goal the civilizing and humanizing of the world."[12]

Hence, it cannot be doubted that Balthasar takes seriously the universal call to sanctity. Yet what about sin? Does he take *sin* seriously? If the reader has been attentive until now, the only fair-minded answer is an emphatic yes. For Balthasar, the way of *sanctity* is the way of the Lamb who *bears the sin* of the world. Since the Church exists to bring the salvation of Christ to all, we must follow Christ's path of "descent" into the world. This entails the willingness to glorify God by bearing sin (our own and our enemies') in and with Christ (Eph 5:1–2).

If, then, Balthasar dares to hope that in the end, every

[11] Ibid., 40.
[12] Ibid., 69.

human heart may let itself be moved by grace to accept the redemptive work of the Triune God (and we can disagree with him on this matter and nonetheless draw a wealth of insight and inspiration from his corpus), still in fairness we ought to see that in him this daring hope is paired with an audacious love best exemplified by the witness of those saints whose vocation leads them to fill up what is "lacking in the afflictions of Christ" (Col 1:24). Saints do more than warn others away from sin. Saints dare to bear sin away on others' behalf. Priming the Christian to respond to sin by demonstrating a love more than human, a love that both "bears all things" and "hopes all things" (1 Cor 13:7)— this is the thrust of Balthasar's mission as a formator.

All this relates to the *credibility* of the Christian's mission to the world. "For as Christ of his free love yielded himself willingly . . . to death and dereliction" for the sake of sinners,[13] so the Christian is called to be at God's disposal in readiness to serve his brothers and sisters without counting the cost. The credibility of evangelical action for the sake of the world resides in its grace-engendered likeness to "the foolishness" of divine love (1 Cor 1:25). Only this form of life "can penetrate the 'secular world' as 'leaven'."[14] The costly discipleship that hazards everything is the mark of authentic Christian involvement.[15]

I will let Balthasar speak from the heart in closing:

> I am the light of the world [writes Balthasar quoting Christ].
> And without me you can do nothing. And, beside me,

[13] Ibid., 27–28.

[14] Balthasar, *MRW*, 57.

[15] Balthasar anticipates protests that he is taking the universal call to holiness too seriously. "It will be objected that such a program of action demands the character of a saint. This may well be; but from the very beginning, Christian living has always been most credible, where at the very least it has shown a few faint signs of true holiness." *Engagement with God*, 61.

there is no light and no god. But you are the light of the
world, a borrowed but not a false light; burning with my
flame, you are to enkindle the world with my fire. Go out
into the furthest darkness! Take my love like lambs into
the midst of wolves! Take my gospel to those who cower
in the dark and in the shadow of death! Go out; venture
beyond the well-guarded fold! I once brought you home
on my good shepherd's shoulders. But now the flock is
scattered and the gate of the pen gapes wide: this is the
hour of mission! Out! . . . Just as the Father has sent me,
so do I send you. Going out from me as a ray from the
sun, as a stream from its source, you remain in me, for
I myself am the ray that flashes forth, the stream that is
poured out from the Father. . . . Just as I radiate the Father,
so also are you to radiate me. So turn your face to me, that
I can turn it out into the world.[16]

[16] Hans Urs von Balthasar, *Heart of the World*, trans. Erasmo Leiva-Merikakis
(San Francisco: Ignatius Press, 1980), 33–34.

APPENDIX B

On God's Impassible Passion of Love

There is an important current of patristic thought that is
open to an understanding of God's impassibility that is consonant with the positions taken by Pope John Paul II, Pope
Benedict XVI, Hoffmann, and Balthasar. We find support
for these claims in the patristic studies of Paul L. Gavrilyuk,
who has focused his research on the suffering of the impassible God.[1] Gavrilyuk makes clear that for the Church Fathers, divine impassibility does not denote the absence of
affectivity;[2] it does not mean that God is aloof from and
unconcerned about his creatures.[3] Rather, impassibility denotes God's perfect control over his affectivity, such that it
is expressive only of pure selfless love. By way of explanation, Gavrilyuk points to the analogy between *apatheia* as a
virtue in Christian asceticism and *impassibility* as an attribute
of the Christian God. "In ascetical theology, *apatheia* refers
to the state of the soul freed from the attachment to sinful
thoughts and desires. . . . Far from being an emotional zero,
apatheia is the precondition for Christian love, purified of

[1] See Paul L. Gavrilyuk, *The Suffering of the Impassible God: The Dialectics
of Patristic Thought* (Oxford: Oxford University Press, 2004). See also his
"God's Impassible Suffering in the Flesh: The Promise of Paradoxical Christology", in *Divine Impassibility and the Mystery of Human Suffering*, ed. James F.
Keating and Thomas Joseph White (Grand Rapids, Mich.: Eerdmans, 2009),
127–49.

[2] See Gavrilyuk, "God's Impassible Suffering", 142.

[3] See Ibid., 136.

all self-centered desires.[4] By analogy, divine impassibility, in the sense of perfect control over emotional states, is a condition of divine love, mercy, compassion, and providential care."[5] The main point here is that if impassibility denotes being unmoved by blameworthy passions, then God's impeccable passionate love can be said to be impassible in the moral sense. To God can be attributed morally impassible passionate love as a super-eminent perfection.

[4] The Fathers are comfortable speaking paradoxically of "impassible passion". Gregory of Nyssa, for instance, in his homily on the Song of Songs, instructs the faithful to "*love* her [Wisdom] as much as you are able, with your whole heart and strength; *desire* her as much as you can. To these words I am bold to add, *Be in love*, for this *passion*, when directed toward things incorporeal, is blameless and *impassible*, as Wisdom says in *Proverbs* when she bids us to be in love with the divine Beauty" (emphasis added). Here Gregory describes this blameless passion as impassible. Love/desire for divine Wisdom and Beauty is an *impassible passion*. Gregory of Nyssa, *Homilies on the Song of Songs: Translated with an Introduction and Notes from Richard A. Norris Jr.* (Atlanta: Society of Biblical Literature, 2012), Homily 1, 25.

[5] Gavrilyuk, "God's Impassible Suffering", 137. Tertullian, for instance, ascribes to God such passions as longsuffering, mercy, and anger, in accordance with biblical revelation. Yet God undergoes these passions in a divine way, in the manner appropriate to him; see *Adversus Marcionem*, II.16.4–7. And Lactantius, writing at the end of the third century, follows suit. He attributes both impassibility and passions to God (again: love, patience, mercy, anger) without contradiction. For assuredly God's passions are different from those of men, since they remain under "God's complete control" (see *De ira Dei* [On the Anger of God] 21.7–8). Novatian, for his part, teaches that passions are possible in God, inasmuch as they are completely harmonious with divine reason; see *De Trinitatis*, 5. For these Christian writers, passions when pure and blameless are perfections of the human spirit and hence can be attributed analogously to God in an eminent degree and without any imperfection. See also Maximus the Confessor, *The Four Hundred Chapters on Love*, I.2, I.81, and IV.91; John Paul II, encyclical letter *Dives in misericordia* (November 30, 1980), no. 7; and Michael Figura, "The Suffering of God in Patristic Theology", *Communio* 30.3 (Fall 2003): 373. For Balthasar's treatment of the notion of the *apatheia* of God as found in the Church Fathers, see *TD5*, 216–23. In addition, cf. H. Crouzel, "La Passion de l'Impassible: Un essai apologétique et polémique du IIIe siècle" in *L'Homme devant Dieu: Mélanges offerts au Père Henri de Lubac*, vol. 1, coll. Théologie, 56 (Paris: Aubier, 1963), 269–79.

This stance is famously articulated by Origen of Alexandria (ca. 184–ca. 253). The reader will recall that Ratzinger/Pope Benedict gives a robust endorsement of Origen's position on this subject, which thus deserves a direct quotation. "The Redeemer", says Origen,

> was moved by compassion for the human race . . . even before deigning to take our flesh; for if he had not suffered, he would not have come to share our human life. First he suffered [as God], and then he descended [and became man]. What is this passion that he suffered for us beforehand [as God]? It is the passion of love. (*Primum passus est, deinde descendit. Quae est ista quam pro nobis passus est, passio? Caritatis est passio.*) And the Father himself, God of the universe, who is full of long-suffering and rich in mercy (Ps 102:8) and compassion, does he not suffer in some respect? Or do you not know that, when he concerns himself with human matters, he suffers on account of men's suffering (*passionem patitur humanam*)? He suffers the passion of love (*passio caritatis*). "For the Lord your God has taken your ways upon himself, just as a man carries his son" (Dt 1:31). . . . The Father himself is not impassible. . . . He has mercy and is compassionate; he suffers a passion of love.[6]

As we saw in the encyclicals of both John Paul II and Benedict XVI, so also here we find Origen affirming implicitly that blameless human passions can be ascribed analogously to God. (As Benedict XVI affirms, "God is . . . a lover with all the passion of a true love."[7]) Plainly, such a move is validated by the Bible itself. For Origen, the paradox of

---

[6] Origen of Alexandria, *Homilies on Ezekiel*, 6, 6. "These last words show that Origen sees very precisely the paradox between God's *apatheia* in himself and his susceptibility in the economy he has established." Balthasar, *TD5*, 221.

[7] Benedict XVI, encyclical letter *Deus caritas est* (December 25, 2005), no. 10.

impassible passion (inculpable passion like compassion and patience) seems to suggest that passion (*pathos*) has less to do with a deficiency than with a capacity associated with charity.[8]

Yet there is more to it. This sort of impassibility—inculpable passion—is not the only kind that the Church Fathers attribute to God. For them, God's impassible way of being passionate is a perfection not only morally, as it were, but also ontologically. Indeed, God's morally impassible passionate love is seen to flow from his ontological impassibility. Saints Athanasius, Gregory of Nyssa, and Maximus, for instance, define the Triune God's nature above all as infinite Goodness. The fact that the Good God, out of his unenvious generosity, graciously pours out being to his creatures, manifests that his nature is without need of creatures to be perfect. God, who is Goodness Itself, has nothing to lose or gain by involving himself with us. Hence God can become wholly involved (for none of God is outside the freedom of his initiative) without being changed, either for the better or for the worse, by that involvement. Furthermore, God's way of involving himself is so sovereignly free that God is not subject to any involuntary influence from the outside. After all, God is *not* a being in the world alongside other beings, whose influence he therefore would have to endure unwillingly. Rather, the negation embedded in the notion of divine *im*passibility is meant to protect the

[8] See Jean-Pierre Batut, "Does the Father Suffer?", *Communio* 30.3 (Fall 2003): 391. Eastern Catholics often quote in this context a passage from Isaac the Syrian: "From the strong and vehement mercy which grips [the holy man's] heart and from his great compassion . . . he offers up tearful prayer continually . . . even for the enemies of the truth and those who harm him. . . . [This he does] because of the great compassion that burns without measure in his heart in the likeness of God." Homily 71, in *The Ascetical Homilies of Saint Isaac the Syrian* (Boston: Holy Transfiguration Monastery, 1984), 344⁻45.

reality and radicality of God's involvement with us while distinguishing it from the involvement proper to mere men who, being natural parts of the fallen world, are subject to external misfortunes and internal (mental and emotional) disturbances contrary to their personal will.[9] Indeed, God's way of being passionately involved with his creatures infinitely transcends the way in which even virtuous creatures can be intimately, affectively involved with others (e.g., by way of long-suffering, mercy, compassion).[10] What is *positively* indicated is that God's affective involvement with us is based entirely on God's utterly free and selfless initiative. This is why, "for the Fathers, divine impassibility is quite compatible with God's providential care, even to the point of participating in suffering."[11] When, consequently, "the Fathers speak of God suffering *impassibly*, they want to stress that God is *not conquered* by suffering."[12] They mean to emphasize that "if God chooses to participate in suffering, he is not overwhelmed by suffering. God retains his freedom and *remains active in suffering.*"[13] They are saying, in short, that "*impassibility qualifies the manner in which God endures suffering.*"[14]

---

[9] "Divine impassibility functions as an indicator of the divine transcendence and as a marker of God's undiminished divinity." Gavrilyuk, "God's Impassible Suffering", 143.

[10] See ibid., 147.

[11] Ibid., 143.

[12] Ibid., (emphasis added).

[13] Ibid., 141 (emphasis added). For the Fathers, God's compassionate responsiveness to suffering is a voluntary modality of the infinite *actio* of his *caritas*. Hence Origen can say: "In his love for man, the Impassible One suffered merciful compassion" (*Homilies on Ezekiel* 6.6). Quoted in ITC, "Theology, Christology, Anthropology", in *International Theological Commission: Texts and Documents, 1969–1985* (San Francisco: Ignatius Press, 2009), p. 225, no. 3.

[14] Gavrilyuk, "God's Impassible Suffering", 143. Gavrilyuk himself endorses what he calls a "qualified divine impassibility", which he finds in the

Most of these points are made by Saint Gregory Thaumaturgus (ca. 213–ca. 270) in his treatise *On the Impassibility and Passibility of God*. God, says Gregory, demonstrates
his impassibility not by proving himself detached and remote, but by the manner of his active participation in suffering. If God suffers on our account, it is in virtue of God's
free determination and initiative; since God suffers by free
choice, he is not subject to suffering but superior to it. God's
sovereign power remains unhampered through whatever suffering God would freely endure—like a salamander passes
unharmed through fire, or like a diamond incurs no damage
under the blows of a sword. In Gregory's words: "God is
the one who is unharmed by every suffering, and it is his
property always to remain the same."[15] Gregory insists that
God does not cease to be God when he freely, out of love,
takes suffering on himself. To the contrary, "God's participation in suffering *transforms* the experience of suffering."[16]
Indeed, this transformation occurs precisely because God's
omnipotent nature is not damaged thereby. Such must be
the case if, by his Passion, God in Christ delivers us from

Fathers. Ibid., 131. Balthasar for his part observes: "Theologians in succeed-
ing ages tended to conceive God's impassibility more narrowly than the Fathers. . . . The biblical 'reactions' of God to human conduct become mere
anthropomorphisms, and any involvement of God in history seems highly
questionable. Now God's pity seems to be located only in its effect in the
world, whereas he himself cannot be touched by the creature's pitiful state."
He then quotes Anselm's *Proslogion* 8: "Misericors simul et impassibilis quo-
modo es? . . . Cum tu respicis nos miseros, nos sentimus misericordis effec-
tum, tu non sentis affectum . . . quia nulla miseriae compassione afficieris."
*TD*5, 222. See also Aquinas, *Summa Contra Gentiles* II, 25.

[15] *St. Gregory Thaumaturgus: Life and Works*, trans. Michael Slusser (Washington, D.C.: CUA Press, 1998), 164; cited in Gavrilyuk, "God's Impassible
Suffering", 141.

[16] Gavrilyuk, "God's Impassible Suffering", 143 (emphasis added). This
stance is not peculiar to Gregory but is also found in other Church Fathers,
as Gavrilyuk notes.

the power of sin and death. This is why the Fathers affirm adamantly that "in order to be redemptive, God's involvement in suffering must be marked by impassibility."[17] Gregory also affirms as much when, engaging in some word play, he describes the impassible passion of God the Son, who willingly becomes human and indeed suffers and dies in atonement for our sins: "For impassibility eagerly rushed upon the passions like a passion, so that by his own Passion he might show . . . [that] the passions were not entirely able to stand against the weight of the power of impassibility."[18] We can restate Gregory's meaning in this way: for God the Son eagerly, out of the pure passion of divine love, rushed to deliver mankind from the bondage of sinful passions, so that by his own Passion as man he might show the omnipotence of his divine passion of love to overcome the power of sin.

This understanding of the impassible passion of God the Son shown by his own Passion as man accords with the analysis of patristic soteriology given by Khaled Anatolios in his article "The Soteriological Grammar of Conciliar Christology" in *The Thomist*.[19] Because of space restrictions, we can present only a brief summary of Anatolios' study of conciliar christology from the fifth to the seventh centuries, beginning with the thought of Saint Cyril of Alexandria.

For Cyril, the person of God the Son is the one "who suffered in the flesh, was crucified in the flesh, and tasted

[17] Ibid., 138. "Impassibility enables God to be involved in suffering to the fullest possible extent. . . . It is precisely because God infinitely transcends all *human* suffering that he is able to overcome our suffering. It is precisely because God has nothing at stake for himself in the experience of suffering, that he is able to love us so perfectly." Ibid., 140–41.

[18] *St. Gregory Thaumaturgus*, 168.

[19] Khaled Anatolios, "The Soteriological Grammar of Conciliar Christology", *The Thomist* 78, no. 2 (April 2014): 165–88.

death in the flesh.''[20] At the same time, Cyril consistently
denies that the Son's incarnate condition reduced the divinity to the level of humanity. In no way does the Son's assumption of the human condition harm the perfection, the
"impassability", of the divine nature.[21]

As he grapples with this mystery, Cyril offers the following clarification:

> He [the Son incarnate] suffers with regard to the flesh that
> is his own, not with regard to the nature of the divinity
> [σαρκὶ τῇ ἰδίᾳ παθών, καὶ οὐ θεότητος φύσει]. The ex-
> position of these things is altogether ineffable, and there
> is no mind that can attain to such subtle and transcen-
> dent thoughts. Yet, following the most correct expositions
> and carefully considering the most reasonable explanation,
> we do not reject speaking of his suffering—otherwise, we
> would be saying that the birth according to the flesh was
> not his but someone else's—but neither do we declare that
> *the things belonging to the flesh* transpired in his divine and
> transcendent nature. Rather, as I said, he should be thought
> of as suffering with regard to the flesh that is his own, but
> not suffering *in any such manner* with regard to the divin-
> ity [νοοῖτο δ' ἄν, ὡς ἔφην, σαρκὶ τῇ ἰδίᾳ παθεῖν, καίτοι
> θεότητι μὴ παθὼν κατὰ τοιόνδε τινὰ τρόπον]. . . . It is
> like iron, or some other such material, when it is put into
> contact with fiery flames. It receives the fire into itself and
> exudes the flame. But if someone strikes it, the material
> itself takes the hit but the nature of the fire is not at all
> harmed by the one who strikes. This is how you should
> understand how the Son is said to suffer in the flesh but
> not to suffer as far as the divinity [ἐν τῷ σαρκὶ λέγεσθαι
> παθεῖν, θεότητι δὲ μὴ παθεῖν τὸν Γἱόν].[22]

[20] Cyril of Alexandria, *Third Letter to Nestorius* (*PG* 77:121D).

[21] See Anatolios, "The Soteriological Grammar", 170.

[22] Cited in Anatolios, "The Soteriological Grammar", 170–71. G.-M. de
Durand, *Cyrille d'Alexandrie: Deux dialogues christologiques*, Sources chrétien-

Plainly, Cyril is intent on maintaining the distinction between the divinity and the humanity in Christ. But, Anatolios insists, "it would be a mistake" to interpret this text as conclusively determining that the distinction of the natures is secured merely by way of separating them into compartments, as it were. Such a view would be content with saying simply that the Son incarnate suffers by virtue of his human nature rather than by virtue of the divine nature.[23] Instead, we should note how Cyril strives to distinguish "the divine and human *modalities* according to which this subject [God the Son] acts and/or suffers".[24] While everything that happens in the flesh happens to God the Son as its subject, "yet, what happens by way of the flesh does not happen *in the same way* [κατὰ τοιόνδε τινὰ τρόπον] with reference to the divine nature."[25] The attribution of suffering, for instance, is not "to be imputed to Christ's divinity *in exactly the same way* that [it is] understood with reference to his humanity."[26] Indeed, what remains to be adequately recognized and theologically explored is that "the distinction of natures is posited *within their union in the single person* of Christ."[27] Certain implications of the mystery of the Incarnation have yet to be drawn out and examined.

Not even the Chalcedonian "definition" should be regarded as bringing to a close the normative logic of conciliar christology. For undeniably, ambiguity remains after Chalcedon regarding the location of the unity of the person

---

nes 97 (Paris: Éditions du Cerf, 1964): 302–514; translated into English as *St. Cyril of Alexandria: On the Unity of Christ*, trans. J. McGuckin (Crestwood, N.Y.: St. Vladimir's Seminary Press, 1995), 130–31.

[23] Anatolios, "The Soteriological Grammar", 179.

[24] Ibid., 171.

[25] Ibid.

[26] Ibid., 177.

[27] Ibid., 179.

of Christ, so much so that another ecumenical council is required to resolve that issue: Constantinople II in 553. Anatolios observes rightly that Chalcedon "is much clearer in affirming the two distinct natures than the location and dynamism of the union". Indeed, Chalcedon "merely hinted that the union of natures involved a unified dynamism of activity: 'the character of each nature is preserved and *concurs* [συντρεχούσης] in one *prosopon* and one *hypostasis*', but it did not clarify further *how this concurrence*, or literally, '*running together*', can be envisioned in terms of the distinction and unity of the activities of the two natures."[28] Hence, the clarifications made at the Councils of Ephesus and Chalcedon represent "a stage in the development of Christological doctrine and not the final and sufficient articulation".[29]

But if Constantinople II overcame Chalcedon's ambiguity by clearly locating the unity of Christ in the second Person of the Holy Trinity (God the Son), it also left open the question of how the two natures work together, concurrently, in the Son incarnate. This question is not treated until the sixth ecumenical council: Constantinople III in 680–681. And the answer given is an endorsement of the theological insights of Saint Maximus the Confessor (ca. 580–662), who sheds light on the dynamic interactivity of the two natures in the person of the Son. Most pertinent to the question of God's impassible passion in Christ is the soteriological principle that emerges from seventh-century christology: in the one subject who is God the Son, the divine nature acts to be united with the human, and the human nature acts to be united with the divine.[30] Salvation is both a divine and human work, which entails more than the sheer juxta-

[28] Ibid., 175, emphasis added.
[29] Ibid., 174.
[30] Ibid., 176.

position of the divine and the human natures. The dynamic interactivity of the two natures in the Son involves the deifying communication of an aspect of the divine nature to a corresponding aspect of the human nature (including post-lapsarian negativities of the human condition) in order to transform this condition without diminishing the integrity and perfection of the divinity. Precisely "this deifying communication itself establishes the *proper analogy* between the two natures and the ultimate fulfillment of human nature as made in the image of God and perfected in the likeness of God."[31]

In a pivotal passage of his study, Anatolios argues incisively:

> The heart of the gospel and its *novum* is . . . the supreme mystery that human nature was united with the divine nature in a single hypostasis without impairment to the integrity of either nature. It is the integrity of the two natures *within their union in Christ*, not the integrity of the natures as such, that has any value with reference to the good news of Jesus Christ. Indeed, if we merely separate Christological predications into discrete compartments representing the divine and human natures respectively, are we not trying to describe the features of the Incarnation in pre-Incarnation terms? . . . That is to say, we cannot talk Christological sense by making either affirmations or negations with respect to the natures of Christ while considering each separately and apart from the other. Christological sense is made only when we talk about *the unity and dynamic interactivity of the two natures in the person of the Word, an interactivity whose content is always the deifying transformation of the human nature by the divine nature*. . . . So, with regard to every Christological predication, it is not

---

[31] Ibid., 186.

sufficient merely to pose the question, to which nature this predication should be applied. Without further supplementation, that is a question that belongs to a pre-Incarnation logic. The mere denial of the attribution of a human predication to the divine nature, while admittedly part of the logic of patristic Christology, nevertheless needs to be qualified by and synthesized with the emphasis on the unity of natures through the hypostatic union.[32]

Indeed, the correct way of stating the question is: "How does this predication belong to the divine person of the Son, who is the subject of both the divine and human natures, such that it refers both to the activity of the divine nature in communicating its perfections to the human nature and the activity of the human nature in receiving these perfections unto deification?"[33]

Anatolios' next move is to apply all this to a statement like "Christ suffered in bearing our sins." In so doing, we should keep in mind the (matured) patristic principle that "any affirmation about Christ can only ultimately mean the communication of the features of the divine nature to the human nature, which deifying communication itself constitutes the single reality of the incarnate Word."[34] Accordingly, we can say that to encounter the sin-bearing Son, Jesus Christ, is to encounter

the mystery of the communication of divine compassion to the suffering of the human nature of Christ. . . . Through Christ, human suffering becomes perfectly transparent to divine compassion such that the incapacity of this suffering is enfolded by the perfect capacity of divine compassionate love. . . . In this way, we can understand Christ's

[32] Ibid., 179–80 (emphasis added).
[33] Ibid., 181.
[34] Ibid., 184.

compassionate suffering as applicable to *both* the divine and human natures, preserving the distinction between them, while affirming their communion or "running together" for our salvation.[35]

Finally, let us turn directly to the theology of Saint Maximus the Confessor. In it we can discern the enduring influence of early Fathers, such as Saint Gregory Thaumaturgus, as well as the benefit of later conciliar christology. This is evident, for instance, where Maximus affirms that Christ as God experienced suffering in a *divine* way because he experienced it voluntarily and free from imperfect motives.[36] Indeed, a hallmark of God's impassible manner of suffering is that God preserves his sovereign freedom and remains active in suffering.[37] If we want to see what this looks like, Maximus points to the Cross of Christ. When the Son, in his humanity, takes the passivity of suffering and—without suppressing its passive character—transforms it into saving action, we see, translated into human terms, the way in which God the Son involves himself wholly for sinners without undergoing change. Beholding the Crucified, we may regard the Son's capacity to convert his Passion into saving action as the human and historical revelation of the Son's manner of *divine* involvement as characterized by impassible passion. Put differently: the atoning power of Christ's human suffering unveils the mystery of the Son's *divine* manner of being impassibly passionate.

In light of both the Incarnation of the Son and man's divinization in the Son, we can say with Maximus that God exhibits a will to anthropomorphism—a divine will that initiates and determines a pattern of covenantal exchange and

---

[35] Ibid., 184–85.

[36] See Maximus the Confessor, *The Ambigua* 5, §18 and §26.

[37] See Gavrilyuk, "God's Impassible Suffering", 141.

mutual *perichoresis* (interpenetration and mutual inherence). By God's gracious dispensation, man, body and soul, becomes a paradigm for God—so long as man, body and soul, is properly ordered and deified. Such is pre-eminently the case with Jesus Christ, true God and true man. As Maximus says in *The Ambigua*: "For they say that God and man are paradigms of each other, so that as much as man, enabled by love, has divinized himself for God, to that same extent God is humanized for man by his love for mankind."[38]

It is beyond the scope of this study to treat comprehensively the problem of the suffering of God. But enough has been said to support our claim (and that of the International Theological Commission[39]) that talk of God's capacity to "suffer" in the face of sin should be understood in view of God's capacity to so love his creatures that he deigns to predestine, redeem, and divinize them "in Christ", his only Son. This capacity of God to love, moreover, should be seen as rooted in the mystery of the Father's eternal generation of the Son as his living Image of divine love.[40] Thus, if the capacity to "suffer" the passion of love belongs to the Father of Jesus Christ, the theological ground of this possibility can best be found by way of an ever-deepening exploration of God's Trinitarian mystery.

[38] Maximus the Confessor, *The Ambigua* 10, §3, in *On Difficulties in the Church Fathers*, vol. I, ed. and trans. Nicholas Constas (Cambridge, Mass.: Harvard University Press, 2014), 165. I am indebted to Dr. Adrian Walker for his insightful interpretation of Maximus' doctrine.

[39] See ITC, "Theology, Christology, Anthropology", p. 216, no. 3, and p. 226, no. 5.2.

[40] Recall that our four guides align themselves with those Church Fathers (Athanasius, Gregory of Nyssa, Hilary of Poitiers, Maximus the Confessor) who see the Father's eternal act of generating the Son as an act of love. Further, they enhance this traditional view by envisioning the patrogen(n)etic dynamic of the Trinitarian Godhead within the framework of a metaphysic of *caritas*, of interpersonal love.

One avenue of theological exploration, we suggest, is the dynamic pattern of *perichoresis* in the Holy Trinity: the interpersonal exchange and interactive penetration of the divine persons (albeit according to the order of the *ad intra* processions). The persons interpenetrate one another without ceasing to be distinct subjects and without diminishing the integrity of their persons. Moreover, they give and receive themselves in love without change to the absolute perfection of the one divine essence. Indeed, the unchanging divine essence is identical with the interactive exchange among the divine persons. It is this unchanging exchange of self-surrendering love in the one Godhead which is paradigmatic (*mutatis mutandis*) of the dynamic interactivity of the two natures in the Son incarnate, Jesus Christ; it is also the divine milieu in which human beings are given a place and called to divinization as "sons in the Son".

Of course in exploring this approach to the mystery of the eternal Trinity, we must rule out every Hegelian-like view that sees God's capacity to suffer in the face of sin as a potentiality that needs to be actualized if God is to become perfect in *caritas*. Instead, we have to think of the Triune God as being in himself absolute and eternal *caritas*. We have to see that if the loving God willingly suffers in the economy of redemption, this can only be a free and gracious (*non*-necessary) expression of God's eternal and immutable perfection as inner-Trinitarian *caritas*, without God needing the cosmic process and the Cross to become increasingly perfect himself.

For the reader who wishes to explore ongoing developments in the doctrine of God's impassible passion of love, see the following:

Anatolios, Khaled. "The Soteriological Grammar of Conciliar Christology", *The Thomist* 78, no. 2 (April 2014): 165–88.

Balthasar, Hans Urs von. *Theo-Drama: Theological Dramatic Theory.* Vols. 4 and 5. San Francisco: Ignatius Press, 1994 and 1998.

Clarke, W. Norris. "A New Look at the Immutability of God". In *God Knowable and Unknowable*, edited by R. Roth. New York: Fordham University Press, 1973.

Does God Suffer? An Exploration. The entire issue of *Communio: International Catholic Review* 30.3 (Fall 2003) is devoted to this subject.

Galot, Jean. *Dieu souffre-t-il?*. Paris: P. Lethielleux, 1976.

———. "La réalité de la souffrance de Dieu". *Nouvelle Revue Théologique* 101 (1979): 224– 45.

Gavrilyuk, Paul L. "God's Impassible Suffering in the Flesh: The Promise of Paradoxical Christology". In *Divine Impassibility and the Mystery of Human Suffering*, edited by James F. Keating and Thomas Joseph White. Grand Rapids, Mich.: Eerdmans, 2009: 127–49.

Hoffmann, Norbert. "Atonement and the Ontological Coherence between the Trinity and the Cross". In *Towards a Civilization of Love*, edited by International Institute of the Heart of Jesus. San Francisco: Ignatius Press, 1985: 213–66.

Ladaria, Luis. *The Living and True God: The Mystery of the Trinity.* Miami, Fla.: Convivium Press, 2010: 429–32.

Maritain, Jacques. "Quelques réflexions sur le savior théologique". *Revue Thomiste* 69 (1969): 5–27.

O'Hanlon, G. F. *The Immutability of God in the Theology of Hans Urs von Balthasar.* Cambridge: Cambridge University Press, 1990.

Turek, Margaret M. *Towards a Theology of God the Father: Hans Urs von Balthasar's Theodramatic Approach.* Bern, Switzerland: Peter Lang Publishing, 2001: 154–88 and 267–96.

Abbreviations

CCC   *Catechism of the Catholic Church*

DH   Heinrich Denzinger, *Compendium of Creeds, Definitions, and Declarations on Matters of Faith and Morals*, 43rd ed., Latin-English, ed. Robert Fastiggi and Anne Englund Nash (San Francisco: Ignatius Press, 2012).

DWH   Balthasar, Hans Urs von. *Dare We Hope "That All Men Be Saved"?*. San Francisco: Ignatius Press, 1988.

GL1   Balthasar, Hans Urs von. *The Glory of the Lord: A Theological Aesthetics*. Vol. I, *Seeing the Form*. San Francisco: Ignatius Press, 1982.

GL6   Balthasar, Hans Urs von. *The Glory of the Lord: A Theological Aesthetics*. Vol. 6, *Theology: The Old Covenant*. San Francisco: Ignatius Press, 1991.

GL7   Balthasar, Hans Urs von. *The Glory of the Lord: A Theological Aesthetics*. Vol. 7, *Theology of the New Covenant*. San Francisco: Ignatius Press, 1989.

ITC   International Theological Commission

MIC   Balthasar, Hans Urs von. *Explorations in Theology*. Vol. 5, *Man Is Created*. San Francisco: Ignatius Press, 2014.

MP   Balthasar, Hans Urs von. *Mysterium Paschale*. San Francisco: Ignatius Press, 1990.

PG   *Patrologia graeca*

ST   Aquinas, Thomas. *Summa theologica*. New York: Benziger Brothers, 1947.

RSVCE   Revised Standard Version, Catholic Edition. San Francisco: Ignatius Press, 2006.

TD2   Balthasar, Hans Urs von. *Theo-Drama: Theological Dramatic Theory*. Vol. 2, *Dramatis Personae: Man in God*. San Francisco: Ignatius Press, 1990.

TD3   Balthasar, Hans Urs von. *Theo-Drama: Theological Dramatic Theory*. Vol. 3, *Dramatis Personae: The Person of Christ*. San Francisco: Ignatius Press, 1992.

TD4   Balthasar, Hans Urs von. *Theo-Drama: Theological Dramatic Theory*. Vol. 4, *The Action*. San Francisco: Ignatius Press, 1994.

TD5   Balthasar, Hans Urs von. *Theo-Drama: Theological Dramatic Theory*. Vol. 5, *The Last Act*. San Francisco: Ignatius Press, 1998.

YCY   Balthasar, Hans Urs von. *You Crown the Year with Your Goodness*. San Francisco: Ignatius Press, 1989.